MUTTER, FALTER

A Chorale for Five Voices

by

Victoria Floor

Other Books By Victoria Floor:

VIA TERRA

80% Cacao

Dee Generation

Trouble With Poets

Crone-icles

Just a Song at Twilight

Create Space
Copyright 2015

ISBN-13:
978-1518792649

ISBN-10:
1518792642

INTRODUCTION:

Annoying as hell! No one likes getting a song stuck in the head, let alone an advertising jingle. Obsessive replaying of endless negative thoughts—even worse. Yet many among us are walking around with these grim hidden tape-loops blaring, and there is little that can be done for the sufferer. Some will pick up mind-numbing chemicals to try to deaden the voices. Others will come up with any imaginative scenario to explain them away, or attempt to counter-attack with positive messages. Some will take it out on their loved ones when the pain becomes unbearable. It's clear, however, that this torturous phenomenon is most prevalent when the sufferer finds him/herself in isolation from others.

When children grow up around such negativity in their elders, it can leave them with a sense of victimization, no matter how otherwise nurturing a family might be. These offspring arrive at young adulthood confused as to the meaning of love, and not knowing how to enjoy life. They may take this habit of negative thinking into their own relationships, thus perpetuating the cycle unto the next generation.

But there IS hope! (There's ALWAYS hope!) The following attempts to escort the reader through this hell of self-defeating internal voices, and to point the way out. Identification is key to helping another. Do not be afraid to identify at any level that you dare...

Chapters

I. Ophelia

Damn. There's not going to be enough bourbon.

Less than half an inch in the half gallon, that's less than half a pint. That won't last until he comes to get me for our one o'clock—
Shit! Only there's not going to be any one o'clock.

You're in Vermont you bastard. Bastard! You're in Vermont with your goddamn daughter. Wait. What day is it, Sun—

No, no. Only Saturday. That's right. You left yesterday. Kiss goodbye on the ear I turned my head car pulled out from the parking lot look out the window now it'll be gone—

No. Don't bother looking.

What time is it? God, it's so gray. Either early or raining. Don't hear any rain. Don't dare look. Wait half an hour or as long as you can. No, that never works. Got to know the truth start planning this day out now. Good, you're still ticking, can't read you though, have to turn on the goddamn—

Twenty past seven! Jesus Christ! What's it got to be so goddamn early for? That's an hour and forty minutes until it opens. And I'm not going to be the first one there. Not going to be one of the ones

1

that line up at the door for those brown uniforms to unlock it and set up the cash register. Goddamn state stores. Why does it have to be so far away? Why couldn't they just have a little corner grocery opens at seven lot of dusty bottles on the shelves could run right out and back.

Fritz and Hannah's in New Jersey. That was a civilized state. "A light white to complement a brie? We have just the thing for you Ophelia dear. Would you like a taste of this new kirsch wasser Fritzi just got in from Munich? And how's every little thing?"

Oh Hannah, Fritz, you must be dead. Why don't you ghosts open up another corner store just for me down there instead of that horrible so-called drugstore full of Blacks grinning over moldy salami? Oh God, what am I doing in this sea of Blacks? Can't walk a mile to the goddamn state store by myself. Not safe.

Oh you bastard. You left me here to this fate; wait'll you come back and find me gone and then read about it in the paper. Raped and knifed. It'll serve you right for leaving me all alone for three days with no liquor. I told you there wasn't enough when you left. But did you care? "You have plenty of cash and you like the walk to the state store." You told me that the other day: "You like the walk—" Oh sure—

Sure, I like the goddamn walk, when it helps pass the morning and I know you'll be here for our

2

one o'clock and I can time it just right and it's not raining. And you know as well as I do I never go to the state store on my walks. I only did that once when I was mad at you and you weren't coming home; you had that goddamn social security appointment. So I walked it. So what? So if I have to I can do it. Put on sneakers and that jacket of yours with the big zip pocket inside just take a twenty no purse. Goddamn sitting duck for that mob out there watching the doors see me come out again with a big bag full of bottles. Just that much slower. Just that much more helpless. Figure she's got change on her; and they can see the booze. Could do it in the street, but might decide to follow her home then what? Get the cash in the pocketbook. Private place for a rape—

Let him find the body here. The bloody body here—

That dream the other night I woke you up…. Oh God, keeps coming back, lean black dog with—

It's too horrible! Oh, the little boy! He's just passing the glass doors. I'm standing there in my nightgown watching the night afraid to go out and the little boy passes by like a little lost beggar and the next thing—

Oh God! That panting in the distance. That awful breathing between teeth. The dog passes by the glass doors the doors are vibrating he passes close and I can see—

The little boy in his mouth, oh God. Boy clutching a dead puppy little legs dangling all broken and bloody little socks and shoes then his mouth—

Oh God! His mouth wide open in the middle of a scream drops of foam on his lips white pearl teeth tormented gaping mouth frozen wide dead. Then the dog sets him down and he walks stiff like his neck is broken and that scream on his face, that frozen scream. And he walks past me. A zombie. His stomach sticks out all bloated and bruised and bloodied and his neck twisted and the door shaking under my fingers as I hold it shut, the glass door in the old house, the night and the pinewoods behind, me in the dark room in my nightgown, the dead boy, clutching the dead puppy, disappearing after the black beast....

Death. It was death passing by my door. It's a sweet smell. Like ether. Like fermenting apples, yet penetrating.... I smell it deep in my gut, beyond the nose, it seeps in, diffuses, blots out everything else.... I know death, Edgar. I'll come haunting you like that. I'm going to haunt you 'til the day you—

You had no right. You and the black dog. Trusty. Trusty you had to be, goddamn canine loyalty.... You could've left me there oh just a little longer. Fool Edgar. You did it. You brought me back a zombie to haunt you. Imbecile. You didn't

4

understand. You didn't understand it was all going to be so simple, so peaceful. I could've been ashes under the apple trees. You're responsible now, Ed. You deserve to be haunted. And you're responsible for the kids. They'll have me around like a bad dream because of you.

Jesus Christ I need a drink. Can't lie here all day. God knows I don't feel well. But have to get up. Get up get up get up. Drag the old corpse up and over there you go. And now for the bourbon where the—

All these goddamn years. Jump up at six. Get everybody's goddamn breakfast. See everybody out the goddamn door. Wash dress powder paint and spray. I couldn't have cared less. Had to choose every day: clothes, shoes, jewelry. Clean up the kitchen slide into the Dodge back out the driveway elevator up to the office. Goddamn Humphrey. You grinning egghead asshole. Face you every day. The nerve to tell me not to drink so many cocktails during lunch. What cocktails? You tell me grinface, what cocktails? If I ever had to, slipped into the bathroom take out the little English flask he gave me. Yes, he gave it to me. And you can't take it away Humphrey-dumpty it's mine and nobody can—

Work all day saving lives. Lives! Damned imbeciles should never have been allowed to be born. Happy moonfaced mongoloids—we should all be so lucky! Helluva lot of good I did for you all my years. Finding you apartments so you could burn to death leaving stoves on poor fools. Fools! We were bigger fools thinking it was all so wonderful dedicated altruistic. Important scientific studies...shit. Where's that—

Had it here last night, didn't I? Wait. Must be in the—

Right, here by the bathtub. Thank God. Looks like only half a cup, maybe two thirds cup. Let's measure it. Christ, can't make this last all that time over an hour to kill only—

Just two thirds cup. Okay. One sip and pour the rest back. Use the funnel, won't want to spill a—

The flask! There's still the emergency gin! Isn't there? I never touched the gin did I? Let's see here. Can't tell how much, pour this in the measuring—

Oh God. Only a dribble. When the hell did I—

TSSSSSSTH. That tastes old.

So there's two thirds cup to go on. Great. That's just great. And what time is it? Seven thirty. Swell. Goddamn early. And raining. Just my luck. Have to go out alone in the filthy city morning cold rain walk a goddamn mile and a half to the brownshirts' liquor fort. Got a big job ahead. Going to be a real working day. Get up get everyone fed see them out the door go get dressed clean up the kitchen. Years and years. Better than this nothing. All this nothing now. Alone and nothing. Nothing to show for all that damn altruism. No medical insurance no retirement none of your damn social security. No wages no savings no—

There's the irony. Jesus! Goddamn lucky mongoloids they get it. They can sit it out for years in front of their TVs, happy clams. And what do I get? Who the hell ever takes care of me? Got to go out there again. Damn it. I got to go fight for it and there are too many dogs out there and nobody's tossing any bones my way. Can't even compete. Over qualified. Overqualified my ass! Too old, that's all it means you know, too goddamn old to invest in and probably a ginhead sicky and why haven't you worked the last two years. Uh huh. None of your goddamn business and you can check my references. Here, I live with one of them. He can tell you everything you need to know. The good doctor. How you doing up there in Vermont? Happy family gathering? And me here in the cold rain got to go out because you couldn't be bothered to pick up any liquor before you go running off. Catch pneumonia. Won't wear anything on my head get wet and frozen drink the whole bottle maybe.

No. It won't work. It's not that easy. You goddamn well try it then. They find you at the last minute and drag you out of it. They make you. Like the alarm clock. Get up. Get their breakfasts. See

7

them out the door like fucking Donna Reed and don't forget to kiss hubby hand him a sandwich crap oh crap. You work like a clock and then you wind down. You want to wind down but you bust a spring and stop dead. But then they haul you to the watchmaker so he can fix you up oh boy. So now what do you do? You try again that's what. You whip your own ass into inane encounters with twerpy interviewers don't know a damn thing about life telling you you're over-fucking qualified which really means you're underqualified for social security so you get ten years to rot before anybody feeds you.

I don't eat a lot. I don't waste energy. Look, no lights on in this gloom. Don't drive the car. Don't go anywhere do anything. Oh, one martini a day at Bradley's, not even a goddamn movie.

So that's my responsibility. Twenty-fifty a week for liquor and I pay it don't I? And I don't get in your way around here. Keep the place clean when I feel like it. Give you someone, some thing, to come home to. At least I take away the empty apartment and replace it with... a kind of presence.

A kind of presence. That's about right. A benign ghost, a sort of shadow, a big semi-immobile blob that sits like a stuffed animal either on the couch or on the chair or waits for you on the bed so you can hug something warm. It's a good deal. You can dissolve slowly and cling like baby chimp to stuffed mommy-doll. I can wait. Oh boy I can wait and wait and—

Just like I can wait 'til goddamn nine o'clock opening hour. I can wait 'til you fade out and by that time—

Shit. It's got to happen sometime soon. He can't keep going on and on. Two heart attacks. What's keeping him going, the bastard? Pure spite! Well, by the time you go, he'll most likely have gone and then I can sell the place must be worth some two hundred thousand—

Sell the place. Of course, sell it. What the hell would I want with it? Stay in this dump. Drink.

Boy, do I need a drink. This is going to be one helluva day to get through. And then there's all of tonight. God knows how much longer tomorrow. Least you could have done is leave me with something to—

Here's to you, Humph. Another one to you, Carl baby. You asses. Kept me up all night with your reports. Here's to you, fuckers all! After, only after dinner dishes done kids in bed TV off Ed passed out. Finally. Oh, then, finally, around midnight, it would begin. Peace. Quiet. The yellow lamp the Chinese vase the photograph color fading....

You were a good mother, Libby. Would you have been proud? Burning the midnight oil and all that at my age and with a family of five shopping list magneted to the refrigerator to prove it. And I would write for you fuckers! I, I, I would take responsibility, committing to paper what you idiots could only keep rattling around in your noncommittal brains. It was my work. I wrote it all under your bloody names. I wrote your articles and did all your other dirty work by day after writing all damn night and you couldn't pay me a decent—

I put your goddamn names on the holy register. Ha! You friggin' phonies, little boys who like to play general with your moonfaced tin soldiers. You played the games. I took the risk for you. Yes I did. Because I had to make sense of it somehow. I got your damn work published. It was I, Herr Doktor mine, in case anyone should ever ask who had the brains, the balls, to commit it to posterity, to put it on white paper. You didn't think that was hard work? Why then did you have me do it? A mere M.A. to our grand PhD's. You can thank me for the publications in French, Czech, German god knows how many— And the letters you got, the praise, the emerald earrings in your wife's lobes, you can thank me for them too. Doesn't do a goddamn thing all day has the nerve to complain to *me*!

Why the hell I even listened. Waste my time listening to that fat blond—excuse me, dyed blond—bitch. Always calling in the middle of dinner. Why the hell I ever gave her the time— Work for you all day and night have to listen to your whining bitch on top of it. All night plugging, sweating, drinking those reports. Did you own me Humphrey? Carl?

Well that's that. It's all over and there are no more scientific papers to face after dinner dishes. And so? What're we going to do with all our glorious free time now? No kids. Only a few dishes. Boy, glad it's just me and you now dirty dishes. Feels like the old days. After they'd all run off. School, work. And it was just you and me, staring at each other, deciding whether you were going to go into the dishwasher. Look at the clock. There is time today. Okay, in you go. Soap. Close the door and turn the dial. Of course there's no dishwasher in this dump. And he has one goddamn it. For one lousy old man. A dishwasher!

When the hell's he going to keel over? Old fart.

Sorry Daddy. Didn't mean that. Here, have a sip. Enjoy the peace and quiet now. No notes. No more reports to face. No reason to stay up all night. No, I realize it now. What a toll. It was on account of those articles. Had to drink. How could anyone— when you knew you'd have to get up, alarm would ring at six for Ed, the children had to be fed and saving for college for three. Ha! That was a joke. Only one went on our dime. All that energy.

And then the meetings: PTA, Board, Commission, League, Citizen's Council. God, when I think of the hours I spent being a goddamn good

11

taxpaying involved citizen. Almost more than all the hours I spent being a goddamn good research assistant, good scientist, good wife, good mother—

Good drunk! I'll take a half sip to that. Easy now. Long way to go yet. I know it. I know it! Jesus Christ, starting to sound like Dolf now. Better move into the living room. Turn on a goddamn light. Whoopee. It's a party. Electric light bulb glowing. Somebody's birthday? What's the goddamn occasion?

Energy crunch. Going to be just like the war. Save up enough ration tickets for a really good time. Turn on three lights, the phonograph, the vacuum, the dishwasher—

I don't have a dishwasher anymore. Yeah, Ed. You keep working for the energy people see what you can save us. Attaboy Ed. Always on the up and up. Goddamn sucker is what you—

Okay, alright, I was a sucker for years. I know it. But I also knew when to call it quits. But not you, Ed. You'll go on and on. At least 'til retirement. Retirement, ha! So you'll be another old dot on Medicare. A burden to your kids. And me? At least I'll have the decency to be gone by then. Oh, I know I was premature the first time. But at least I've had practice. And you, Ed, frankly, lack the guts. Easy living. That's your bag. Creature comforts. You're just like a goddamn cat. And if the kids roll you over to change your diaper you'll find exquisite pleasure

in the sensation. Kids schmids. How about nurses?
Pimply faced, ignorant. Nursing home? You don't
think, Ed baby, you'll be put in one of those homes?
Your kids aren't going to have any one-point-two
acre six bedroom suburban deals by the time you—

They'll be lucky to have a one-point-five room
apartment way things are going where's that leave
you? Ah, but you'll have money put aside. And for
your goddamn sea burial too. You really think the
kids'll do that? Scatter your ashes over the ocean?
They'll have to rent a boat. Or at least stand on a
beach in an offshore breeze. Oh Ed! You and your
Conrad. And Daddy and his Shakespeare. And his
ash collection. His mother and three wives all
scattered under the apple trees. How nice. And
what about me? Sure, oh sure. You kids going to
bother sprinkling me around when there are no
more apple trees? On no you won't. Because I'm
going to sell them apples! Don't give me any crap. I
raised you, now leave me alone. They're my apples.
I sell the house for a cool two hundred thousand.
Like hell! Who's going to buy it? Taxes alone cost—

There'll be nothing for me. TV soap operas
and cheap—well, maybe their authors don't think
they're so cheap—women's novels and, oh, of
course, bourbon. Box, books and booze you say.
The three eternal B's. They're all I got and I'm going
to use them and use them and abuse them 'til I'm all
used up and they'll find me by the stink weeks later.
That is if Paula still lives upstairs.

Paula thinks she's looking after me. Why? Is this the alkie's legacy, the concerned citizen? Am I turning back on myself? Can't they just be universally unconcerned? A little negligent? I know what the hell I'm doing. Leave me alone. I need peace. I need to be alone. Need to concentrate. Feels just like those nights facing the typewriter, waiting, foldtop desk, yellow lamp, her portrait with the pearls, all waiting. And I'd come and we'd have it out, wrestle it out, for hours, 'til the bottle was low, the sky paling and I could lie down for an hour before—

Bzzzzt! His alarm and the next day and the next slide under the steering wheel Humphrey comes in with the dirty work.... You'd call me at lunchtime. Maybe we'd meet at a restaurant. Go to the park. Once every other Tuesday, you'd call me at work and we'd—

The kids come home housework dinner then Ed the dishes TV drinks Ed bedtime face the typewriter and the briefcase and all those damn notes....

AHHHHHUUUUMMMMN. Slowing down. Sleepy. Take it slow and easy now and maybe drift back into semi-consciousness. How to make time move? I just don't feel up to this today. The rain. My neck aches. What time is it?

Quarter to eight. Well, that's better. And where the hell are you? You're supposed to be here.

Taking care of me. What the hell else do you have to do? Alright. I know. I could have gone. Maybe I should—

No. You're right. We need to take breaks. We've got a long way to go together. Unless you get killed on the highway coming back. Oh, no such luck. I'm stuck here with you. You're stuck with me now. Ed's got his sacred divorce. Screw him. Bastard better sell the house and give me my half quick. You hear that Ed? You and your goddamn procrastinating. Jesus! I lived with that for twenty-seven years so damn slow about everything. Can't you just do it and get it over with? Do I have to live in constant suspense? What if something happened to you? Would I still get my half of the money from the house? God. You've got to give me something Ed what the hell am I going to live on what if I have an accident what if I have to have an operation or if someone breaks in here and robs us or if Dolf dies and I have to go out there all of a sudden pay all his bills 'til the estate's all straightened out—

Dear old Daddy couldn't care less. Never gave me a damn thing, now he's going to die and I'm going to be left with a bloody mess and nothing to live on for months—maybe years—'til it's all straightened out. Nobody's going to be there to help. I don't know a blessed thing about—

Have to hire a lawyer I suppose. And with what? Can't even take care of myself. How'm I supposed to take care of Dolf now? At least he gets his benefits. I don't get a red cent. Work all those years with nothing to show for it. Now I've got to get a fulltime job. You need a job to get any benefits. Half a year, maybe, if I can hold on, then be eligible for medical. Maybe it takes longer. Who knows? I'm trying aren't I? God knows I've been looking. Go through the want ads every day send out dozens of resumes make hundreds of phone calls nobody ever calls me back. Overqualified my ass! You go out and try it now, Edgar. At least you weren't laid off in the middle of the Second Great Depression.

If only he'd die soon. I'd have the house to sell. There must be someone with the cash to buy it. I'm not settling for anything less. Two hundred thousand dollars it's worth. And all the antiques! Maybe I could auction them off for another four or five thousand. Take my time selling off the antiques for the best price. Live in the house awhile 'til the divorce money runs out. It wouldn't be so bad if only Daddy weren't so, so tenacious.

Oh Daddy, I don't want you to die. I'm just getting desperate, and you've had a long, good life— all those cruises, three wives— Jesus, what have you ever given me? That house is all I've got. It's my heritage. You think I'm going to keep it for sentimental value? Well not if I can sell it for two hundred thousand I'm not! You realize how long I could hold on? Maybe move to Florida, like Janey did, or the South Carolina coast, somewhere sunny.

St. Thomas. I could end up there. Maybe even have a last fling with some old retired, whatever. Don't you see Daddy? I tried. I did my best to kill the issue. I tried not to outlast you. I just wanted out. No return. But—

It's all goddamn Ed's fault I'm still here, Daddy. They wouldn't let me die. And I tried. God knows, I was hoping to get away with it. Hid the car and everything. Okay, so I was stupid to go to the pinewoods. Next time I promise I'll go to some busy city stretch out on a park bench—

Shit! And all I'd have to do he here is step out the door with pearls on and they'd do it for me.

Look Daddy, Ed, you might as well face it. I'm going to be around a while longer than you might have expected. And I plan to spend every last minute of it as close to a state of inebriation as possible—assuming I'll have the money to keep me in liquor. It's the least you could do. And it's not much to ask, is it? After being such a dutiful daughter, dutiful wife, you could just set me up and leave me alone. You go your way and I'll go mine. Jesus! The two of you, taking up so much property it's a crime! What a waste, two solitary men in oversized houses. What do you do, Ed, sleep in a different room every night? No, you probably haven't been upstairs once this whole time. Place must be covered with spiders' webs and dust, clothes in heaps in open closets bathroom sink dripping green stains kids' junk scattered everywhere that hideous wallpaper peeling Sam's mattress on the floor covered with cat hair—

Ed, you bastard. You neglected me for years and years and years. Oh, Ed, why couldn't you? Why didn't you love me like I loved you? Didn't I take care of your needs, sympathize with you, work my entire life around yours, do your dirty dishes, your laundry, for years and years while you just withdrew and faded into a potbellied conservative, Archie Bunker—

You're pretty damned conservative. And very damned dogmatic. You know, Ed, your ideas are boring and repetitive, unchanging. You're a drag, Ed. You didn't used to be. You liked theater and restaurants, even new movies when they interested you. You read lots of magazines. You were up on most everything. But you didn't have anything to show for it. You couldn't flaunt it. You lacked the imagination. You fell back on your worn-out clichés. Everybody was getting sick of it. You never had the guts to really express yourself with passion. Never had the balls to ask for a damn promotion. Always came to me and bitched. But you never had the guts to tell it to Barruco, or Swensen, or any of the creeps that could've done something for you. What the hell could I do? I agreed you deserved it. But you had to fight your own goddamn battles. I had my own twelve thousand a year insult to live with. Jesus! And it was you that was being exploited! What

18

about me? You could've damn well said so. I did. All the time. Lot of good it did me. I was trapped by my damn degree. You could've gone further than your B.S. but like with everything, you put it off, found excuses, procrastinated. And what happens?

They lay you off. Swell. So now we're surviving a year on my lousy twelve thousand insult. Kid in college. Mortgage. Bills bills bills bills bills—

And you take your sweet time getting another job. Sit on your ass in your undershorts reading *National Geographic* all day while your dutiful wife goes out to support a family of five on a lousy twelve grand—

Mortgage ate that up. So you get your goddamn job, finally, and of course we have to move give up that house we'd loved, the town, all our friends, my political commitments, my job, my Tuesdays with him. Was there ever any question? What about Sam? What about Trusty and Cleo? We were still a family, weren't we? What did you expect me to do, break it all up then and there because my husband gets a job in another state? What the hell had I always done before? What the hell do all good wives do? Naturally they go along. Start a new life. Ha! There's always another suburb. Another shopping center to get used to. You can always get another low-paying job. Somehow. Doing something—it doesn't matter what. The kids adjust quickly. Sam did at least. He's always been great at getting along making himself popular in any new neighborhood. He was sad to leave his friends. We all were. But he at least made new ones. Girlfriends too. And it wasn't that far. He could take the train up on weekends to see his old buddies.

For crissake, Ed, it all made sense at the time. How should I have known everything was going to be so horrible there? I was willing to give it all up in hopes of a change for the better wasn't I? I was being adventurous, wasn't I? It was I did all the packing and unpacking moving and reorganizing setting up a new household. I even got a job in three months. Better than you did, Ed. Everything was going to be hunky-dory, remember? I even said so once or twice. You were frustrated. But new jobs take a while and you don't know all the games yet. So. We were learning together. A new phase.

Goddammit I was miserable! How could I have known I would miss it all so much? Ten years. After all, Ed, ten years is a long-time investment in a community. I guess I overestimated my ability to adapt.

If it hadn't been such a godawful place. Jesus! That suburban sea goddamn maze I'd get lost in it those highways wrapped around everything the air pollution a dirty ring around the horizon the small ugly lawn the woods scrabbly and tiny after what we'd been used to.... We were taking a loss. I didn't want anything to do with those idiots and their bridge clubs garden parties, cooking groups. What the hell—

Weren't even any intelligent people. No one at either of our jobs. Certainly no one in that lousy development. The humiliation! People barging over with their Welcome Wagon casseroles sticking their noses in smelling us out goddamn bunch of redneck beer drinking football worshipping idiots. You think I was going to get cozy with those creeps? Were you, Ed?

You didn't have to. You'd come home from work. Didn't have to deal with them. Well I did! For three months. Not so much as a job to go off to. Alone in that halfassed house taking things out of boxes nosy women coming over those lonely bored-stiff—

You can't imagine, Ed, the wasteland! God, those suburbs. The worst I'd ever seen. Desperation, Ed you don't know a damn thing about it. Wretched deserted women alone going nuts all day kids at school nothing to do. Bored? Bored? You haven't known boredom like that, Ed. It's like you're scared to death to finish the shopping because you know you have to come home to that empty house drink and watch soap operas. That's what you do, Ed. You spend a good solid four hours drinking and watching soapy TV before the kids come home.

Don't you think I lived for Sam's return from high school? And then what was I supposed to do? The kid had his friends. Wanted to go off with them. Another two hours, more like three, and you'd finally come home.

So, I got a goddamn job finally. You don't think I wouldn't take the first thing I could get? Jesus! It's not even Humphrey, Carl or the rest. Match my past salary. Big goddamn deal. With prices down there wages should have been...

That idiot outfit! Well, hell, it was something to do. Some money coming in. I couldn't stand that Jack Creeley, oily little dandruff-covered rat-faced—God, he made old Humphrey look like a prince. The stupid work they gave me. I felt like subverting it. I couldn't work for a goddamn bank. I couldn't have cared less about that crap... Okay. It was a job. I was working. Going through the motions. Life restored. Only by that time, Ed, by that time, you know, I'd had a taste of it and I knew. I knew what was waiting for me as soon as that six month stint ended. I knew and I was terrified. Going back. The neighbors. The obscene phone callers. The delivery men. The TV. The remaining boxes. The silence. The empty mailbox. Hours upon hours upon hours of blankness. No friends. No familiar job routine. No Vera or Jessie to chat with during lunch. No him.

God I missed him. We only met every other Tuesday, but he was always there, in his office, a phone call away. Local phone call that didn't show up on the bill goddammit! Your emotional impotence. His accessibility. At least then the office hours were mine. I could meet him for lunch. We'd start with a couple of dry martinis... . No one had to know. I'd dress that day. I'd care. The pretty pink one he gave me with the buttons down the back he liked to slip his hand between—

Oh, Ed, that's what I missed most of all. That's what I gave up, for you. For you and the lousy family, what was left of it. Oh Sam, not you. I wasn't going to leave you. Not ever. I couldn't leave my last baby, my Sammy. You couldn't have expected me to choose back then. Give up Sam for him? My only child, now that the girls were gone? That was an unfair choice. That was no choice, Ed. I would have laid down my life, thrown myself under a truck. I couldn't leave Sam. He had to finish high school at least. Go off to college. That was two years away. It wouldn't have mattered if he'd already been gone. But he was only fifteen and needed a normal family a complete complement of parents for crissake. What the hell was I supposed to do?

And I got a goddamn job. So it ended after six months. You think that was going to stop me from taking it? I would've taken anything, collected tolls, garbage, unpaid bills—

But how can you work when you know the job's going to end any minute? Something more permanent. They always held it out like a carrot. Something more permanent hell. They wouldn't hire me for another two years. Remember, I was overqualified! A threat! Could've gotten any old halfwit, been a lot more comfortable, right Jack? Banks! What the hell did I care about banks?

So there I was again. And I kept looking all the time. But in my racket, you see, Ed, they don't hire you until the last possible minute, the money's so tight. Charity money, Ed, not corporate, not defense. Nonprofit organizations Ed, there's a big diff—

You never paid any attention. It was enough to say you have a wife with a scientific career. You were proud of me for a while. Shit, you must've been a little proud. As long as I wasn't worth more than you. As long as I was limping along on those rip-off salaries making some man somewhere look good to his fucking superiors! Alright. Aright. Alright.

I need a drink. Just a sip. No. Holdout. Will need a stiff one before I go marching out into the rain. Goddamn rain. I need a drink.

***

Rainy days were the best. I could stay home and watch TV and not feel so guilty. Felt like a day off. No neighbor's going to venture out in a hard rain. Had my bourbon. The box. The boxes, Jesus, that interminable unpacking job. I didn't give a damn. Get out what I needed left the rest in the so-called attic couldn't be bothered miniature hibachi how often were we going to use that? Dinner parties? What dinner parties? Who the hell was going to come all that way for a dinner party? Some friends. Friends of convenience they turned out to be. Nobody wrote. Nobody visited. Oh, I had Margot on the phone a few times....

Charming Margot! Tells me her problems poor little Smith girl never had a real career never could respect herself poor, poor Margot—sick of your crap took it for years endless outpouring of sympathy, concern, listening, listening. You think I could call you when I was down? Hell no. It only worked one way and you knew it Margot. You bitched and I listened you looked up to me and admired me—shit, for what? For being your goddamn doormat? You were wrapped around a gin bottle for years. I knew that Margot. And now I understand. I can really understand you now, crazy isn't it? But now that it's my turn, where are you? You're all born again! Jesus! I can't even talk to you, Margot, I've lost all respect—

Ed you liked Margot though. Didn't you? You and Margot kissy kissing under the piano what was I supposed to do? Dickie? That little shrimp? Came up to my elbow! You think we were supposed to— that I was supposed to—eat shit Ed. There wasn't one of them I wanted. You can have your cocktail parties.

There was only one I wanted then. We went to Margot and Dickie's cocktail parties; you were there at the door, grinning at me, when I arrived. And no one knew! Oh, you kissed me against the bathroom door so long, long ago. Those were the best times. Now I can't remember enough—

You seem so old and frumpy now, so uninteresting. Could it have been you? All those years? Keeping me alive. It was the arrangement, not you yourself, perhaps. It was the way it worked. All those innocent mutual friends. The lunches. The phone calls at work. The park oh the park. Feeding the ducks you made me feel like a college kid, I was a coed and you my professor. Under the big black umbrella, smell of spring mud.... Oh, I don't know, it all seems so long ago now.

If you're so much older, why don't you make me feel younger? You've cooped me up here. You and your Rights for Retirees League. Got to be old and proud now or you're shat upon is that it? I get to be your staunch defender as you slide into senility god bless old age goddamn prostateless—

You really get a kick out of it, death romance crap. I can tell you, it's no romance. It's the plainest, simplest thing. You just take a handful of pills with a liberal amount of bourbon, see, then you lie down somewhere and quickly black out, see, and then, if you're lucky—which I, of course, am not—you never have another care in the world.

It would've been so simple. So easy. You could have gone off to work as usual goddammit, Ed, you didn't have to get involved. It was none of your goddamn business. You had no right! Oh why? Why did you have to ruin everything?

Tired. How much longer—

Eight. Be open in an hour. Got to go out. Out in the freezing rain god forsaken friendless aching drizzle soak to the bone catch pneumonia no money for a doctor die here show you all—

Cold. I need a drink that's what I need. Get dressed by the time I—

No, better wait. Hold off just a little longer maybe it'll stop. Just a tad now. Got to save enough to see me out the door. That's too much. Pour half of it back. This is all your goddamn fault, leaving me like this no liquor you could've thought of me for once. Nobody thinks of me.

Well, thank you, Ed. Thank you for this wonderful life you saved. Life of nothing. Alone.

Day like this when Libby died. At least she wasn't alone. You can't imagine—you and your goddamn—your mother's still alive! Cancer-faced monster. Jesus, how she hated me. Well, see where it got you, Iris? Turned against me from the very beginning. The resentment! Her darling Edgar. Made me sick. She's rotting now. It's your turn to watch your mother—

It's not pleasant, Ed. Cancer. All she would eat was eggdrop soup. Eighty-two pounds. Wait'll you see your rotund little mother drop to—

Skeleton. She'll be an empty-socketed skeleton staring—and you'll have the pleasure of—

She'll be prattling her religious crap. At least my mother wasn't so full of self-righteous fundamentalist—

Lot of good it'll do her. Look at Libby.   She wasn't, never had been, a practicing Jew or anything else. Never assaulted you with her crackpot beliefs like your mother did me. And your kids. She was good to you. All of you. Libby loved you, Ed, she never thought anything but the best of you. She never made a martyr of herself the way your mother always—

But she doubted. She told me that in the end. It was too late of course. She said she'd wished she'd had something to believe in. Sure, it might be nice. If you could really believe you were immortal like your holy mother.

Well, I doubt that'll happen to me. No religion for crissake, where would I have ever gotten religion? Maybe if I'd married Jules…. We talked about it. I would have had to convert. To become a real Jew. Libby wouldn't have stood for it. If I'd married Jules I'd have been a Jew all this time. Maybe I'd have felt—

Well, certainly everything would've been different. For one thing, I'd be living in Scarsdale, not in this dump. Rich. Closet full of Bergdorfs, Saks. Like the hand-me-downs his redhead wife gave to my daughters. Would've been his daughters, if only. Libby wouldn't let me bring a Jew in the house. A rich one. Going to be an architect. And she wouldn't let—

Well, I should have anyway. He wanted to. "Won't you at least think about it Fella darling?"—his uniform smelled of starch, the train….

Gave me his army undershirt when he left. I wore that shirt all through the war. Saved all the letters. Burned them finally. Yellowed army-issue blue ink tied up in red ribbon….

Burned everything. Why keep it? Everything's gone now. Too fast. Too bloody fast. What a rip-off. Everything taken away at once. Bang. It goes. Your uterus shrivels up and dies kids grow and leave you husband kicks you out job ends no home no love. Oh Jules! Leave her. Come take me away. Take me to Florida on the night train. Take me sailing. I'll be so good this time—

How did it go? We'd been together the night before. But I can't remember that. Just getting into your roommate's truck. Old pick-up with the wooden sides and that crazy rubber chicken hanging from the mirror.

That's right. We'd been in your friend's apartment. We woke up early and it was gray and foggy and we got in the truck with that stupid chicken. It was early damp and drizzling and we drove out of town past the campus. Was it a weekday? Were we skipping classes? I think so. There was that certain illegal thrill to it all, that sense of wild abandon, freedom....

Okay, we got in the truck and drove out in the drizzle. We were drinking beers from bottles, and you sitting up so straight at the wheel—a little truck driver singing Cole Porter songs. And I was even singing a little too—damn the offkey: "Give me land lots of land under starry skies above, don't fence me in. Let me ride through that wide open country that I love, don't fence me in...." We giggled. Oh, it felt so good! Two nectar-tipsy, pollen-dusted bumble bees careening about the landscape so free, so un-nettable riding on sheer appetite, slipped right out of town. Left the world behind. Out into the spring rain. Early spring, I remember, the grass when we got out onto the sea road was green. That early spring green, so bright suddenly among the browns and grays. And the windshield wipers conducted and drips traced the glass like notes in flight sitting beside you so cozy in the raw wet world that hungry gnawing spring dampness bare trees still that neon green carpet—

And we were laughing! Remember laughing? And it was enough to be sitting next to you. I didn't dare touch you. Just wanted to hear you sing. You had a delightful voice, you know, and you were very good at imitating Sinatra. We splashed down that dirt road and across the salt pond the water almost washing over at that one low place then out on to the point. The foghorn must've been blowing. But the wind would snatch it away. I remember the wind. And we got out and climbed down the slippery, mussel-covered rocks to the water's edge and stood and admired the sea. We both loved the sea. The same. Exactly the same. We stood there and loved the sea together. And then I must've gotten bored with the sea because I wanted to put my arms around you. I was slightly behind you. We were in our pullover sweaters and our khakis and mist and sea salt were glistening on your black curls and I wanted to grab you, or better, I wanted you to take my hand and pull me beside you and kiss me, but we didn't dare. And you didn't dare break the spell, then we—you must've started it—picked up some pebbles and tossed them and that broke the tension and we joked I think and we knew we were lovers at moments like that.

I knew it was all play to you, even that pitch at the station. Every boy in uniform was doing it, so naturally.... I guess I was just the right girl at the right time.

I never really took you seriously, Jules. When you came back with Ava it was no surprise. Of course, I'd found Edgar by then. I kept you, though, where I kept all my little trophies, in the box in the attic, the overflowing box. Your letters in a neat stack tied with a red ribbon, something you gave me, Jules? I can't remember now. Your old yellowed teeshirt silting away along with the other snapshots, letters, dried flowers oh what a pretty offering all gone up the chimney. It's all over now, there's nothing left to give you all. I'm gone, the body's gone boys, there's nothing but this putrefying hulk here, wouldn't drag it to the thirtieth reunion invitation sitting on the desk should throw it out—

No way! I still have my pride. Not going to let anybody see me like this. Thank God it's gone. Good riddance I say. I can go anywhere in this disguise. Untouchable I am, like those holy street people now I'm one of them. Living offal, a human offense. I've earned my rotting time upon the tree. You bees have swarmed long enough; you birds have pecked me with your bony beaks. I'm brown, fermenting, twirling on the last fibers of my stem; happily bloated I'll make a pretty squish when I fall—

I'd had it with little pretty boys by that time anyway. You were my fate. A truly brutal man come to tame me. Come to silence the siren with sheer force of prose. Thank God you saved me from the poets of my life!

You'd seemed so old, so enormous after Jules. Looming in front of me, I sometimes noticed a little dandruff—

I thought you were ancient, ancient. How absurd. To think you were ever really that much older, that I ever had the slightest fear of you. When you'd get mad at me in the beginning and the power would build and you'd want to come smashing down on me, I wasn't really scared. It felt secure. I knew I had you under control. I'd clam up and grin at you. I couldn't speak when you got like that. You hated that grin. Wanted to slap me, didn't you? Well, why the hell didn't you, you coward, bloody impotent coward! Scared to be a man in the last analysis. I should've figured you out then.

We had that horrible scene and you made me feel like such a whore, such a monster for trying to seduce you, but that was your problem, not mine. That's probably why I ended up with old Ed. You were the first one—and the only one, for that matter—who ever rejected my sex offering. It drove me crazy when you did that! How could you. Didn't you know what a valuable piece of ass I was? I had the whole campus wrapped around my little—just like I'd have Bob, later, and Eddy, and Dave and Paul and Roger and, and, Jerry and Steve, and of course, Alan, who gave me Sam, and who almost cost me my life—that was a great moment for you, pulling that knife on Ed—

A rare moment of passion for you, too, old Ed. Pretty much shot your wad. Really, all downhill after that. All you could do was steam. Steam 'til you passed out drunk. Nice Ed. If you couldn't take it, why the hell'd you have to stick around? God knows I didn't need you. Certainly not once I had him. It's like you were addicted to me Ed. Too weak to pull out. Same old Ed. But you--you were such a man to me. You old Captain Kangaroo with a martini you—

Rain rain rain rain shit! This isn't going to let up. It's not going to stop by nine o'clock. I'm going to have to go out. You could've picked some up. You were out that way when you went to get the paper on Thursday. Jesus. You knew we were low and you were leaving me for three days and nights how could you be so damned inconsiderate? I pay for it. It's my money. Now I'll have to go out there and get soaked or knifed. Why do these things always happen to me? Now I'll have to take your black umbrella.

Remember the day it rained and we walked through the park under your big black umbrella? It was spring then. The rain was warm, not icy. We went down and fed the ducks in the rain. You

34

wrapped me in your black London Fog and worked your hand inside my blouse and bit my neck where it paralyzes and called me your treasure reaching up under my skirt where I was like the warm mud soaking into your shoes your mustache tickling my earlobe splatter of raindrops on the umbrella I held it trying to cover our backs in case anyone should pass.... We were so free then. All the time in the world. What happened? Why do I hate you now? Oh, I don't hate you so much I suppose. Don't have the energy to hate you. Numb, that's all. Indifferent. Worse than hate. What happened?

It's because I had to move here, isn't it? Because you liked it better when we weren't stuck with each other and you could play the free bachelor. You could never take it. Intimacy. Dirty word, *n'est ce pas*? Look at Kitty, Susan, Teresa, Jody—did I forget one? Jesus! You couldn't stand it after a certain point. When's my time going to be up? When are you going to extricate yourself from me? You seemed to have no trouble walking away from four wives and seven diverse children. I should be especially easy.

Or is this it now? Are you going to stay up there in Vermont in that woods where there isn't even a telephone, where I couldn't even reach you in an emergency? You going to hole up there 'til I get sick of this and move out of here? Don't kid yourself. I'd love it if you'd stay up there. Just send down the rent checks. I can take care of myself. I can handle

35

it. Here, see, I'm handling it just fine. Come back from the liquor store, build a little fire, finish that book, have a little drink every hour or so, "and it went right to my head, wherever I may roam, on land on sea or on foam, you can always hear me singing this song, show me the way to go hoooome—"

Give us a wee shot, Bartend. Just a drop. That's good. Looks like a full shot left. What the hell time—

Quarter past eight. Fine. Leave at nine. Nine sharp. Something to look forward to. Something to do. Those great parties after the plays—

Freddy and Alan and I in the back seat. Show me the way to go home. And: "There is a tavern in the town, in the town, and there my true love sits him down, sits him dowowown—"

Could always stop in at that dark bar on the way. No, can't go in there. That's a Black alkies' bar. I'd have to talk to them. Jesus wouldn't that make a funny picture? "Drinks his wine just as happy as can be, and never, never thinks of me, thinks of me."

Like you, you bastard! Some big lover you turned out to be! Telling me you can't live without me then running off to visit your daughter first chance you get. How the hell do I know where you are? There's no phone up there. Could've used that as an excuse. How do I know you don't have another—

Just like two years ago. That cockeyed floozy with the big tits—

I'll never trust you. You say yourself you're unreliable. Well, I know that, goddammit! Could've gotten me my liquor before you took off with the car. That old piece of junk. Why didn't you take my car when I offered it to you? No you'll just break down and—

My car? I'm not driving that car! I'm not touching it. What if anything happens to Dolf? He's bound to have another heart attack any minute. I expect it every time the phone rings. Mabel's voice: Your father's in the hospital, but don't run out, he died instantly, we found him at the bottom of the spiral staircase—

I need that car. I may have to go there any day. I can't depend on your old jalopy. Maybe you think it's fine, but I wouldn't trust it in an emergency. I'll need a car to get out there, take care of things. I'm the only one. It all falls on me. Christ! I wish he'd hurry up. Every time the phone rings—

I'm not calling you any more, Daddy. You got your maid, so screw you. Spend all your money on maids and kids to mow the place. You don't need me. That's right. Stay there by yourself and die of a heart attack let Mabel find you. I'd much rather it that way. I don't want to go through it again. Not like with Libby—

You! Don't judge me about my father. You can't imagine how painful! You were damn lucky not to have any parents. You never had the responsibility. Wouldn't have done a damn thing for them if you had— Look at those seven kids you've littered behind you, never send them a lousy dime—

I used to go there and cook for her. All she ever wanted was eggdrop soup. And I'd take it up to her. Up the spiral stairs, my hands shaking, little china bowl rattling.... I couldn't bear it. Wasted away like that. Her eyes. Yellow. I couldn't face her. Oh, but I did. I saw it through to the gruesome end. And then Janey too. That was almost worse. She was so weak—

Christ, I wish you'd hurry up, Daddy. How long do you think I can hold out after I get my divorce money? It's not going to be that much. Ed'll only get forty thousand for that house after mortgage. That'll give me a lousy twenty thousand. Know how long that'll last in this city? And the liquor taxes! Shit, I should move back to New Jersey!

Can't afford to live in this lousy hole much longer. What the hell am I doing here anyway? I'm not in love with you anymore. You run off to god-knows-where leave me to go out in the rain get soaked, catch a cold. You call that taking care of me? Your treasure? God, how could I be so foolish, fall for a cheap line like that? What the hell am I here for? You don't need me. Your treasure. Ha! You can take your goddamn treasure and—

I don't give a damn about our romance. It's over. You kid me along. I know it's over for you too. You can't live with me. You need your goddamn independence. Well what about my goddamn independence? You think I couldn't make it on my own? You think you are so friggin' desirable anymore? You're a fucking old man. You don't even have a goddamn prostate. Even Dolf still has his prostate. You've got white hair. You're on social security. What the hell, you're not going to be around that much longer. You think you can take me for granted. You're going to need a nurse soon yourself. You and Dolf. You act like it's a goddamn invasion of your privacy, but when you're flat on your backs you'll be calling to me. And you're going to have to beg. I'm not playing nursie for nothing.

I took her eggrop soup because I loved her. Because she was my mother. But I don't know about you. You can call one of your ex-wives. Call your daughter. Call one of your sons.

And Daddy, you'd better have that heart attack soon. I'm not going through it all again with you now. If you live long enough to get cancer—

I'm sick of your attitude. You won't admit you're a helpless feeble old man. You're not going to find another wife, Daddy. Who'd be crazy enough to marry you? One whiff and they smell death in that house. You're going to end up like Old Hank prone in the living room stinking up the whole place unable to roll over—

God, all the people that've died in that house. Grandmama, then Hank, and then Mrs. Alcott, and Libby almost did before the hospital, and Janey, and then Rosy—

I couldn't live there. Don't want to have to. Just want to get rid of the place. And all that junk! What does one do? Haul it to an auction? I don't know anything about antiques. I don't know anyone there except Mabel. How helpful can she be? She's practically blind, for crissake.   Some of that junk must be worth something. Don't want to have an experience like Ed's mother with that conman lawyer sold her husband's stamp collection for one fifth of what it was worth—

Probably get ripped off. What the hell do I know about antiques? I wouldn't know how to get them appraised. What does one do, look in the yellow pages? Some day I'll be in that house all alone, you'll be—

Christ, I'll have to get you cremated won't I? And then you'll want the goddamn ashes scattered in the orchard. Oh, I can't do that. Maybe one of the kids—

Yes, let the kids. It'll be good for them. They've always been so protected from it. I wouldn't let them see her when she was that bad. She'd agreed. The kids mustn't see her like that. I saw her. Her own daughter. If I could, they could. We should have let them. At least the girls. Not Sam, though. He was too sensitive. Only one that cried at the crematory chapel, poor kid. Nobody'd explained anything to him. I have to admit, it came as a bit of a surprise when the coffin sank through the floor like that.

I didn't know it was going to happen myself. The man looked at Dolf, he nodded, there was a buzzing sound, then it started sinking through the floor, a steady whir of machinery and down it went, straight to the waiting ovens—what a fate for a Jew! Then, with a soft bang, the floor boards closed again and that was that. Well, we'll have to do it again with you Dolfi, you goddamn—

I'm not keeping your ashes around in a lousy urn until apple blossom time. No way. Let the kids do it. They all act so sentimental about the place. Well let them pay the goddamn taxes on it then! Let them keep up the lawns and the flower beds all overgrown now, put new roofs on the barn and guest house, fix the front fence. Let them paint it and clean it, get rid of all the accumulated lifetimes of junk. I can't even face it. There's still a trunk or two of Libby's up there, and now all Janey's stuff they never came and got. Why the hell they took her silverware and not her clothes; if they'd wanted her valuables so badly they could've taken her junk too. Why should my father—

They were only married two years. And she brought a lifetime's worth of stuff. They didn't even want her homemade dolls. You'd think they'd have some sentimental value for her granddaughter, but no. The dolls are still there in the basket in the closet. I don't know what to do with them. If the kids don't want them, I'll have to throw them away. Breaks my heart, too. She'd made those dolls for me, the summer I went to live with her and Harry, the summer Libby was in Washington with the Red Cross and that nice crippled British guy with the tickly red mustache—what was his name? I think it was Howard, but, no, maybe Harold, or Howarth? Oh, just let it go…. Daddy, you were overseas. You wrote me funny letters, remember the one about the French can't-can't girls, and your funny little drawings? Funny, Daddy I missed you then, oh, much more than I missed Libby…. Janey was a second mother, always, in some ways I loved her more—

Certainly as much. She couldn't handle him though. Libby always told him to shut up. But not Janey. She couldn't. She was too soft, too goddamn sweet. I can't control him, she said. He never listens to me. No respect for me whatsoever. When did he ever have a kind word to say?

Kind! You wouldn't know kindness if it bit you! You thought you were such a saint when they were dying. Well, it's a good thing they each got a few hours of peace in the hospital finally—

No, that's not quite fair. I must admit you put up with a lot. You were good about cooking for them. And you brought Janey's meals on those tiny dishes. She ate practically nothing then. But still, you did cook for them and—

Christ, I had to fight you to do their laundry though. It's not worth it. You die out there alone, you old fool! Let me know when it's over. I've had enough of death. I've got troubles of my own. You don't want me to interfere with your death? Fine, I won't interfere then. That's the last thing I'd think of doing. Hell no! You can die out there all alone. I'll wait here for Mabel's call. There's nothing to do but wait anyhow. The kids can go look in on you if they want. I've had it. All you want to do is yell at me when I'm there. You won't let us come and help out—

He'd drive. He's got his jalopy. We could stay in the guest house. But no. You want to stick it out alone. You just do that. Die out there. They won't find the body for days. Wait'll the maid comes. Wait'll Mabel makes her once-a-week check. You could be a week old and stinking—

Who the hell will care? I don't feel responsible. Not if you won't let me, Daddy.

Ah shit. I'd better go to the bathroom. This place is so depressing in the rain. Dirty grimy windows, can't clean them, smog would just dirty them again right away. What am I doing in all this filth? Look at this bathroom floor! I'm not going to wash it. You can damn well do some of the cleaning—

You don't give a shit, that's your problem. You're just like Ed. All of you. Dolf! Look at the pigsty he lived in before he got his maid—

Filth everywhere! The dust I found under the piano was incredible! Well, I'm not doing any more of it—

This is your pad; you built up the dirt in these tiles here. You can damn well get down on your knees and scrub it if you care. I don't care. Why should I? It's not my apartment. Shit, no toilet paper. That's right, it ran out last night and I checked the cabinet—

I don't give a damn. Don't care what I smell like living alone. Who the hell's going to smell me? The guys in the liquor store? They're used to stinky old street bums, hardly going to notice—

Look at this soap, all black. You could damn well rinse it off after…. You old men with your gnarled hands solid black under the fingernails, worse than little boys!

Why bother with the hair? Let it hang loose. But I won't be able to see. Gotta see. They could come up suddenly from the side and I might not catch a glimpse before it's too late—

Okay, that's better. Put the other barrette in. There. At least that'll keep it out of my eyes when it gets wet. Goddamn rain. Whole day's going to be so damned depressing. Well, I hope it's raining on you too. Hey, maybe you'll come home early because of the rain—

Maybe it's snowing up there and not raining. It could be snowing. Then you'd have to start back early to be sure to make it out. You'd do that wouldn't you? Or would you call and say you were stuck? It's snowing so hard I can't get out. Oh, you bastard! You would wait too long and then tell me that. But how would you tell me? There isn't even a goddamn phone up there! You wouldn't even be able to call! Oh, for crissake. I'd better get an extra fifth. God only knows how long—

How much cash do I have? Oh why does this always have to happen to me? You could've foreseen it. You don't give a damn about me. You should have taken care of it before you left. You're the one who likes it here so goddamn much. What the hell are you doing up there?

It must be snowing in Vermont if it's raining down here. Great. That's just great. You won't make it home tomorrow. And what will I do all that time? I'll get sick and no one will find me. You'll come back and find me lying there by the bed. It'll be all your damned fault. You won't care. You don't care what happens to me. Nobody ever gave a goddamn about me. Let her die. Why didn't you, Ed? Why the hell didn't you let me? You were always saying I should go ahead and do it. Well I tried, didn't I? I tried to do it and you had to get in the way. The one time I almost succeeded at doing what everybody all my life has always wished I would—

Two hundred and sixty-five and don't bother with the change. I guess that'll be enough. Unless, of course, there were an emergency—

Nobody really cared; nobody gave a damn whether I lived or died. The kids don't need me. The kids'll never need me again what the hell is left? Won't have any grandchildren. They'll never have any children. They won't even get married. Why should they? What the hell did it do for me? I should never have bothered. I should never have bothered going on after they told me I was—

But lots of people get depressed. And they go on. It seemed like something I could live with at the time. Alright, so I lived with it. I controlled it pretty well, didn't I? I functioned. Held a job, took care of you Ed, and your children and your house and did plenty of other things besides. Went on and on, coping, managing. I took care of it myself. I had to. Nobody did a bloody thing for me. Worthless doctors. I suffered it out, though. I was brave. Wasn't I brave, Ed?

Oh, you wouldn't know. You were so spoiled rotten by your mother. You could do no wrong. Everybody always loved you. You just drift right along. Nothing bothers you. You don't give a damn for anybody but yourself, that's why. You never took care of the children when they were sick. You only had yourself to take care of. Oh, alright, you worked, you paid bills, big deal.

Big deal, Ed. You drove off every morning and blissfully forgot about us all. Could forget about everything. Come home and down your three martinis so you could forget about us even more. You just disappeared into your cloud when you didn't want to be bothered by any of it. You didn't have to live with it day to day. Oh, I suppose you'd condescend to get involved with us on weekends—

What's the use? It's all over and done with now. You got rid of it, didn't you? Your problem. It wouldn't go away but you managed to get rid of it. You divorced it and it went away. You don't have to face it anymore. Congratulations, Ed!

Oh you! You get the problem now. You've been slipped some damaged goods, dontcha know mister? You'll come back from your happy little weekend in Vermont and it'll be lying here on the floor dying of pneumonia and you'll have to deal with it. Or maybe it'll already be dead and all you'll have to do is dispose of it. Well, you'll have to deal with that then. Nobody's going to help you. The children won't bother to show up. They'll be off with their friends and boyfriends. No, they wouldn't come. It's all your baby now. You wanted it then. You don't want it now. And you'll be glad to get rid of it. You make me sick! Just go running off for the weekend when you know damned well I'm not going to make it on the little bit you left me with, two hundred sixty-five and change; you know I can't survive—

Have to go out into that jungle. Why the hell you have to live here—

What am I doing here? It used to be fun. We'd meet for lunch in a nice restaurant. You'd buy me martinis, take me for walks in the park. You always brought flowers. You never bring me flowers now. How quickly it all dies! You don't love me anymore. You don't even care what happens to me. Go off and leave me—

***

I can't go out there. They'll knife me. They'll knock me down and rape me. In an alley. In the rain. And it'll all be your fault. As if you gave a damn. Of course you don't. You're like all the rest now. Waiting. Just waiting for a chance to get rid of her...

Where the hell else do you think I have to go? I can't go to Dolf. He's an old man. He's a senile old man with two heart attacks behind him. He's kidding himself if he thinks he's going to find anyone else to marry him. He's had three wives. What the hell more does he expect? He won't let anyone take care of him. Stubborn bastard. Let him die there alone.

I'll get the phone call in the middle of the night. I'll be the one who has to drive all that way alone in the middle of the night and take care of things. It'll be pitch black, probably raining just like this, or snowing, and besides, I won't be able to get the car out of the parking lot, everybody'll be blocking me in, and I'll have a flat because one of the vandals here will've knifed the tire, and there I'll be, standing out in the cold and dark and snow with my father in the funeral home and I won't be able to find anyone to help me. And that's what I have to look forward to. That's all there is left for me now. Whoopee! Lucky me! Jesus Christ, what a lot to live for.

What a life, what a friggin' joke! And I tried to get out of it. God knows I really meant it that time. Oh, Ed, I hated you so much. I wanted you to find me. Sure I wanted you to find me. When it was too late. Then you would've been sorry. What a bloody mess. You self-righteous—

Bastard! You bastard! You could've left well enough alone. Why did you have to louse it up? Leave me to this miserable fate. Stuck up here in this wretched apartment in the middle of this filthy jungle full of Blacks I don't know or trust—

No one cares about me now. You've made it impossible, Ed. The kids won't come to see me here. First you have to save me, you big hero, then you turn around and abandon me! You fool! You idiot! Why the hell did you have to interfere? You wanted me to do it. You said so enough times. You should have been glad. You should have let me. Even when you found me you could've waited. A little longer and it all would've been so unnecessary. Goddamn divorce! So, you finally got what you'd wanted all those years and hadn't had the balls to do anything about.

Naturally, I had to set it all up for you. I had to get it started. You never would've done it—you could never do a damn thing without me pushing you. You can't motivate yourself, so goddamn lazy. You make me sick with your lazy, procrastinating, cowardly—

Well, you got your damn divorce, thanks to me. And now I hope you're miserable because you won't be able to do a goddamn thing now that I'm gone. You'll just sit there and drink and eat chocolate and peanuts and get fatter and never do a laundry or the dishes and the house will fill up with your goddamn newspapers and magazines and catch fire some night when you're passed out drunk. I hope it does! I'd like to think you'll burn up in that house now. You and all the rotten furniture and the kids' junk—

I hope to hell it burns to the ground because I never want to see any of it again. I never want to see you again. You can do what you want with the goddamn house now.

I never answered your lousy letter because I don't have to do another damn thing for you. That's your tough luck now, isn't it? You divorced her, and now she's not responsible for making you get anything done anymore. Simple enough for you? I'll never have to get involved with anything of yours ever again. You wanted it that way. I don't exist as far as you're concerned. You get rid of me, you can get rid of my things too. And all that junk in the house—

I'm never setting foot in there again. I don't care what you do with any of it. That's your problem, mister, all yours. Good luck! I know you'll never get it done. You'll sit there and sit there night after night martini after martini and nothing will get done and you'll never sell the house and I'll never see my twenty thousand—

But that's not my problem now. You want me to starve? You want me to die because I can't afford to go to a doctor because you can't sell the house and give me my share? That's on your conscience, baby, not mine. You think you're free of me, but you're not. Not legally. Not 'til I get my half of the money for the house. And if I drop dead because you don't sell the house, that'll be your own damn fault. I don't care. What the hell should I care if I drop dead at this point? It's all over for me, baby. I don't have to prove a goddamn thing. I stand on my record. I have my accomplishments. My conscience is clear. I did enough for the world, now I'm going to sit back and enjoy the one thing I love. I'm going to drink all day and all night and stink if I want because there's nothing left for me. I've done enough.

I've had my lovers. Do you have any idea, Margot, what it means to be desired by a man....?

You ever have any goddamn romances, eh, Ed? Wake up! I asked you, did you ever have any goddamn romances? Well I thought not. What the hell's wrong with you? You didn't want to try out anyone else? You afraid or something? Such a coward. So scared of taking action. You never got anything out of life because you never dared to get off your fat ass and live!

Oh hell. What does it matter? You're happy just lumping along, going nowhere, doing nothing, being nothing, so smugly self-satisfied, your mother's own self-righteous goody-goody, never take risks, never really live your one life. You'll regret it. You'll look back in your dotage, a fat, dull blob, and you'll wish you'd tasted it like I did.

Oh, when he'd call me at work and we'd arrange to meet next Tuesday and I'd have that to look forward to and hold in the back of my head all day and night and dream about at night when you were passed out snoring and I had the yellow lamp and the typewriter and the bourbon glass—

You had your business trips too. You could've taken advantage of the conferences you went to. Jesus, even I had the sense to get a little something out of my conventions—

UUUUUM, a little taste will take me back—

Bourbon Street, those old-fashioned lamp posts, three of us leaning on one together out in the air, smoky bar behind us oozing saxes loud and yet muffled by the scuffles, voices and tinks of glass, his sweaty red face swings into mine breathes out a bourbon blast: "Ophelia, let me see you home?"

"You should let us both see you home, old boy," you chime in from the other side of me. I sneak a peek at you and your eyes are winking, face unflushed. I feel a hand pat me through the red mini-skirt, through the black silk slip, above the garters, for a split second, I wondered, but then, it was obviously yours. He couldn't have possibly….although he tried to edge you out. Taking my arm and swinging me, practically smack into a car—

"Lessss go. He can take care of himself." And I had to laugh. It had been so wonderful sitting there between the two of you, first one foot on mine, then another, then one hand here, a thigh pressed…I began to lose track whose was whose, and I loved you both. Equal. The same. He was so funny, and charmingly competitive, hot, and carried away, lost in the moment, in love with it too much, interpreting every note for me…. And you, so cool. You and your pretended aloofness while a hand snuck in under my blouse, and you couldn't wait 'til he left for the men's room, could you?

I had you both literally drooling in anticipation, didn't I campers? It was all leading up to this, the final showdown, and now he was about to pass out on me, and I'd wanted him, too. Now you were going to win, but it wasn't fair! He'd fought so hard and really won my heart, if you'd won my mind. I had to hope…

Maybe I could sober him up. Go to you first, then find an excuse to leave after he'd had a few hours to sleep it off, maybe then…. Well, you had the nerve to threaten to cut out on us! Like you didn't need me after all. Right! What were you thinking, make a show of going across the street to that strip joint, pick up some whore? You were red hot for me, and you'd never let him beat you out. Somehow, I knew you didn't mean it. So you came with us in the taxi, and we got him in his bed.

Poor Martin! You were so beautiful, yet so frail! Couldn't hold out another minute. I wanted you so. Wished for a moment he would leave and I could stay with you. I'd have lain quietly beside you, could have mopped your brow all night, waited for you to come 'round…. It was no good. He had me then.

You had me then, and yet you continued to play it coy, you beast! Threatening once more to leave us there together. Well, perhaps you should have, I wouldn't be here now—

But you surprised me. Closed the door behind us, the lock clicked. You snatched off the lights and pulled my wrist hard, over by the window, pulled the curtains, I was sure he'd wake up—didn't even stir. Then you tore my blouse off so roughly, I was sure a button fell, but somehow, no. You really impressed me with your one-handed dexterity on the brassiere, but then a man with four wives….

And you guzzled me, so noisy, all I could think was poor Martin, he was going to hear you. He'd come to and try to break us up, maybe swing at you, end up flinging himself out the window when he missed—

And you were rough and fast and growling, deep animal tones, I'd never had it like that. I was as scared as I was thrilled, as reduced as I'd been inflated. You made me feel like a little girl, your hand rough as bark now stripping my black stockings, now cupping my crotch, threatening to tear those expensive new lace panties I hadn't even had a chance to try out on Martin yet—

But the really beautiful, the really ingenious part of it was your ending. You knew, you bastard! You knew all the time that I'd go back later for number two. So what do you do? You slimy bastard, oh, God, I admired you for it—what a gesture! Thank god you didn't hurt him when you threw me on the bed. He never woke up! You zipped your fly with a flourish and—oh, God, I can still hear your cynical "Sweet dreams…."—the lock clicked behind you. I pretended I'd passed out in Martin's arms. I was too pulverized to move a whit.

Why the hell not? Men do it. Women can do it too. Oh, but not Edgar. Not holy Edgar. What the hell's wrong with you, you scared bunny? Well, you'll have plenty of chances now. Oh, but you'll make an idiot of yourself. You'll go after some little twenty-three year old secretary and be the laughing stock of your department for months until she embarrasses you in front of your boss or somebody

and you slink off tail between your legs. You won't
even know how to get started having affairs without
me!

OH, GIVE ME A DRINK!

You know what your problem is, Edgar? You
need a woman prodding you. You've always had a
woman telling you what to do. Your mother. Your
goddamn mother did all your thinking and directing.
Bought you all your goddamn clothes 'til you were
fifty. Such a mama's boy.

So naturally I fell right into her role. I could
tell way back in Idaho you needed me to give you
pushes. You needed more than encouragement.
You needed somebody bossy, somebody giving you
direct orders. Okay, so I did it. I played along. And
then when I'd get sick or depressed and was
helpless, you'd look at me like some sort of freak,
like some colossal disappointment, because I'd
ceased to function as your mommy-prod. You never
knew how to help me, to comfort me or to do a
damn thing for me without me telling you exactly
what to do and how to do it. You needed me
directing and supervising even from the hospital bed.

When the children were being born I wrote
you long lists. I bought all the groceries way ahead
of time and froze casseroles so you would all get fed.
And still I'd come home to heaps of dirty laundry and
dishes. You were useless to me. Utterly useless.
Frieda was a bigger help but she could only be

counted on for some things, especially when she was small and the other children even smaller. I needed someone who would help me, who would be my partner, who would share my load. Not to push me. I never needed that like you did. I could motivate myself, discipline myself. All I ever needed, all I ever asked for was a little cooperation. All you had to do was occasionally think of doing something on your own and do it, without having to be given full instructions. But no. You got so damned lazy.

I was sick of it. Sick to death of it for years. I lost respect for you, hated you, even though I still loved you sometimes. You never hated me or loved me. You were too friggin' selfish to know I existed half the time. You just kept me around to keep you going: to get out the door in the morning and to bed at night, and out the door in the morning. I tried to help you get up the nerve to ask for a raise or a better position, but you could never follow through. You never had the balls to get anywhere yourself. If mommy weren't there telling you it was okay to do it, please do it Edgar, you never did it. Like a stubborn introverted brat who was always sneaking off to his treehouse to play with his model airplanes....

Oh, Ed, you helpless baby! I had three children, but none was ever such a baby as you. Such a little prig, too good and too lazy to live with, you were always right, you were always sane, you were always healthy and you were always nice. I couldn't stand it! Naturally I was crazy compared to you—sick, wicked, sinful next to you. Your own friggin' Christian mother wasn't any help: "Oh, my Edgar can do no wrong. Edgar is right dear, you must listen to him, you must obey him, Ophelia, dear, he is your husband, Edgar knows what's best because I brought him up that way...."

You go rot. You and your cancer face. You can go to your dear little Edgar now, Iris! I hope you do go and live with him. I hope Nora gets hit by a truck on Fifth Avenue and you have to go live with sonny-boy. Oh Jesus, that would be divine justice! You go live with him and be his daily torture, lecture him on drinking, on religion, drag him off to church each Sunday, drive the bastard crazy for me, as only you Iris, and your Christian martyrdom could. I hope that thing eats its way through your eye right into your brain and you squirm for years as your nerves get all chewed up. You can make Edgar read the Bible to you night and day—

Oh, you make me laugh. You wanted my children brought up to believe that nonsense so they could grow little harmless skin cancers into great big killers with the help of God. Boy, how stupid. You could at least have waited 'til something got you from the inside out. At least you'd be something one could look at instead of a damned bloody Cyclops. For all your prayers and scriptures, teachings and readings—

Hell, I'm going to enjoy your dying. If I'm lucky enough to hear about it. Of course I'll never have to see you again, thank God. Hey, at least you've given me one nice benefit, Ed. I'll never have to look Iris in the eye again, thank the lord! Never could stand your mother, Ed. You knew it. You used her to further undermine me. Naturally I was crazy next to her, the righteous bitch. Tells me how to raise my kids: "Don't vaccinate them, oh, you know that's just poison you mustn't take their temperatures, there's no need for a cast, his arm will heal, the Bible says—"

Bullshit lady! Your mother's going to come live with you and ruin it for you now Ed. Well, you two deserve each other. Mumzy can have her precious wittle Edgar now that I'm through with him. How do you like your blue-eyed boy, Iris? He drinks too much, eats too much, picks his nose, spends hours in the bathroom reading magazines, wears the same dingy shirts, the same drab suits he's had since the fifties, speaks the same worn-out lines, too. Lucky woman gets you this time around!

And at least Daddy will die hard and fast with another heart attack soon and leave me the house and there you'll be with your ever-rotting mother hanging on, driving you crazier than I ever could. If only Dolf would hurry up. Especially if you're never going to sell the house, give me my half. At least I'll have my daddy's place for security. It makes me so nervous. Any day now, any night, the phone will ring, it'll be raining and the car will be all blocked in—

This is never going to let up. What time—

Jesus Christ. It opens in twenty minutes! Alright. I'm going to have just a sip now and then I'm getting dressed. Just a tiny taste. Leave the last big one for going out in this crap. Look at it! Rain rain rain cold wet filthy dog of a city. One helluva nice life you gave me, Ed. Condemned to this. Now it'll be some Black punk's knife in the back instead of a peaceful, pillful sleep. Oh, thanks a lot!

AHHHH. TSSSSST. That's all now. Maybe I should get two big bourbons and one small gin— better make it a fifth—refill the flask and still get smashed. What else is there to do? Nowhere to go, no one to talk to. You're not even here to play Scrabble, let alone go for our one o'clock—

Nothing on TV today. Even less tomorrow. No soaps. No game shows. Almost finished the last of my books. Library closed tomorrow. Nothing to read. Not even a paper. Could buy a paper at the corner drug—

No, no that would take too much time. Would have to face another cashier. What the hell do I care what's happening in the world. Won't be anything new in the job listings. Nobody's going to call me back. I'm never going to get a damned job. Who the hell would hire me? Too old. Too qualified. That's a nice way of saying it mister. You're all a bunch of hypocrites, liars, can't call a spade a spade. I haven't got the chances of a spade in this holy city. Can't even go on Welfare. Can't get social security for another fifteen years. What the hell am I supposed to live on, will somebody please tell me that?

Might as well wear these pants again. Who the hell's going to see me? What do I care what I look like now? The dirtier the better. Don't even have any clothes that fit. How in God's name am I supposed to buy clothes? With what? What money do I have? You won't sell the goddamn house, I'll have to go around in these 'til they fall to shreds. Could somebody tell me how, for crissake, am I supposed to get a job when I don't even have any decent clothes to wear to interviews?
This shirt of yours—

Coffee stains on the sleeves here. Great. Why don't you wash your damn shirts once in a blue moon? Just because you don't care—

Did you ever think I might? You're balder than my father. Charming, really charming, aintcha? Not going to outlast me; then what the hell will I do? Can't afford this place alone. Guess I'll have to find some efficiency somewhere, under the trolley tracks no doubt. Boy, wouldn't that be lover-ly. Dolf'll go on and on after you're gone and I'll never see the money from that house. Don't want the house. What the hell am I going to d do with all those antiques? Have to auction it somehow. Taxes are terrible. Can't pay the damn taxes. Nobody'll want to. Won't get much for it if I do get to sell it someday. What if I need a doctor? Well, that'll just be too bad, now won't it? You don't have to concern yourself now, Ed. You're a free man—

Better take this ring off, and this bracelet, don't want to tempt them. Don't want to die without the ring. Well, what difference will it make anyway? Better the kids should have them. Damn, this knuckle! There. Feel naked without my ring. The one thing in the world you ever got me that I really wanted—

No, no kid's going to get it. I want to take it with me. They can burn it too. Some damn undertaker'll rake it out of the ashes. What the hell do I care what happens to it?

Ought to hold onto it though. Probably have to take it to a pawn shop soon. Maybe take the emeralds out, pawn the gold. Buy bourbon—

Don't need to comb this, just get it back out of my face. There. Oh, I can't stand looking at her. A different person. I don't know her. She came in the night. The other one's never coming back so don't bother looking for her. There. Great. What a slob—

Don't you remember? Don't you remember how it was? How wonderful every day was when it was just us two? Just you and me, my pretty bright baby? The mornings we spent—

There was so much to do. We'd get you up and put your little clothes on, and make Daddy's breakfast. I'd let you pick out the eggs. Daddy would shave and we'd set the table and put the pretty eggcups out. You loved those eggcups. Especially the one with the funny face. That was your special eggcup, and we'd put it at your place. And then Daddy would kiss us both and we'd smell his shaving cream, and then he'd go get in the blue Pontiac. And remember how you always waved to him from the living room window and he waved from the car as he backed out the driveway, and then you'd look at me and chirp: "Well, mommy, what are we going to do today?" and I'd say: "Well, first we're going to do the dishes," and you'd help me bring the dishes from the table, "And then we're going to do the laundry," and we'd go down to the cellar together and you'd play with the big cardboard bricks that Daddy and I spent all Christmas Eve putting together for you, and then maybe we'd go out into the yard and weed the garden for a while, or go over and visit old Mrs. Gallagher next door and she'd give you fresh-baked cookies and we'd have tea in the sunny kitchen with all the African violets, and then maybe we'd go home and dust and vacuum the downstairs, you had your little carpet sweeper, and we'd chat—

You were the best friend I had. The best person to talk to. We'd chat all day together, and I never got bored, you were such a delight to me. And then I'd read to you after lunch and we'd take our naps together and then maybe we'd go shopping in the afternoon and you'd ride in the fold-out seat in the shopping cart—you loved that—or you'd play in the sandbox while I read the *Times* magazine.

And we planted tulips around the mailbox together; you had your own little trowel Libby bought you. You loved to plant things. We put in those spider plants outside the cellar doors, you remember the sweet, sticky spider plants? Of course not. Well, Mommy does. Mommy remembers every single one of those days. Every one was happy. And we'd get excited when Daddy was coming home. As cars went by you'd run to the window and come tell me in the kitchen, and I'd be making something special for Daddy because we loved him then—

And then he'd lift you up and tickle you and he'd kiss me and we'd all sit down on the couch together and he'd talk to us and ask us what we did that day. And Daddy would read to you at night and then we'd put you in your little kewpie doll pajamas—of course if it was winter then we'd put you in your yellow bunny-sack with the feet, and you were a little yellow bunny from top to toe. And you had your rabbit and your blankie too.

Remember your rabbit? How you wouldn't go to bed without him, and sometimes you'd put him somewhere during the day and we'd all have to go on a rabbit hunt, and we'd always find him eventually, and you'd spank your rabbit and tell him never to hide from you again, do you remember? Your rabbit and your blankie—the one with the pink roses on it. Libby got you that blanket at Saks Fifth Avenue. It was real silk quilt. I still have it in the trunk in the attic—

And all your toys and books, and your little shirts and blouses and the red velvet dress your grandma Iris made you for Christmas—

Remember the Christmases we used to have? When all three of you were little and it would snow the night we'd drive to Libby and Dolf's and you kids would be all huddled up in blankets in the back, and we'd drive though the snowy night and you'd be asleep by the time we got there and you'd give sleepy kisses to Libby and Dolf and we'd put you right to bed, the girls in the little bed that used to be Dolf's when he was a boy and Sammy in the trundle bed we'd pull out from underneath—

You always thought that trundle bed was something special. Well, it was. And the next night they'd have the big party and you all got to come down and say hello to everyone and you were always so sweet and charming and everyone always said so, and we'd let you have some of the eggnog and the marzipan candies we'd made together and let you admire the Christmas tree and play with the little unicycling clown on the string, and then it was back to bed with you, and Dolf and I would hang the stockings and fill them and we'd clean everything up after all the guests were gone and there would always be boxes of chocolates and fancy fruit cakes and petitfours people had brought, and finally we'd go upstairs to bed and it would be snowing out and we'd unplug the Christmas candles in the windows and turn on the electric blanket, and we'd go in and check on you one last time and you'd be curled up asleep, Sam in the trundle bed, and we'd cover you up and kiss your curly sweet-smelling little heads—

Damn you kids! Why did you ever have to grow up? All of you! You think you're so clever. You can all go to hell. You had no right. It was none of your goddamn business. I knew what I was doing. You had no right to interfere. You think it's so easy. You try it. You try living with a depression no one and nothing can help. You try living when it's all over and never coming back and you're all used up and sexless and nobody wants you, nobody cares—

All you have to look forward to is death anyway, so why waste all that time and energy? Why use up that much more of the earth's resources? Why take food from starving babies? Why bother, when you're not getting anything out of it and apparently neither is anyone else? Your husband doesn't care. Your children don't care.

Your children don't even remember when they did care. Neither does your lover. They're all so busy running around leading their own selfish lives, it makes you want to puke! All they've meant to you, all you've done for them—

Well, I could see it wasn't suddenly going to change. Sam was leaving and he was the last, and Ed, you and I would have stopped talking altogether and I couldn't have stood it another week. You drag me away from everything I know and love and when I don't get too excited about it you turn around and threaten to leave me, tell me to go drown in a lake. Some loving husband you are, some good provider! So what if you can feed a family of five—then only three and a dog and a cat—if you can't get it up to show any feelings for anyone? Big provider—you couldn't even provide a wife's basic needs for happiness. You didn't love her. You were sick to death of her. She was nothing but a big goddamn drag to you. You were hoping she'd just quietly go away....

But then oh then, you bloody coward! When she did oblige you, you had a little change of heart. Conscience struck, didn't it? You couldn't have that on your conscience. Oh no! You wouldn't be able to forget her so easily then. If only she'd gotten away with it. She was only trying to do you a favor, Edgar. Couldn't have gotten a cheaper divorce. Wouldn't have cost you more than the gas in your car to go to the morgue and identify the body—

Oh, and your time for that. I guess you'd have to take off work. You think they wouldn't've let you take an hour out to go down and identify your wife's corpse? You would've been afraid to ask for it!

"I need an hour to run down to the morgue."

"What for Ed?"

"Got to make sure it's my wife they've got down there."

"Well, I don't know, Ed, there's the budget meeting at ten, and we want you to give that report, it's very important—"

Look, you idiot, I did the smart thing. I knew it was hopeless; look at me now. I knew this was the way it would be. I looked ahead and saw this and wasn't so sure I wanted it. I was right then: it stinks. I don't want it now either. It's miserable. So now I'm a prisoner of it. I can't even get any more pills. I can't afford to go to a doctor.

No need to try it now anyway. Booze'll do it sooner or later. Won't feel much in the meantime though. Christ, won't be feeling much if I can get out there and get the goddamn bourbon before I start going up a wall here—

Thank you, Ed, my savior, my big deliverer from the jaws of death. Thanks for the wonderful life you've left me to. You've taken care of everything now, haven't you? Got a clear conscience now, I'm happy for you. Anything happens to her now it's not your responsibility. You're a free man, Ed! You don't have to think of anyone but your pudgy self, don't have to talk to anyone when you come home, nobody asks you to fix them a martini, nobody asks you to help with math homework, no dog asks to be taken for a walk. That was too goddamn awful wasn't it, having a wife and kids to come home to, a nice clean house with dinner on the table? That's not what you wanted out of life I suppose. You wanted yourself. Well, you've got yourself. You can fuck yourself now, Ed.

Well, I can't wait any longer. Go out in the goddamn rain catch a cold get knifed. Got to do everything myself nobody ever thinks of me or my needs. Nobody'd think of taking care of me. Hell no! I'm the one who has to think for everyone else, take care of everyone else. Nobody ever did a goddamn thing for me. Think I'm so bloody strong, regular cornucopia: Give give give. Take care of the house and the kids the clothes the shopping the meals the dishes the sick kids, the mongoloids the psychologists—

Here's to you worthless parasites! You helpless women talk my ear off—what have you ever given me? You dump all your troubles on my head for years, think I never had any of my own? Oh, I never expected anything from you. You were all just jealous because men found me so attractive.   You

think that was all a bowl of jelly? They were just a
bunch of horny parasites too—

Goddamn it, nobody ever thinks I might have
needs, I might have limitations of my own. Oh,
heaven forbid! She can't have problems, we need
her. The League needs her, the Board needs her, the
Council needs her—she has to give, give, give, that's
her role in life. She gives, we take, that's the way it's
always been that's the way it'll always be.

Even you. What the hell do you give me
now? Okay, so you pay the rent. Big deal. You're
only biding your time expecting to cash in when Dolf
dies and leaves me the place. The joke's on you
buddy. He's going to outlive us all. You're wasting
your time playing vulture. Why don't you just drive
off for three days and leave me here to die of
pneumonia out in this miserable—

Leave me here to get raped and knifed on the
way to the liquor store. Hope you and your darling
daughter are enjoying yourselves. Probably getting
snowed in together right now, oh won't that be cozy.
You'll find me dead if you don't come back tomorrow
like you promised. Come back to a stinking corpse—

Well, where's that filthy jacket of yours? I'm
not wearing mine out in this weather. Why don't
you ever take it to the cleaners? Expect me to,
naturally. Take your big black umbrella too.
Nobody'll see me—don't give a damn what I look like
anymore. Glad I'm ugly. For the first time in my life,

71

finally, I don't have to hear it anymore. No more broad, dame, cheesecake, doll, no wolf whistles—

Here's to the goddamn men in my life! TSSSSST!

Well, that's that. Don't care if I leave one lousy light on. You can worry about the goddamn electric bill, it's in your damn name. It's going to cost a lot when I get sick, and where the hell do you think the money's going to come from? Your goddamn Social Security pays for your prostate operation, what the hell do I have—

Goddammit! When are you going to get this lock fixed? I can't open the damn door without a lot of—

OH, HELLO PAULA—

II. Iris

OOOOOMMMMM.

What a sweet smell!

Of course. The lemon tree's begun her bloom...

Yellow light. Must be late. Nine-thirty. OOOOH MY, did we sleep late. What day is it? Saturday? Yes, that's right, only Saturday. No need to get up for church. HUMMMM, such sweet blossoms has my little lemon....

A toasty warm sun meadow high grass hill behind Farnum's, blue pinafore crickets jump splotches of purple, Lily comes running two red braids, sweet grass blue sky forget-me-nots—

Shall we go to the window and look at those white flowers peeping out of dark shiny green?

OOOOH what's this? It's stuck to the pillow, darnit....

Oh Lord Jesus, what have I done to offend Thee now? I only wanted to peek at the little white blossoms. Oh, smelling them, I'm like a hungry cat moving in my sleep, dreaming, licking my chops—

OH. OW! It's really glued on here. Keep calm, Iris, keep calm now. Peel it slowly. Slowly—

OOOOOH, why oh why? What have I done Lord Jesus? Why do you punish me so for ever and ever with this dripping, oozing humiliation sticking onto a pillow like a barnacle now—

Pull in short, little quick, like a bandage, pull—

OUCH! Quick. Once more. OOH! There now. 'Twasn't that terribly bad. Let's see what's on the pillow case.

Only a little crust. No blood. Two drops here though. Oh why oh why oh why? Jesus help me one more day....

Let's see it now. That handkerchief...

Ah, yes. A few drops. Torn open a little here. Not flowing though. There. That takes care of it. Stings a little that's all.

That's enough now, you know you're not supposed to look at it for too long.

AHHHH, SCHERZO! YOU FRIGHTENED ME! WHAT ARE YOU DOING SHOOTING LIKE A ROCKET UNDER THAT BED? POOH POOH POOH POOH. YOU LITTLE SCAREDY CAT! C'MERE YOU, COME OUT NOW, MUMZY WANTS TO PET YOU. C'MERE. COME TO MUMZY, THEN WE'LL HAVE A LITTLE BREAKFAST.

OH, BE THAT WAY THEN. I'VE NOT THE PATIENCE FOR YOU THIS MORNING.

AAAHHHUUUUMN! I'm hungry. I'm going to make some nice eggs and toast and I bet there's still some of Helen's apricot preserve, AND YOU MAYN'T HAVE ANY YOU LITTLE SILLY CATKINS, IF YOU DON'T COME OUT FROM UNDER MUMZY'S BED, YOU LITTLE DEVIL!

Don't you want to come out to the lemon tree with me? It smells so good....

OOOH, such a headache! Came over so sudden, better lie back down, dizzy. Oooh, my, what a shooting pain, turn that pillow over. There.

AHHHH OOOOH, there it goes again. Maybe it's the light's too bright...

UUUMPH, roll over again get up and draw the curtains—

Dizzy, I feel dizzy—

What! This thing's jammed again. OH, YOU DARN CURTAIN—

Pull the shade then. There you go. Must be fouled somewhere. When Nora comes I'll have her take a look up there. Oh, when Nora comes....

Nora, when are you coming like you promised your dear old Mumzy? Didn't you tell me at Christmas that you were considering...

That job's not worth the energy. You put so much of yourself into it and look what you get out— headaches! Headaches and phone calls in the night and plumber's bills. You're always complaining about them, Nora. Why don't you just pick up and leave the whole lousy bunch?

Scherzo misses you, Nora. And who's going to drive your poor l'il ol' Mumzy to the grocery store after her license runs out? Oh, they're not going to renew it this time when one look at me...

Know I can't pass the darn eye test. Not going back to that nasty Sergeant What's-your-name with your big pot belly and reeking of cheap cologne. Oh I just hate it when men put that junk on; Edgar, I hope you never...

Nora, now you must be about to give up. Heating bills enormous this winter, and who's going to lend the money these days? Why, even the government money's running dry and they're not going to budget any more for the likes of your outfit. Oh, leave it all, Nora! Leave that lousy little radiator sizzling city dirt smelling paint peeling apartment brown door second floor....

Tisn't even safe. You have that cat burglar. And what about the little girl from across the hall? Trina—oh, yes, I remember her name, Trina from across the hall number six, or was it seven—that left her fourth lock undone and he still gets in past three. You girls are crazy living alone like that; I've been telling you that for years Nora. Come to Mumzy. Come to this clean quiet safe... smell the lemon tree you love the garden so and somebody has to tie up those roses and you said you'd do it last time but then we went shopping, oh yes, there wasn't time.

And you could drive me and have the car to yourself too, take it out to the beach if you want. Room for plenty of friends take a picnic, I need not go along. You'll have plenty of free time, I shan't be a pest. All I need is the shopping, and the garbage once a week, and maybe you could type up the accounts for me, make everything neat for when we go see Mr. Potter.

Couldn't have more than a couple thousand, mostly from that electric company. Shares probably no good, and we'll have to check those mutual funds. All the children have theirs now; I've nothing more to give out. We'll see how we're doing, Nora, and maybe we'll be surpri—

OOOH, that smarts! Keep it turned on the left side then, that's a bit better. No, no aspirin! ASPIRIN'S POISON. Mother was right. And we were all such healthy girls. Except Camelia. Only fifteen! And then all the rest, one by one they went. Now they're all gone, every one, all your beautiful rosy-cheeked young ladies, Mother...and we never took aspirin, Mother, not that I know of. I certainly did not!

A headache is due to any combination of things: body aches, fatigue, eye strain—no, it can't be that—infection...lots of things. Aspirin just enlarges the blood vessels to ease the pain. Anyone can't live with a little pain....

Why, life is pain. You can't get away from it. God sends us pain to humble us, to remind us that we are still imperfect, that we lack spirituality.

Look at Ophelia. Edgar tells me she's drinking herself to death. Spends every day in a semi-coma smashed out on booze, how she abuses the Lord's greatest gift, the filthy—

No, no, she was a sweet girl when I first met her. That day Edgar brought her over to the house on Appleby Street, she was so attentive. Nora liked her instantly, and that was the first time any of Edgar's girls had really taken the time to talk to little Nora. Well, she was almost seventeen at the time, hardly a child, but in her way, retiring, shy, withdrawn....

Oh, you crystal white gowned thing, your silk slippers—I used to sew the ribbons on myself. You were so serious. You've always been the serious one, Nora dear. Much more serious about yourself than Edgar. Always working, lessons—lessons every day of your life—dancing, dancing dancing. Hours of hard, grimy work. You couldn't have slaved your time away in a factory working any harder.

Nora, little china doll. You were little once, before you got too big...how could we have known? I wasn't especially tall, your father was a little above average height, but we couldn't have predicted at twelve, even at fourteen...

You were a late spurter, Nora. Edgar shot up at ten, maybe twelve at the latest. We couldn't have discouraged you. And your teacher was so confident things would change. Solo parts, and modern dance, and at least the center chorus girl...

Did you ever take the devil's aspirin for your sore muscles, Nora dear? I'd never ask, but would you? I can never be sure you really believe. Oh, we go to church together and you make me promises, but once you're back in New York you have your own life—how could I know if you were sincere? Oh Nora, I don't doubt you were. When you were with your Mumzy...

You were so good to me, always, never gave me reason to worry or doubt.

You told me about your friends in the dance world. And I met many of them, coming to visit you, that stuffy apartment always smelled so bad...like cabbage and old fly paper.

And they seemed like sweet children. I never wanted to know too much about their personal lives. That was your own business. And that Russian girl, that darling little blue-eyed thing, what was her name? Nataly? No, not Nataly—well, anyway, she had a husband and a baby eventually didn't she?

And it was only that pair, Ginger and Tommy, or was it Timmy? Whatever. They were a little strange....

Oh, Nora, you and your big heart, always adopting those strays. Stray kittens, stray dancers, you'd take anybody in. You were full of the best Christian charity, off in that skyscraper jungle. A little missionary. I like to think of you that way. Your free hours, exhausted as you always were, spent comforting a friend. Always a listener, the one they came to, the one they trusted in, took refuge with...

What was that little girl's name the last time? The one whose boyfriend she said was locking her out of the apartment? You put her up for six weeks. She slept on your couch, that crummy thing. Poor little girl.

Was it because you were so much bigger, and they were all such miniature little things? Tiny dancers. Ballerinas all. And you, the bending willow. Nora, dear, I can't doubt your faith in God Almighty. You've led such a straight life helping your neighbors with the rent strikes—a community leader, too. And then your work with the poor little Black Children...

You see, Nora, I remembered to say Blacks like you told me to and not Negroes. I always say Blacks now, just like on the TV. Everything's Black. Black, black, black! Well, don't they know that Negro just means Black in Spanish? So what's the big deal? A Spanish appellation changed to an English one?

Why, if everyone weren't so terribly uneducated these days, they'd know these things. Now kids in California are supposed to have Spanish mandatory in the public schools, if I'm not mistaken.

We always had a choice: French, Latin, Greek and Italian, wasn't it? I took French, like most of them. Never was very good at it. Don't think I continued it in college. No, surely I never bothered. Of course I could have learnt Norwegian from Harold for free, but...

Oooooh, the time we went to visit your parents! I never complained, but Harold, that was very uncomfortable. All of them talking a mile a minute at me. Unable to say a word. A prisoner. At your mercy for two whole months! Thank God for Edgar, if I hadn't had him to talk to...

Who wants to learn Norwegian anyway? Who could you talk it to around Memphis in those days? It was enough for you to speak English as well as you did. You amazed me. When I met you, you were still stumbling over the simplest phrases, your accent was something terrible! No wonder they wouldn't let you work without an assistant to translate for you—well, just to give the orders in clear English. But you picked it up remarkably fast.

That first year in Baton Rouge ("red pole" in French, of course), remember our little language lessons? Oh, you'd get so mad at me, go running around the house slamming doors like a big baby!

But you had to be taught. And you should have been glad I'd the patience for all those lessons. I really should have been a teach—

OOOOH! That shooting pain again. Oh please, Almighty God—

Mathew eighteen: nine: "And if thine eye offend thee, pluck it out, and cast it from thee: It is better for thee to enter into life with one eye rather than having two eyes to be cast into hell fire"; Mark nine: forty-seven: "And if thy eye offend thee, pluck it out: It is better for thee to enter into the kingdom of God with one eye, than having two eyes to be cast into hell fire."

AHHHH-OH, a mite better. Yes, that's better now. Oh, I can forgive you, Harold, it's she I'll never be able to—

But you were in a weakened condition. You were unable to resist that temptress, that Jezebel. Why, you narrowly escaped with your life, by the grace of God. Two years flat on your back, helpless and she comes along—

And I couldn't save you alone. I tried, God knows, Harold, I tried to keep you from her, to keep our little family together. After all the hardships I'd been through, after all the waiting, all the responsibilities. For two years Harold, I'd been alone. I'd had a lot of practice. We were all waiting for you to get well, everyone prayed for you, you could've had the decency to—

For Edgar's sake, if not for mine for your little son's sake who needed a father. Although I don't think you ever loved your son enough. After all, Harold, you hardly got to know him. Such a good little kid! So helpful, always helping his Mumzy round the house. We'd dust all the furniture together...

Oh Harold, maybe if you'd been there to watch him grow. It wasn't your fault. I do, I have, forgiven you. But not her! How could a woman—

Home-wrecker! And a small boy. She knew all about us, about me. Whatever you told her about our private life... Oooh, Harold, I can't bear to think of it. The humiliation! Why, everyone in town knew of it long before I did anything, showed any sign. That whole town talked behind our backs.

You didn't care. You were above it all, you thought you were better than all those people. Well I'll tell you something, Harold, there were some good neighbors in that town. They looked after me. That Mrs. Little's visits. I knew she was a gossip, but she was a comfort too. Harold, you couldn't have imagined how alone I felt. And Edgar, and tiny Nora, left, abandoned, without a father. They grew up never really knowing you. Well, Nora was an infant for Heaven's sake. A beautiful baby girl. Your own lovely daughter you never wanted to know. Oh

Harold, how weak you were God rest your soul. And as for your floozy—may she roast!

Edgar, you poor fatherless boy. A boy should have his father, to pitch balls to him, to teach him things. Why, I gave you half your education. You were such a smart kid in school, Edgar. Straight A's every year, and it was hard for you with us always moving around so much. I remember you so proud one day, bringing your grades home to Mumzy. I baked a cheesecake, your favorite. Do you remember? Do you remember all the good times we had together, Edgar? Despite your papa gone, and then all the hardships? How I always used to cook with chicken fat because butter was too expensive, and sewed all Nora's clothes, and most of yours….

Oh, my Edgar! Your father left you, and now your wife leaves you too. Twice you've felt the pain now…. Come. Smell the lemon blossoms with me. We'll sit on the veranda. Oh, Edgar, why did she treat you so abominably? I could kill—

I never would have thought, Fella…. Why, she was such a conscientious wife and mother in the beginning. I used to think of you two as happily married. Then she suddenly falls apart on you. Why? What happened? Because you moved? Was that all? I can't believe that was all there was to it.

Edgar, I wish you'd tell me what happened. You let on she's taken to drink. But was that before, or since? And what's this Barbie tells me about a suicide attempt? Why has she got to be so demonstrative, so dramatic?

You always gave Fella your full attentions. Didn't you tell me once that you'd spent thousands on doctors and hospitals—that she had the best psychiatrist money could buy? Of course, they're all quacks anyway, but if she'd wanted one…

You're better off without her. Good riddance, I say! A wife like that. A drunk. A mental patient. Who needs it? The kids are better off with their father. Frieda and Barbie have left home, Sam's in college now, they don't need her anymore, and you'll look after them. You've always been so generous, sending Frieda to that expensive school, and you wouldn't even let me help.

Edgar, you're better off without her. She was such a confused girl. I knew it all along. Oh, she played up to me alright, she was very attractive in the beginning, but as soon as she got her hooks in you—boom! I'm sent to the back of the room. Mother-in-law. She takes over and where do I go? She could have shared you with me. She cut me right out and we'd been so close, you were all I'd had for so long…

She didn't want me to come and visit you even. I could tell. She always treated me abominably in her home. And you, poor dear, trapped in the middle. I know you felt badly. But little Fella had to have her fits, had to always be in charge.

Dominant, pushy Jewish women. Her mother was like that. Libby always ordered her Dolfi around, and in front of company,

"Oh, Dolfi," I can hear her still, "Shut up! And bring me that ashtray, will you?"

Now I rather liked Libby. At least she always treated me with due respect, unlike her ill-behaved daughter. And I was quite fond of Dolf. A regular German professor—and a Shakespearean scholar—I liked that. He'd a certain continental flair….

But those Jewish women. So domineering! Have to run everything. So demanding, have to be queens in their own castles. Start out spoiled princesses, every one, of course they expect to grow up to be queens.

Like that little snoot—what was her name? Peggy, Peggy Feinblatt, Feinstein, something like that. I shall never forget it. The way her parents used to fuss over her! Why even as children we thought it was just too much. Every time Lily, or Camelia, or one of the sisters and I would go ask her to come and play, her mother would have to do her hair first with pink ribbons in fussy little bows and make her put on a clean pinafore and then give us girls a lecture on what Peggy mustn't do:

"Now Peggy, don't you go running around berry-picking getting stains all over and tearing your clothes, and don't let the girls take you off into the woods where you might fall and hurt yourself...."

The way they treated her, you'd think she was some sort of holy treasure. And her mother was always saying—and right in front of us, too—how beautiful she was. Why, she wasn't half so lovely as Lily! I think I was much more attractive than she was. But *my* mother never told me so like that, never made me so conceited about my looks....

Oh Lord, thank you for the sign, even if it means I can't look happily into the mirror now. I confess, I did gaze into it too long. You called upon my vanity. It was vain, vain youth. I knew it was vain of me, trying to preserve that young girl beauty too long, past the point You allow, Lord. I know, somewhere in one's sixties one has to admit...

And I had to learn to accept, didn't I Teacher? You had to show me that there was another way, another form of beauty. A beauty more pure than the milkiest skin, than the shiniest most fiery hair done up in such long, silken braids.

It was too soft, wasn't it? That's why it couldn't last. Like a delicate fruit, my peach skin. Harold used to call it that: peachskin. It was peachskin, even softer. And a peach is a very soft fruit and liable to rot.

You didn't make me rot. No, My Lord, it's not rotting. It's shining! Shining with beauty. Beauty through strength, through cleanliness of spirit. The eye, plucked, entering Heaven's open gates with full speed. A clean, straight shot.

I'm marked with Your sign. Your holy sign to St. Peter. And it's a mark of bravery too, that I, of so many born sinners, had the strength, with Divine assistance of course, to pluck it out.

The plucking has been slow. Imperceptibly at first. You wanted me to learn the lesson thoroughly, and of course it takes many years of study. And I have studied, Lord, faithfully, every day, as You have revealed more of Your message to me.

This eye has been sore offended. Had to see, had to face the naked, pitiful truth: You two, running off to hell hand in hand. My husband. The father of my two babies. Babies you never cared for, never loved, never took a father's pride—

Okay, Harold, you were weak and fell to the temptress. And though it took me a few years, I'll be the first to admit, I forgave you, Harold. You are forgiven. And I told you so, in my letter. And you'd said: "Thank you, Iris." Thank you….

You poor, pathetic thing. Couldn't read God's clear sign to you. Falling off that scaffolding. He nearly had to kill you to make you listen. And still, you were deaf to the voice of the Lord. And so He, our Savior, chose me, once again, as His messenger to you. He gave me the strength to forgive you. And then, I believe you did see the light and heard me for the first time and wept for the emptiness of your life.

The life you could have had but denied yourself. The rich, warm loving family life with Edgar and sweet little Nora, a darling daughter, a rare and beautiful child. Harold, your heart would have been made whole just to see her, running to me with her little basket of blackberries, pink pinafore, a ray of golden light, always honey, sunshine. You would have been healed by Nora's clear child-light alone. But you had to live out your mistake. And we all forgave you in the end and were sorry you died as you did, a lonely broken old—

But her, no, I couldn't forgive her. I couldn't, though many times I called for the Lord's help. Harold, it was torture to my soul. I suffered much, trying to forgive her, always trying to find the spot in my heart where I could lay her down in peace, side by side, within me, as I had you. But I'd never find the spot. Oh, I prayed for the strength to forgive your little hussy, your conniving Jezebel, that town floozy in the red dress....

She actually wore a red dress! God needn't have marked her so clearly for me. I didn't have to see her. But you made us meet, Harold, and that cinched it. I couldn't throw off the devil of her image. It was too powerful. Red dress. Painted lips. She was such a monster. You couldn't have picked a better devil in that town, Harold. You really had to make it obvious where you were going, taking the very serpent by the hand. I couldn't—

Oh Lord! I wrestled with that devil, but I couldn't kick her out. Even after Harold was at peace, resting safely within my bosom, she was writhing there, a snake, chewing her way through my body. It was as if the image of her had stuck in the back of this eye somewhere and was torturing me, offending me, hurting me, and I couldn't get at it. Until You came, Lord, to help me pluck it out.

That day I fell outside the church. Why did you have me fall that day? That tiny cut was sure to heal. I never bothered about it. But it turned out to be a sign. It wouldn't close. You'd left it open to let that devil dance her way out, was that it? You opened the skin, just below the eye to let her escape from me.

But that demon! She was too large. She wouldn't come out the little innocent slit You made. Oh Lord, no! She was too great a monster to quietly skip out in the night; after all, she'd tortured me for almost forty, no more than forty years. It's incredible to think. What a lifetime of suffering, quietly at first, but then, when it got too excruciating—

That day. I'd gone to church. Once again, I prayed for the torture to end, to find forgiveness for the woman who took my husband away from me and left me to raise a family so alone, to raise them and see them off into the world to end out the rest of my mortal days alone. Widowed, prematurely, by a living man. Oh, it wasn't so simple, I know.

Then You sent me Stephen, and for two years I had a man beside me again. A good man, Stephen was a good man, but oh, so selfish. A man for a man's sake.

It wasn't the answer, was it Lord? He didn't really give me anything. And he certainly couldn't love my children. Of course, they were grown, they didn't need Stephen as a father.

Brave little dears. They'd grown up with me alone. And we didn't need a father, did we?

We were so contented, weren't we Edgar? Your Mumzy was mother and father and teacher to you. She kept so busy being all those things. You weren't deprived, either of you.

And Stephen passed away. What did he leave me? A mess of papers and bills and debt and worthless stock. All this junk. These etchings. Nobody wants etchings anymore. They're worth, well, hundreds of dollars apiece and nobody will buy them. They're out of fashion now. Fine work. Well preserved. Why, the frames alone...

You sent me Stephen because I'd prayed so long for another man, for company, in my dotage and You couldn't have known—well, of course You knew, Lord—I was the one who couldn't have known what bad condition he was in... We did have several pleasant moments, but soon I was alone again....

And it all seemed so unfair. Oh, I knew I was selfish, Lord. I knew I was missing much of Your glory because of self-pity when I went to church that day. Self-pity (like Ophelia, the wretch). I was drowning in self-pity when I went to church that day and prayed for the thousandth time to be freed from her image, from the torture of that vampire in a red dress, haunting, laughing, big painted mouth—

And I was meditating, I remember clearly, upon the lesson, it was about the loaves and the fishes. And I was thinking: All you've got, Iris, is spiritual hunger.   You need to take the Lord in deeper so that He can feed you. Take that seemingly empty basket of a life of yours and make it full of bread and feast upon it. You'll have plenty for the long years, lonely years left, if only you'll make room in your heart. Kick her out! Now's the time!

I remember so clearly saying it to myself: Kick that shedevil out and let her go. There will be so much more room for the Lord to feed you. Your spirit needs nourishment. That demon's been eating up the Holy Host, the word of the Lord, faster than you can digest it.   And you must be strong. Strong and whole, to enter Heaven.   And it came to me then.

There was a rumbling sound. It could have been thunder. But the day was clear. It could have been an airplane. But I asked Julia and she hadn't heard anything. I know I heard it. It was very loud. Just like thunder. Anyway, that was the sign.

And I felt suddenly dizzy walking out of the church. I wasn't all there. Then I heard her voice. She was saying her weekly goodbyes, oh, ever so profusely, making such a scene, as usual, shaking his hand, blocking the way when other people were simply trying to leave.

That fat fanny! Oooh how I'd come to hate that Gloria Miller person, that fat toady, always putting on a show, like she owned the church, like she had private rights to Dr. Henry and nobody—

Not even me, when I'd just received a powerful sign. When I was feeling light-headed and needed to talk with him, oh, for just a moment. He was the only one I had, the one mortal man that could help me. And you—your big rear blocking my way! And I waited patiently. And Dr. Henry couldn't see me standing there. You kept your big head right in front of his. And he was shorter than you.

Oh Gloria! I was feeling so dizzy, trying to focus my attention, trying to hold on. And then it got so hot standing there. I suddenly felt so hot, needed fresh air. More than I needed to talk to Dr. Henry, had to get a breath—

Started down the steps and—boom....

Then he noticed me alright, helped me up. And Fat Fanny, leaning over me, making such a scene, jabbering on so, jabbing that damn handkerchief in my face. I couldn't hear what she was saying. I hated her so much at that moment. I just wanted to get away, to get home and think. I had to recapture the Lord's message that came in that rumble from the ceiling. I had to have it straight before I talked to Dr. Henry.

It's so clear to me now, Lord, after so many years. Fanny's—I mean Gloria's—death made me realize it. You would have left that little cut to heal, perhaps, if Gloria hadn't blocked my way, if I hadn't felt so much hatred for her that day when I fell on the steps and got that little cut on my cheek.

Hatred. Poison. I was full of it. The hatred for that slinky red devil, submerged all those years, came out that day against Gloria, and she was wholly innocent, really, though she was blocking my way to Dr. Henry, the one soul I could appeal to for help and understanding. I needed him at the time. And Gloria, you'd kept him from me! And so I let some of that hatred leak out.

And God was watching me. I knew it, because I'd just heard the rumble. He was present. He saw it. He saw a glimpse of that hideous snake living inside me. And He decided: Here's a good woman, she deserves to go the Heaven. We'll have to poke a hole to let that devil out.

Oh, you took your time escaping, you fiend! Are you gone yet? Or are you going to drain out and out until the last? I suspect you're still in there, a little part of you. Though I don't feel it much, the pain anymore, the resentment. Oh, it's definitely eased up. My heart has lightened.

Oh, I've enjoyed many more years of study. And the congregation respects me now, because Dr. Henry, bless his soul, had understood. And he helped me to understand how I had been chosen and was one of God's examples. And he said I had received a holy sign. Oh, he was a good man.

Dr. Cook is nice, but he's not you. You are in heaven now, and I will join you. In my gossamer white-gowned hands upstretched to you, you'll take my hands and we'll walk side by side in the path of pure gold light….

You taught me to see the path, and I'm on it. Oh, I'll stay on it….

There's the lesson for today on the table by the sofa with my reading glasses. I should get up and study awhile. First though, we'll make ourselves some breakfast.

SCHERZO! WHERE DID YOU GET TO? MUMZY'S GOING TO MAKE US A LITTLE—

WHOOPS! That's not a good idea, Iris. You're not in very good shape today. OOOH, I thought it was gone. That awful pounding! Oh please, Lord—

Relax. Just lie back. Relax. That's better it doesn't hurt lying down. You probably need to sleep, oh, just a wee bit more, and wake up again and the pain will have vanished. That often happens. I wake up with a terrific headache, then fall back to sleep, oh, no more than fifteen minutes, and it's gone, like a miracle. I don't know why, but ours is not to reason...

***

WHERE ARE YOU SCHERZO? COME TO MUMZY. Oh, close that eye you've got left, you old fool. You know what the room looks like. Everything's right where you left it….

I'm not afraid to die now. Not very much afraid. Oh, you know me, Lord, brave one minute, trembling the next. I know I'm almost ready. I'd like to see my children first. It's been such a long time. And now that Edgar's free…

He wasted, he *devoted* so many years taking care of her. And what was wrong with her? She didn't have cancer. Ophelia never had anything wrong. It was all in her head. Always imagining things. And then her self-pity! Always dragging my poor Edgar into her problems. He had enough of his own, with his job, all the bills he had to pay—the houses you two lived in weren't cheap. Oh, I'm glad you had them. Always had to have woods behind. Acres of woods, 'for the kids'. Fella, you were always putting things in terms of the kids.

That rainy cold day you insisted, *insisted* that we all go to the zoo. Because you'd promised the children. You'd promised the children they would go to the zoo. Well, it was cold and raining. The little girls couldn't have cared less. Why, little Barbie was only a year old. What could she have cared for the zoo? You made such a fuss, Fella. Such a tantrum you threw that day. I shall never forget it. Why, there was nothing for us but to bundle up the

99

children and drive all the way into town in the pouring rain….

Well. Enough of you now. You had my Edgar for almost thirty years. A long time. Longer than his own dear Mumzy had her own son at home. And you didn't appreciate all the love and care…

Thousands of dollars in doctors' bills he had to pay. Thousands and thousands, all those hospitals. Oh, he's written me all about it. You and your demon rum—a cancer on Edgar, eating up all his money, his patience, his kindheartedness, his strength. He tells me he's put on too much weight. Well. No wonder, what he's been through these past few months!

Good riddance I say! And now he's free. He can begin to look after me, enjoy his own life for a change. It's been five years since you came out and stayed with your Mumzy, Edgar. Five years. I would have given you the money. I told you. Nora comes every Christmas now, and usually once in Spring or Summer. Last year she took a week off in August and I sent her the fare. Well you promised me…

And now that you're finally a free man, there's no excuse, Edgar. I'm not going to beg you. I still have my pride. I'm not even going to mention it again. Never again. Won't write you so much as a reminder to keep your word. It's up to you now, son. And I'm sure you'll find it in your heart…

Those kids of yours, they're all gone now. Where did you say Sammy was going to college? Oh, I'll have to look through that pile of letters. Sam never writes me. How should I know what he's up to? He must be eighteen by now or nineteen. No, nineteen-fifty-nine, that would make him...

Eighteen. And Barbie. Here she is, only two hundred miles north and I never hear a word. She might as well be on the other side of the continent. They've no respect, Edgar. You should have brought them up to at least have a little respect for their elders. A grandmother has a right to see her grandchildren. To share in their lives, to watch them grow...

I send you kids your birthday checks, don't I? And I haven't forgotten once, not once! And you used to draw me the cutest little cards when you were in grammar school. For Thanksgiving and Christmas too, when your mother would let you send them. Oh, I know she discouraged it. She wanted to come between me and my grandchildren, Edgar's children. She had no right. Why, you would have all come to see me much more often if not for Ophelia, isn't that right Edgar?

If only she'd turned out a little better. Oh, she took fairly good care of your children, but she was incapable of providing your most essential needs. A mother should see that her children get a religious education. What did she know or care about religion? She was half Jewish, after all, and she couldn't have brought you up Jewish. Libby wouldn't have stood for it.

I always liked Libby; she was right to reject her parents' heathen teachings. She could have been a good Christian. She had a good heart. Doted on those grandchildren. Well, she got to see them all the time. Thanksgiving, then Christmas, right in a row, and every summer too. She had the joy of them. Saw them grow.

But not me. Not all the way out here. You brought them out here to see me exactly once, and before Sam was born. And it was up to me to come see them, alone, on airplanes, all that way. And then just to be met by that—

Fella hated it when I came. I could always tell. The children behaved well enough but Fella always threw her fits. Right in front of me. No respect. No self-control. I tried to stay out of the way, Edgar. I never interfered in your marriage, not once did I get myself involved. I always knew you two would have to resolve your own problems.

And the children would come and sit with me for a little while. But they were always running off. Kids are always running in and out. Can't stay still. Can't concentrate on one thing.

I remember, I tried to teach you girls sewing. We'd work at it for a few minutes and then whoops—you'd find some excuse. The telephone would ring, or a little neighbor girl would come by and take you away from me. No wonder you girls don't make your own clothes; you could save so much money! And some of the patterns now are really very simple, and extremely fashionable. And you look at this junk! That's what it is nowadays, pure junk! All made so sloppy. Well no wonder, in Philippines and Hong Kong and Japan. Those flimsy, cheap synthetics.

Remember Nora, we looked at dresses that time for you and we decided we could do so much better buying the fabric and making them ourselves? Nothing fit you well. They make everything too small in those Oriental countries. Women there are so much tinier, they don't understand American fits.

And we found that orange velvet remnant in the sewing cabinet and there was just enough, with a little flap in front of that nice deep blue paisley print from the old dining room drapes. Oh, we had such fun, didn't we? You always told me: 'Mumzy, I'm so glad I don't have to think about shopping in New York. Everything's so terribly expensive.' Well, don't I know it? The things here—always so marked up! Who in the world buys all that junk?

It's nice to look at I suppose. We always did love window shopping. Remember, you'd take me down Fifth Avenue, but we had the good sense not to buy anything. You take some of those things that look so fine in the window displays and they turn out to be no good.

Remember those fancy sandals you bought that time? Well, you learned your lesson. Oh, oh, it seems so funny now, the way they simply disintegrated in the rain that day. Where were we going? Ah yes. You were taking me to Myra's church and we had to park so far away….

Well now. Shall we try it again? I think I should probably need the bathroom by now. Maybe that has something to do with—

OH SCHERZO, YOU'VE COME OUT HAVE YOU? WELL, TO WHAT DO I OWE THE PLEASURE YOUNG SIR? YOU LITTLE NUISANCE. GET OUT OF MY WAY NOW, MUMZY'S GETTING—

OOOOH---

UPSIDAISY, THERE WE—

OOH, that pounding. That's a little better now Iris, bend and stretch. Out of Mumzy's way Scherzo. Go to the bathroom, maybe that'll help it.

That ladder's going to be the death of me. Always afraid it will come crashing down on us walking this dark hall. Got to get that boy back, that Scotty, what was…

Elsa said she'd send him next Saturday. But wasn't that *this* Saturday? Now let's see. I talked to

Elsa just the other night. Was that Thursday? It was right after Nora called, so it must've been. No, wait a minute, the news was on. Was that the day the toaster broke? No, now just a minute. The news was on that night I had the toaster out on the table to remind me, and I don't remember it being there when the phone rang...

Anyway, it must not be 'til next Saturday. Oh, I hope he finds a dead one up there this time. There's only been that one, and we put so much poison out you'd think if there were any more up there...

Funny. I haven't heard them lately...

What? Oh, Iris, you forgot the toilet paper after all! There's no spare roll down there anymore. Tear these tissues in half then. Don't clog the plumbing. Write a bigger note to yourself this time, and read it. That was the one item...

Well, I'm not going out again now. This Kleenex will last 'til next Wednesday. Honestly, Iris, sometimes I don't know what to do with you. You and your roof-rats. Out of toilet paper when you wrote yourself a special note. Broken toaster just sitting there for days. Got to look in the Yellow Pages. Had that thing for almost thirty years now. Why it would suddenly collapse like that?

Well, if Nora were here, or Edgar.... Oh, they're such clever children. Both of them trained in electronics. Can fix anything. Why, Edgar fixed that watch of mine that time in Poughkeepsie. How do you like that! Talented children, could save me so much trouble and expense! Now I'll have to find one of those thieving repairmen, take my toaster away for weeks, tell me it's too old ought to buy a new one.

Well, I happen to be quite fond of that toaster, mister, and it's served me just dandy for more years than you've seen on this earth. Now fix it! And while you're at it, have your friend there bring it 'round to my house when you're done. I'm an eighty-year-old lady. Now must I go driving all over this town risking my safety just to...

We'll look in the Yellow Pages after breakfast, ALRIGHT SCHERZO? Mumzy can't go on making her toast in the oven, it's terribly wasteful you know. We mustn't waste electricity or water now. We're very conscientious. Not like those yellow-house people with their six sprinklers watering the street. Oh, I find that just so abhorrent, when we may have another terrible draught like last summer. Oh, they'll never learn.

Yes, there's today's lesson, I know you're waiting for me. I'll be getting to you shortly. Must review this entire week's readings, for tomorrow is Sunday, and we must enter the Lord's house prepared. Oh, there's so much to do today, and I'm not sure I really feel up to it. This headache business.

It's better, but I feel so tired. Oh, and for no reason. I slept well last night...

And there's the unpotting to finish. Look what a mess out there. I've got to get those plants in soon. Why, the lemon tree is blooming already. Ah, look at you my gorgeous pet! I'll take the lesson book outside so's I can smell the blossoms. Can't let them go by without fully appreciating...

If only Nora... You love them so. Come share them. Oh, it would be so wonderful! And you could fix the toaster too....

Alright, enough now Iris. The day is late and you still haven't eaten. NEITHER HAVE YOU PUTTER-PAWS. I KNOW DEAR, MUMZY'S GETTING YOUR FOOD NOW. JUST YOU BE PATIENT. OOOH, THAT'S STINKY. Mash it down a little. And now, a drop of hot water. Wait for the water to get a little warmer.

SCHERZO, YOU GET DOWN NOW! YOU'LL SLIP IN THE SINK, YOU POOR LITTLE CLAWLESS THING. Why, don't they know it's cruel? The poor things. They can't walk properly. And they feel so helpless and insecure, like you, you little devil, hiding under the furniture all the time, running whenever anybody comes. And the way you look after the birds, oh so longingly. You poor cripple. HERE, EAT YOUR PUSS N' BOOTS. AND HERE, LET ME FILL YOUR WATER DISH.

So indecently cruel to declaw a cat! If people are so worried about their furniture they have no business keeping cats in the first place. Why, of all the cats we had: Popeye, Elmer, Robespierre, Tom Swift... Oh, there were so many, I can't remember now. And not one of them clawed up the upholstery. And you know why? You know why foolish people? Because we trained them not to be destructive. And we provided scratching posts for them.

It's so simple. People don't take the time or trouble. And it isn't any trouble really. They just don't bother to train a pet, instead, what do they do? OOOOH, the cruelest thing: They mutilate the poor defenseless creature. Oh, I just find that the lowest—

Almighty God, thank you for delivering this poor orphan into my care. Look how he eats, so timid, always on his guard, because he has no defense but to run and hide....

And now, what about you, Iris? Oh, I'm not hungry. Well, you've got to eat something. A little toast maybe with some of Helen's—

Ah, yes, here 'tis. I knew there was still some at the bottom of the jar. Must ring up Helen one of these days. She's been so unwell. I hate her complaining. If only she could trust in God more, she could handle that pain a little better. It's only arthritis.

Well, now, there's bread and butter up here, ah, but no toaster! Oh, why must things always fall apart? For thirty years I took you for granted, and now you're sitting on the table there, utterly useless. I hate to heat up the whole oven for a lousy piece of toast. Oh, it's a warm day, I don't need to toast it. If only this butter would spread a little better. I hate the way it crumbles and tears the bread. Where's another knife? I need that long one, reach the bottom of this jar. Yes, that will do. There's only enough here for...

It's a good thing you aren't here, Nora. There's not enough of Helen's apricot jam for the two of us. And I get the very last lick. I'll miss that too. This store-bought grape stuff is so unappealing. I'm not going to buy it anymore. It's just become a bad habit. They hook you with their advertising gimmicks and before you know it you've made a bad habit out of buying something. I never really fall for it, but I can't think of any other reason for getting that grape jelly again. I'll have to use it up gradually though. Can't waste anything.

Is it in one of those flower-printed glasses? Oh, yes, that's why I'd been buying it now. You get the free glass. That would have made a set of four. Fine, we'll have four more matching glasses thanks to the grape jelly.

Who's going to take all this glassware? Why just look at those crystal wine glasses. Those were my sister Violet's, or were they Daisy's. No, not the red ones. The red ones were definitely Violet's. And all in perfect condition. A little dusty. One of these days I must wash it all again. Oh, but that's so tedious, and I don't trust myself with this one eye now, what if I dropped—

Well, Nora, that's another job for you here. You may have it all if you want, everything's yours of course, though, if the girls ever get married I'd like to give each a piece or two, maybe some of that china. There are at least four sets up there, just sitting on the shelf, unseen, unused.

They should be starting families soon enough. How old is Frieda now? Let's see, Edgar's going to be fifty-four, and Frieda's thirty years...

That makes her twenty-four. Hmmm, she should be settling down soon. She has a beau, so Edgar tells me. I think he said his name was Gregory. Yes, Greg, he said. I like that name, Gregory, what is it, Scottish? And of course Barbie's been living with that boy. I don't approve of that. But if her father has no objections I suppose...

Oh, I never interfere, never tell them what I think. What good would it do? They have to learn for themselves. They have to make their own mistakes just as Edgar did. How could I have foreseen the troubles he would have with Fella? And she started out such a nice girl. There wasn't the least indication.... And I remember, I tested her. No one was going to take my Edgar's hand without first passing a thorough....

And she did. I thought she was very attentive and thoughtful. The picnics we'd fix together...

I even thought she liked me. I was fooled by her charm, just like Edgar, poor dear. I'm so glad...

Well, I mustn't gloat; she obviously was defective to begin with: The product of a Christian and a Jew, clearly irresponsible...

Now, I was very fond of Libby, really. She commanded a great deal of respect somehow. Very dignified. And of course Dolfi is really a dear thing. And quite the Herr Professor. Always did remind me of Uncle Franzi. But they never should have married, or at least they never should have had a child. So contrary to Nature! Why, even the Jews teach it: It's forbidden to marry a Christian. Libby knew that. Her parents must have brought her up that way. And yet, she rejected their wisdom.   A Jew marrying a Christian!

It's a doomed combination. You can't mix races. Look at those black and white couples. You think their children have an easy time of it? It's so unfair to inflict that on a child. The child's not responsible. And look what happens in cases like Ophelia's: The father brought up Christian, the mother brought up a Jew; now how are they going to decide what religious education to give the child? Obviously, they chose to ignore the whole issue.

By neglecting a child's basic needs—and religious training is one of the most essential—you're bound to create a problem-adult. And what about my grandchildren? Why, if it weren't for my efforts...

Naturally it was all her fault. Edgar would have seen to it they went to Sunday school at least. I seem to remember Frieda did go for a little while. But wasn't that one of those liberal churches where they don't make sufficient use of the Bible?

They are basically good children, despite their handicap. I do believe they are basically good. At least they've never been in trouble with the law like so many from this area. Drug smuggling in the high schools. Oh, their poor wayward souls! I hope you kids never try any of that marijuana poison—why that's the Devil's own snare to lead innocent children off the path of righteousness!

I did my best with you kids. Maybe you'll discover God on your own now. That's what I pray for. It's the one hope I have: That you may discover your own souls and begin to care for them, as I have, and as Nora and Edgar were brought up to. Even Edgar's got a terrific faith. How could he have survived all her tortures otherwise?

Should I have an egg? That toast—no, it wasn't toast was it, just plain bread, but so delicious!

And I really must telephone dear Helen. Maybe she has some more of that preserve lying around....

Oh, Iris, you Devil. I do feel better though. Perhaps the headache was due to hunger. I ate a good meal last night. That chow mein was excellent. Always fills me up. And I had ice cream for dessert, didn't I? Ah yes, here's the dish. Hate facing these every morning.

Edgar, you must have to do your own dishes now too. Or do you eat out all the time? Oh, I can't imagine that you do. You like cooking. You always have. Liked to help your Mumzy. Oh, you were so cute....

Remember when I first taught you to fry an egg? That was in Mississippi. Do you remember what you said? Ooooh, I'll never forget it. You looked up from your high stool where we were standing by the stove and you said, 'Mumzy, why does the egg want to spit at me like that? Am I hurting it, is that why? You always taught us spitting was bad manners.' And the way you said it, such a serious little face, 'Am I hurting it?' and then such an angry tone, 'Spitting is *bad* manners'.

You were only three or four, but you could fry your own egg. And weren't you proud? You never let me do it after that without your help. 'Mumzy, why does the egg want to spit at me like that?' AH, AH, OOOH, MY, such a cutey you were!

Well, shall we cook Mumzy an egg this morning then? A 'spittin' l'il egg just for her loneself? Let's see, there are seven left. That's more than enough. I can have one of them, in a little chicken fat.

More people ought to know about saving chicken fat. That Jewish baker in Idaho, he knew. I'd never consider cooking with anything else, especially baking. And it saves money too. I should have enough here for several dozen batches of cookies. So when you come, Nora...

Just a teaspoon now, you don't need much. And this little fry pan is just perfect for me. Now don't you go and give out on me; I've had you all my life. Weren't you part of Mother's things once? Wherever did you come from? You're a mystery, little pan....

And turn it to number three. We don't need it sizzling, just bubbling. And how about salt? Only a tiny shake. And get the pepper in here. I like to pepper while it's cooking. Some people think that's terrible, but really, I find the flavor's better. Oooh, you lemon tree, my little princess! I'll open this just a crack, get the smell....

Um. That's delicious. After breakfast we'll take today's lesson out. I should really do the unpotting first. Well, you're not even dressed yet Iris.

Ooooh, it's bubbling. Crack this. Fine, now slide it in ever so gently.... Perfect! Though the yolks are awfully pale. You can't get those good farm eggs at the supermarket anymore. Remember the ones in Indiana when Uncle Gus had his chicken business and you liked to go out in the morning with the basket?

Nora, you were afraid, you were only two or three, but Edgar, you'd burst in the kitchen door with the basket, a big grin on your face, sometimes a few chicken feathers sticking to your clothes. 'Look Mumzy! Fourteen!' And those yolks were deep orange, bright, and round and firm as little golf balls. There's nothing like a fresh egg. Oh, this will have to do today, this cheap imitation....

Don't let it get leathery now. One, two, three, ally-ooop! Ah, that was perfect. Now turn it off, there, this little plate...

Oh, it's still got chow mein on it. Let me get another down. So many plates, cups, that whole English tea set, in perfect condition, and taking up so much space. I'm afraid if we ever have another of those bad earthquakes—

Well, the girls will just have to come here and pick out what they want. I'm not running the risk of shipping any of these pieces. A fork. This little salad one. You can't have my gold dessert forks, girls, those are Nora's, I already told her. And they're the most valuable things we own, that's why they're kept in the bank box. I couldn't bear the thought—

They can break in here and take these etchings if they want. Oh, stop grinning, you hideous monster! Why do they make fine etchings of such ugly faces? No wonder the things won't sell. They aren't the most wonderful subjects to live with, those dreary churches and street scenes and the gnarled grimaces by old what's-his-name. They're supposed to be worth something. Perhaps a museum would take them. I could declare it on my income tax then, or could I? I'll have to ask Mr. Potter next time…

I know what I forgot! For heaven's sake, Iris, what is wrong with you today, got up on the wrong side of bed, left your thinking cap in the closet? You finished your egg and didn't even miss it. Well, you don't need it. Just another habit. It's got no nourishment. Maybe it's a good sign….

Ah, but now I'm thinking of it, I do want some Sanka.

Got to put the stove back on then, fill this pan up. Edgar, I hate to think of you doing all these things alone. Oh, I know you can manage. You've told me yourself how you like to cook. But day after day, meal after meal, dish after dirty dish—that's a woman's job. Women are trained for it early in life. You could fry an egg but you didn't have to do all the planning and shopping and cleaning up, dear. That was Mumzy's department. And now you're a bachelor again, you'll have to take care of yourself.

Now, don't go buying junky foods just because they're easier to prepare. Those dreadful TV dinners. You wouldn't fix a TV dinner for yourself, oh would you dear? And plop down in front of the TV with a beer can on your belly like that fat Archie So-and-so. That show is disgusting, really, Edgar, you'd never allow yourself to degenerate so....

Oh, I can imagine you with a sink of dirty dishes. You might not even do them once a day, as I do. And what a dreary picture, to think of you coming home after such a long day at your office and then that terribly long commute back to an empty house with a sink full of unwashed dishes. That's no life for a man. A man who's worked so long, so hard for his family, deserves better. If only you'd invite me out there, I'd take care of you. Ooooh, I'd spoil you again, have such a nice meal on the table every night when you came home. And you'd have a companion to listen to you...

Ah, but you want your own life now. I understand. You both want your own lives now. Nora never seemed to mind living alone; maybe you'll find you like it too. You'll have a lot more time to yourself without the kids and Fella vying for your attention. She never did take much interest in your life or work, did she Edgar? Always me, me, me, talk to me, comfort me, listen to my problems. Wasn't that how it was? Don't I know it! I used to see it every time I visited you two, all this bickering, the complaining. She always had to drag you into the bedroom to yell about something. Well good rid—

Are you boiling? Yes you are. Now for a mug. The one I always use—ah, in the sink.   Well, I'll just rinse you out, and this spoon while I'm at it. Now turn the knob to "off." Just a rounded teaspoon. And let me see how much milk we have left...

There's less than half a quart here. Well, we may have to run out before Wednesday, Scherzo. You want more, you hungry thing. NOW JUST A DROP OF MILK FOR YOU. We're running low, and you know Mumzy hates to go out for groceries if we're not going to do a complete shopping. It's so wasteful. The President says we must conserve energy. All these housewives constantly running out for this and that. Starting the car, you know, wastes twice the energy. Once you get it started and run it awhile it's much less wasteful. You should do all the shopping at once. They're so stupid though, and careless. And they'll be sorry one day. I won't be around to see it, thank the Lord. They'll just have to learn the hard way.

Now, sit back down here admire my lemon tree. How big she's grown. I wonder if she's poking too far over the back fence. I haven't heard any complaints. Well, they aren't likely to object, they haven't got much over there. Remember the time, Nora, we stood on the ladder and peeked? It was really quite dismal, only that one mangy hydrangea and all that bare dirt. Some people just don't care. And it's so easy to grow things. I'd offer them some cuttings, anything, I've got so much here. Especially the forsythia. I really would like to get rid of some of that Nora, that's a job for you. I should start a list. Goodness, there are so many things!

I wish you could give me a definitive answer. If you knew how I hate the waiting. If only you could commit yourself now to a date. It would make it easier getting your vacation schedule planned, as you yourself said. You must let me know soon, everything depends on...

I mean, it does help me to know. I have appointments to make. And if it's going to be August again this year, that's when Mr. Potter takes his vacation. Now you know that. And we'd have to put it off until Christmas. I simply must get my accounts straight. I don't even know how much money I have now with the stock market so unpredictable. And that Dairy stock, that may not be any good anymore. But there's nothing I can do without you. Oh, I can get it out and look at it, but without your help...

You know I can't see that fine print so well. Why make it hard on me? It's all for you, Nora, if you took any interest in it.

Interest in it, that's a joke, get it? Interest in it! Oooh, I'll have to remember that for you. Stop flitting around out there. You're not going any further. You're getting too old to find work as a dancer. Honestly, I wish you could see it as well as I do. Oh well, it's your life. I never interfere. You and Edgar have to work out your own problems. Oh, I'm always here when you need help, but I'll wait until I'm asked. I'm not like some nose-poking parents.

Well now, are you satisfied Scherdy-cat? I am. I'm just going to do these dishes and then get dressed. My goodness, it's getting late, and we have a lot to do today...

Oh, you were something in that uniform! Especially in this one, before they cut off your beautiful curls. With that grin...

Edgar, you'd better not be drinking anymore, now that she's gone. I know it was all her influence. You told me you'd had a drinking problem well, maybe not a problem—she certainly had the drinking problem—but that it made you put on weight. Now that's not healthy. A man of your age. A little weight, certainly...

You can't expect to fit in your old navy uniform now. I used to wash that thing. I remember. You'd come home, a big bag of dirty laundry...

It was so heavy. Doesn't look like it weighs anything on you, but I remember washing it, the blue dye would run out, and it weighed a ton wet, pure wool. They made you wear wool in the tropics?

You had a white one too didn't you? Maybe they only made you wear the woolen one when you were stationed in Maine. I don't know. What does a woman know about these things?

You'd better lose some weight, Edgar. If you're fat now, you know that's bad for a man's heart. Drinking's bad for your heart, Edgar. Oh, come out here and let Mumzy take care of you for a while! You're in a state of transition. A man can't be expected to suddenly do everything for himself after so many years of marriage. You're bound to suffer. I don't want you to have to do all those dishes and all that laundry and all that cleaning and then have to keep up with such a big yard too!

Why don't you invite Nora down for a few weeks, help you fix up the place? She always did love helping rake the leaves and prune the dogwoods at your old house. Remember that Thanksgiving? Even I was out there raking. Why, I always think of that as our leaf-raking Thanksgiving. All we seemed to do...

Oh, there was a turkey, I suppose, but all I remember was the raking, raking, raking; everyone out there, Sam a baby, raking, then the girls running through the leaf pile.

You know, you were so lucky to live in the woods like that, and in New Jersey too—you've always had so many trees, so much forest around you. Why, I always wanted a place in the woods.

And the closest I ever came—no, I never had a house in the woods like you, Edgar—the closest we ever came, me and Nora, was that summer in Carolina. That was when you were off in the war. I wrote you about it, the big pine woods, sun filtering through so toasty and sweet-smelling, felt like you were walking on a feather bed. And a deciduous forest too, full of oak and poplar and beech...

I remember all the campers went leaf-collecting, and we mothers, we counselors as they called us, pressed the leaves between pieces of waxed paper for the girls' scrapbooks. Such beautiful woods! And endless. You could get lost in them. Oh, I never felt such extraordinary power. The sun shafts the floor of bright copper color as if God himself...

And mushrooms! Edgar, you would have gone wild seeing all tho—

What's that? Must be the trash collectors. No, no Iris, it's Saturday, they came yesterday. Now what could that be? Oh yes, now I recognize it—the recycling truck. Oh dear, and I forgot, they said they were coming on Saturdays from now on. Why they had to change it from Mondays—

I'll have to get used to it. Darn it I don't have any of my bottles ready. Well, you won't get anything from me today. Oh, they're moving on, good. I'll have to remember to get the bottles ready by Fridays now. I always used to do it Sundays, after gardening. Oh, I'll never remember. Maybe I should write myself a note. I'll have to remember to do that next time I'm in the kitchen. I'll write a note and tack it to the garage door: Bottle pick-up Sat. A.M.s. They gave us that slip of paper. I never saw it again. Must have thrown it out. Why they couldn't have stuck to Mondays....

Really, this recycling business! Of course, it's a very good idea, I strongly support it.

Why, when we were young you always returned the bottles: milk bottles to the milk man, soda bottles to the drug store, and of course everybody kept his own canning jars. Jars were never a problem. Everything was so sensible in those days. You got your vegetables from the market. I used to take a basket, Mama had that great straw basket. I'd fill it so full I couldn't carry it by myself. That one day Jimmy Fitzsimmons helped me....

***

He carried my basket home. Oh, I was so tickled. Jimmy Fitzsimmons! Why, he must've been at least five years older. He was so nearly a man to me. And we had to walk all through Fourth Street and all the way down Palmer Avenue side by side. He didn't say much. But he did say to Mama: "Your daughter here's got eyes bigger than her muscles." He said that. "Your daughter here's got eyes bigger than her muscles." Just like that: "Your daughter's eyes—"

Oh, how I blushed. I ran in while he was still standing there holding the basket. It had been so painful, walking all that way through town, everybody staring at us—well, it certainly felt that way to me. Jimmy Fitzsimmons! Married that big Louisa, moved out to his grandfather's place on the hill. We'd pass it on the way to the meadow with all the blackberries....

Oh, the time Violet and I—oh, and Violet stepped on a snake in her bare feet—ooooh, how we screamed all the way down the hill, don't think there was a single blackberry left in the bucket. Oooh, and how we shivered for weeks! I can imagine it now. Even though it was Violet who stepped on it, it was as if I'd felt it too. The big black wriggly snake, oh, and my toe was no more than a few inches away. Violet shouldn't have taken her shoes off. She was older, and should've known better. She was always doing foolish things like that. The rough one.

The time she fell out of the tree and broke her arm—such a tomboy! Oh, I was a bit of a tomboy, too but I didn't have the build that she had, I didn't have all the muscles. I don't know where Nora got all hers. Certainly not from me. And Harold wasn't exceptionally big or muscular. Oh, maybe in his prime. He was strong. The day he carried me all the way down to the beach...

Oh, I mustn't think of that. No, as much as I loved you, Harold, I mustn't think of you in that way. Never again. No Harold, never again.

We must fight the weakness of the flesh. Fight it. Fight it! I'll never be weak like that again. I was foolish. I was sinful and foolish then. And selfish. Oooh, how selfish I was! But no more. That was all before the children, anyway. Not once since Nora was born did I give into temptation, to folly. Oh, why did you turn out to be such a weak man, Harold? So weak! So helpless against sin and perversion. You were so easily victimized. And though I used all my strengths, Lord knows, I tried to save you, but a man can't be saved unless he finds the Lord for himself. He can't be led by the hand to Christ's love. He has to be called, alone.

Oh Harold, Lord have pity on your soul. You were never called. And we'll never find each other again—your poor lost soul, whirling, whirling, eternally flapping like a bat in the blackness, never resting. Oh, dear Harold, how I pity your weary soul!

You'll not find the peace I seek. Christ died for us, nailed to the cross. Fully conscious he was. The way I intend to go. I want to experience the Agony. I want to be awake, and have all my brain. Surely, it will be glorious! Oh, I mustn't even try and imagine it. Sometimes I get so involved. You can't anticipate it, the vison, the light, maybe even the voice! Oh, nearer my God to Thee, nearer my God to Thee!

I hope it isn't too much longer. I want to be fully conscious, I don't...

Not like Libby. Oh, that was a terrible thing Edgar said they did to her. Just terrible. And she had no one by her side helping her fight to keep awake, helping her along to the final ecstasy. Why, Dolf was there. Had he been a good Christian, a knowledgeable one...

He may be a good one but he certainly must lack the education...

He let them do it. He should never have let them give it to her. A person in such pain will plead and cry out, but you mustn't, oh, no, you must not give in to them. They are the weak ones at such times. We others, the ones sitting beside...

Dolf, I'm really surprised you let them! A Christian, you must be aware of the Glory of the Agony, the Being at One with Christ, to find Him at last in the Agony—oh, it's too glorious not to see.

You deprived her, you know. You robbed her of the most precious experience of life. Evil, evil drugs! Oh, how I abhor them. Satan is surely among us. Doctors, agents of the Devil! Oh you can go to the Devil for your x-rays, if you must have them, poisonous damaging rays piercing the body—oh, I'd never! But if you must have them...and your surgery—

You let them take off first one breast, then they lop off the other breast, and what good has it done you? Did you really think that was adding years to your life? Oh Libby, you were, perhaps, too young; you felt it was before your time, you let them confuse you with their fancy talk. It's all deviltry. It's all the devil's language. No wonder people are mystified by it, fascinated by it; they think it's powerful: strings of initials thrown at you that nobody can understand—as if incantations ever cured a man! They think it's magic, well it is. Black magic. The devil's tool: surgery.

I'd never let them go poking around in there, and for what? Cutting some of it away isn't going to do anything. They could take all this area here, they could take some skin from my arm or a leg and patch over it, they could probably fix it up almost like new and put a glass eye in for effect so I could look almost normal. Like Libby and her sponge breasts—you couldn't tell, she always looked good. But what's the point of it? It's just more vanity, just cosmetics. I don't want thousands and thousands of dollars' worth of cosmetics before I die, now what good would that do? The cancer wouldn't be stopped. They can't control something that's in God's hands alone. They are blasphemers, all of them. It's blasphemy, and sinful vanity. God still and always has the final say. Young and old, middle and teenaged, it's up to God...

My, my don't we sound like we're in Sunday School? Now Iris, you won't repeat Libby's tragedy. You'll have no one threatening you with a needle, no one's going to put you out like that—like an animal who has to be put down. Only Nora will be there. Oh, and I hope Edgar will come. And then I want Dr. Cook and Miriam. Miriam was so good with that old Mrs. Trader. She's supposed to be quite excellent by all accounts. And it will come faster here. They put you in those hospitals like Libby and they stick all those horrible tubes into you and pretty soon you're a drugged vegetable....

Oh, if they only knew! If only they weren't so needlessly afraid. Well, a little fear is only natural I guess, but there's the wonder and the glory of it too. I wouldn't miss it for the world. To join at last with my Lord, at last at last, my true Darling! Oh, I've waited too long for you, kept myself—look, see how I've kept myself for You, and worn Your badge, the sign You gave me? Oh, remember Lord, the thunder clap and the fall? You were with me then as I lay on the steps, whispering in my ear. Oh, I felt so close to You, You alone!

Am I not beautiful to you, my Savior, beautiful dripping, this wound, this hole in my face? I gave up my vanity didn't I? I know I was vain, oh, I know it now. All those years of brushing each other's hair. First the sisters, then me and Nora.... Oh, and all the mirrors! See, I've kept them to remind me of my sins. See Nora practicing her plies in this oval one? Oh she was just a kid. Please spare her, Lord. She was never vain as I was. She was only working, poor dear, she wasn't admiring herself; she had to use the mirror, it was a tool, all dancers us them. They also use the televisions now, or so she tells me.

TVs can be mirrors too. Oh, I think of it every time I watch the darn thing. It's like the monkey cage at the zoo. I only watch the educational shows. I like the ones with animals. The animals have more dignity. The one about lions last week! Oh, I shall never forget it. Such beautiful creatures, didn't you think so Scherzo? REMEMBER THE LIONS, KITTY-WITTY? REMEMBER THE BIG CATS ON THE TV CHASING AFTER THE ANTELOPE AND THE ZEBRA? COULD YOU HUNT DOWN AN ANTELOPE SCHERZO, AND POUNCE ON IT LIKE THAT? OOOH, THEY'RE FAST AND SPRINGY! YOU POOR THING, YOU CAN'T EVEN CATCH A ROOF-RAT WITH THOSE MUTILATED PAWS!

You're kind of like Libby without her breasts, aren't you? Not-a-cat. You're not-a-cat without your

129

claws. Libby was not-a-woman; she told me. I shall never forget it.

We all went there with the children. It was Thanksgiving. The place was lovely as ever. Libby always gave a nice Thanksgiving. And Edgar and I did the goose together, and she chopped the chestnuts, poor thing, that's all she could do she was so weak. I thought it just terrible the way they'd butchered her. And for what purpose? What earthly good did it do her? It didn't stop the cancer, probably just sent it on its way faster to another part. At least I can control mine. I can keep it from spreading....

And then they poison you with chemicals, more chemicals, and you get so weak, like Libby. You can only chop a few chestnuts. Edgar and I did all the stuffing and sewing and basting. Edgar, you snitched at the skin you bad boy. I noticed that. I didn't say anything in front of the others but I knew it was you. Naughty boy! Oh, Edgar, come to Mumzy, we'll cook us a goose here, just you and me.

No, Dolfi, you were wrong to let them drug her. As much as she may have pleaded. You should have been stronger. It was bad enough she had to suffer the extra tortures of the hospital. But she never had her reward—the Glory—and now her soul is left unenlightened, she remains forever in the dark. I am sad for her, Dolfi. I always did like Libby, even if her daughter was a rotten wife to my son, a rotten mother to my grandchildren. Spoiled, that's what she was. Spoiled rotten. When you have only one child...

You should have had another, Libby. You could have waited awhile. I waited eight years for Nora, and that was just perfect. If Ophelia had had a baby brother or sister to help take care of as Edgar did, maybe she would have learned early not to think only of herself. Maybe she would have learned that you don't always get your way, that sometimes everything doesn't work out exactly the way you wanted. Always had to be just so. Always had to have everything your way.

Alright already, we let you have your way. Did I ever put up a fuss? I never tried to fight you. You were always so stubborn. "We have to go for a drive in the park, the children want to go for a drive in the park...."

The children! Always the children. Nobody was fooled, Fella, it wasn't the children making demands, it was you. Always you. You should have heard yourself sometimes. The children were better behaved. I never heard them whining to their father: "We have to go for a drive in the park."

You never asked us, you always told us what we were going to do. I'd be perfectly happy sitting with Nora and the children, or walking with Edgar in the pinewoods looking for mushrooms. That's when we were closest, a family again, just like in Kentucky, in Carolina….

And it was so rare we could all be together. You always had to break it up, didn't you Fella? You always had to come and order us to do something else, go somewhere else. You'd get the kids in the car and we'd be forced to go. I'd be so content just sitting there and you'd insist we get up and go for a drive. And then what would happen? Why, something inevitably happened.

That time we got caught speeding on the highway and had to pay a very expensive ticket. Oh, and then there was the time you'd sent us all to the museum, all the way into the city, and none of us, I don't think, really wanted to go but you'd insisted so, and put all the kids in the car, so of course Edgar had to drive us all in, and you know he must've been upset. You two were always fighting. I knew it, I could tell. Of course I never said anything. And off we go and bam! What happens? The little boy gets hit. And Edgar was only going twenty miles an hour. Oh, it wasn't his fault at all. I saw him run out after that ball, my eye was still good then and I saw him clearly from the right. There was no time, nothing you could have done to avoid it. Poor Edgar, how they tortured you! Didn't you tell me they wouldn't let you talk to his parents, that their lawyer didn't even have the courtesy to tell you the boy was alive and not seriously hurt? You poor baby. Two weeks I think you said it took, and all that time going to work, living at home, in such torture, and all because that Ophelia, that self-centered brat, insisted we go to the museum just then. I'd had a premonition it was not God's will that we go.

She would have thrown a tantrum if we hadn't sped away. "You have to go to the museum now." Just like we had to go to the zoo, "because I promised the children." Promised the children! The children were too young to know the meaning if a promise. Barbie was just learning to walk. I had to take all the breakables and put them up high. I remember she tipped over the coffee table, and that's when the alabaster vase got cracked, and it's not worth one tenth of its former value now. Well, you can hardly blame a child, but her mother should have been watching her. She expected me to do everything. All she wanted to do was go running round to the beach, to the park, to the zoo, and never cared what happened here in my house.

You see it now Edgar? Wasn't I right? Oh, I never said anything. I never interfered. You had to learn the hard way. You had to find out for yourself. She fooled us in the beginning, but it didn't take long after that. The first time—the only time—you all came out here I was convinced of it. But what could you do? The children needed a mother then. I know, you did the right thing by waiting. You suffered for years for the sake of the children. You learned a lesson from your father. You knew what it was like to grow up with only one parent. And Sam would have felt it.

Maybe the girls would have been alright with their mother, but as for your son, a son needs a father. You were right to put up with it as long as you did. God will reward you my son.

Well, you're rid of her now. Only now see how foolish you were to waste so much money on all those doctors? Obviously they couldn't do her any good. I know all about alcoholism. They came to the church, and I must say, I was impressed. They are absolutely right. Only by accepting the Good, by calling on divine assistance, by admitting it—first they have to admit their sinful weakness, the body is the temple of God, they've no right to abuse it—only through God is there any hope of salvation.

And what was Fella to do? She's no religion. She'd no knowledge of God. Her parents deprived her of that. She could have come into the fold late in life as so many do, but it's much more difficult. Of course, she didn't have the strength.

She's a very weak woman, Edgar, a victim of the devil's temptation. You were right to finally call on the A.A. people, oh, I was glad to hear it, but I didn't think it would work in her case. And it didn't work. Now, you see, she's got to find out for herself. No amount of suffering for her did a bit of good. You only injured yourself. And now you must look after your own health. Ah, but you had a good mother who planted the precious seed for you. You have your Bible now, and I know you will turn to it in times of need. You must look to the Bible, Edgar. It's the only message that saves. You'll find such wonderful advice….

I could put you in touch with someone in the church there to help you with lessons. None of us is that strong, Edgar, we all need help, and there are trained professionals to guide you to the best readings for your needs. Oh, I'd do anything I could for you, anything….

Where's my pancake? Oh, here you are. What were you doing over there? I think just a little right here won't be too close. That part looks like it's healing a bit, it's not half so red and sore. Lipstick, I don't need any today. Such good skin we always had, Nora. Didn't I teach you to take good care of it? And I like this new cream you gave me. I hope you bring some more, I'm almost out. I like this one better than that cucumber stuff, although that smells so nice. Well, we'll try a bunch of them next time you come. Don't go buying any more of that mink oil now, that was too expensive for what it was.

There. That's the best we can do. Now where are my glasses? Oh, and my girdle. Have to remember to sew that. I'd really like a new one, but this will have to do until you come. We'll go to the mall and you can help me decide. They make so many different ones now. I need one with garters though. Those are hard to find. All you girls wear that darn panty hose now....

A mother's responsible for what goes on in a child's mind. At least you kids were always healthy, and never spoilt. I kept your minds clean of silly thoughts. You were such cheerful, obedient children, always eager to help your Mumzy; no lagging, no whining like the kids today—always begging: "Mom buy me this, Dad get me that." So spoilt! So completely spoilt rotten. Why, a good licking is what—

We were a good team, weren't we? We made out well. I've no complaints. It's a woman's duty to care for the family once the husband's gone. She has every right and responsibility to handle the finances. She has to make all the investment decisions by herself and look after the stocks and bonds. Oh, I didn't know what I was doing always. Those men with their fancy talk about this or that mine, this or that dairy, this or that railroad shipping company.... How did I know what to believe or how much to buy or when to buy it? I did my best. I tried to be sure, to check up on them as much as possible, but I lost some. It couldn't be helped. I'm no stock broker.

And then when Stephen died, God rest his soul, and they practically stole that valuable stamp collection from me—

How could I have known what it was worth? He never had it appraised before he died like I'd suggested. Oh, that was so terrible! I lost thousands. And nobody will take these etchings. Hundreds and hundreds of dollars they're worth, and no one wants etchings these days. They want big splashy things. Nora's told me. She knows what's what in art if anybody does. And they don't want etchings. Perhaps a museum....

But Fella, you spoilt those children. You put wrong beliefs into their little heads by fussing over them as you did. Oh, I remember, I remember it well. When Frieda was small and she was just walking, why, every time she stumbled you'd run and pick her up and cuddle her. Now any good mother knows you mustn't do that. No matter how much you love your child you must let them go when they fall down and cry. Pick them up briskly if you must, and remind them there's nothing the matter. Naturally, if you look worried about them they're going to worry. That's how you get all these nervous kids these days. Always sickly, their mothers cram them so full of drugs, and then they wonder why the kids want to try marijuana at night with their friends. And you know that leads to crime. Drugs are a crime, a crime against God and Nature.

Oh, Edgar, I wish she'd been a more spiritual woman. She was too weak, oh, obviously, always too week to do the hard tasks expected of a good mother and a good wife. She could only be a mediocre mother, and I suspect she was a terrible wife much of the time. After all, her parents brought her up very poorly. It wasn't entirely her fault. She was never taught to believe that God is Good. In her dark mind of shadows and confusion there was no source of good, nothing she could trust in, nothing she could draw strength from. How can you expect a child who never sees the light of Divine Truth to grow up healthy and strong, and to know what to do when she has children of her own?

Oh, I tried to show her the way. I told her it was useless to fuss over them so. Why, I could see that God was going to protect them, and she could never see it. She simply didn't believe they were going to survive their little scrapes and falls, always running them to the pediatrician for more shots, shots, shots, drugs, drugs, drugs. So many drugs pumped into their helpless little bodies, it's a wonder they aren't all addicts now.

I suspect they do try marijuana, but I pray they'll soon outgrow it and turn to the path of Truth and Righteousness. Oh, I pray for your babies, Edgar, for my grandchildren you gave me. They've had it tough having such a mother. Maybe now they too will see that she was no good for their father, and that as his suffering is ending, so will theirs.

A curse on our family. I sometimes wonder if she wasn't sent to test us all, to bring us all back together after you'd turned off the path, Edgar, and strayed for some years. And now you see it. You see where error and sin get you. I'm glad you've seen the sign through her. Now maybe you'll start taking care of yourself again. I can help you. If only you'd let me. I can help you begin to think clearly again and to accept more Spirit. Come out here and I'll take you to Dr. Cook. He's done such wonders for me, I'm sure he'd be glad to talk to you now.

When you were with me, though, Edgar, you were a much more spiritual young man. Remember the time you lost the car keys in the water at the beach and we weren't going to be able to get home that day? And we looked up and down in the sand, and then you realized you'd had them in your pocket swimming and we thought there was no chance they'd be found, that the sea would surely have buried them in the sand or carried them away? But you said to me—it was you who reminded me that God was always taking care of His children, that He was surely looking after us that day—yes, you were the one who said it, I'm sure of it now, you said: "Mumzy, I know where I was swimming. We could look in the water and maybe we'll find the keys in the sand."

And so we went in, you and I, and we searched the very sea floor and lo and behold, there they were, right down at my toes! I shall never forget it. God took me straight to them. He used my son to remind me of my faith, and we were rewarded with certain proof of His goodness that day.

And then, that other time not long after, when we were driving home from your Aunt Daisy's, you remember? There was that awful blind curve in the road ahead, and just as we were coming up to it I had a vision. I clearly saw it. Something was coming fast around the curve, something big and black, and as we headed toward that bend in the road the blackness in my mind's eye grew stronger and stronger and the feeling came with it that we were in danger and God was trying to send us a warning through me, and I almost didn't recognize its meaning.

I remember so clearly, we were coming right up on that dangerous bend in the highway when the blackness and the sense of something big and evil came into my mind so strong, I said to you kids in the back seat, and I'll never forget it, I said to you: "Something's about to happen to us if we try and go around that bend. I'm going to pull over." And just as we were safely off the road that enormous truck loaded high with telephone poles came screaming around the curve on the wrong side of the road, tipping over and scattering telephone poles in all directions... And if we'd gone any further, a single inch further, we would have surely been hit, and that would've been the end of us.

But once again Divine Spirit was watching. We were in His hands. He guided us to safety through a clear vision of evil around the bend. Thank God I had the power to receive His message. Like a telephone, I was the wire that carried His voice to my hands and feet and maneuvered our car off the road just in time. It was almost as if my hands and feet were acting before I understood why. I was explaining it to you kids, but it was already taking place.

I remember it all as though it were last week. His power entered me and I was no longer the mistress of my own limbs. I was completely an instrument of Divine Good. I knew I wasn't strong enough to see around that curve, but He helped me to see. He sent me that vision and caused my hands and feet to follow the Spiritual Mind, not my own inferior one. And so we were saved. I clearly was blessed.

But then, later, after you kids were grown and gone and I'd married again, for a time there, I began to get weak. I began to forget my responsibilities to study and fell out of the habit. I thought I was happy, but I was blinded by worldly pleasure. I'd been so long alone, fighting so hard for myself and my family without a man, and then suddenly, there was another man, and for a time it seemed my struggling and fighting were over. I leaned back and relaxed. I got too comfortable, let down my guard. And so, naturally, the Spirit in me began to shrink and my powers grew weak.

And when he lay dying of that lung disease, I was unable to save him. My powers of faith had decreased beyond the point of doing any one else any good. Poor Stephen. And this too was a sign....

Of course it was. I only saw it too late. God was reminding me to stay on the path and not falter just because I was surrounded by weakness and decay in others. I hadn't known him but five years. His moral life before we met may have been terribly corrupt, for all I knew.   It was too late by then. And I was too weak, it couldn't be fought. He succumbed to his own wrong beliefs, and then at last I saw the sign and realized what I had done and vowed to never waste myself in vain pursuits of morally weak men. What good, after all, had it done me? My own father dies before I'm born, my husband leaves me for a floozy, my own son leaves his mother's bosom for a weak and craven woman who torments him for years before he sees the light, then, the only other man in my life succumbs to a meaningless lung ailment at a time when we're both too weakened from our selfish enjoyment of each other to fight the devil in him and win.

Weak men! Morally, they're much weaker than women. Women have to be stronger, they're the first teachers. They are the ones who first serve as conductors for the spirit into the newborn. Even before their children are born, mothers are carrying messages of Spirit into their very wombs to feed the unborn and give it strength to survive the first test of birth. Oh, and my babies were so strong and healthy, and they were never sick—oh, maybe for a day or two—but they always healed up quickly and no quack pediatrician ever touched them and no poisonous drugs were ever injected into them against their wills and therefore they rarely, if ever, fussed and complained and cried when they fell down and skinned a knee. They knew they were in the Best hands. They never feared the foolish illusion of sickness, and certainly not that of death, because they had early and constant training, you see, because I cared enough to teach them. Even before they were old enough to speak their lessons had begun and never ended until they left home and were on their own in the world. Each had to make his own mistakes, as I did, and had to suffer in his own ways, as I have. And yet, neither of them has fallen prey to sin or sickness.

Edgar, your children don't appreciate Divine Truth. They must be confused by what happened to their mother; they need help and guidance. But, oh, they're so far from me. And now, with this eye, I don't think they could look at me for long or listen to me. They'd have no respect for the teachings now, seeing me, they wouldn't understand it was a Divine Badge of Honor placed on me, a reward for my years of study and openness of spirit. I was a receptor for Spirit many times.

That day in church—that was the biggest task of all. I was to carry a most important message, a message that would be forever etched on my face for all the world to read it clearly like a billboard. And it's had to grow bigger and clearer. I am a chosen instrument of Spirit, clearly, or He wouldn't have demonstrated it so many times by sending me visions in moments of need, as when he led me to the keys on the ocean floor, or saved us from that killer truck, or the time when as only a girl I stepped over the snake in the meadow when Violet, who had taken berries out of my basket just a few minutes before, was caused to step on the snake. OOOOH, I can still feel it now in my toes!

And He was always sending little signs through me. Sometimes the clouds would form letters I could read, like the time they made a clear forty-five when Edgar was in the navy and I'd been worried that the war would never end and then He made the forty-five in the clouds over the apartment in Jacksonville and nothing could have been clearer to me. I was probably the first person in the States to get the news.

And now He's graced me with this great message, something to serve mankind, I'm sure of it. I've worn it for nearly twenty years now and it's never pained me. It's almost no trouble to keep up, just have to mind the tears and the blood when they start flowing, and it does stick to the pillow now

144

sometimes when I roll over, but other than that, I can practically forget about it.

It's a small cross to bear, and the message is a great one, more powerful than any He's sent me before. I can't pretend to read it now. In my imperfect state I still lack Divine Mind; I still can't quite make it out. Sometimes I think it's a warning to the vain. I suppose I suffered from the sin of vanity. I remember how I worried once that Harold had left me because of my looks. Oooh, I was so broken-hearted. I was making up any number of wrong beliefs then. I could not accept that he was so full of depravity, the father of my children, that he could run off with that, that—

She even wore a red dress that day, and painted her lips that nasty color too, and wore high spikey heels that most decent women didn't wear in those days. Bouncing black curls, and that cheeky grin, her red dress swirling as she whisked her back to me, showing off that little round rump of hers—

Oh, and then I went home and cried and cried, looked in the mirror. Yes, I confess I, I remember staring red-eyed in the mirror, asking myself: "What does he see in her? Am I not attractive to him? I'm still young, beautiful..."

I remember, I was vain, vain enough to think I'd had something to do with his misbeliefs, that I was somehow responsible for his error, for his sin!

145

Oh, but I suffered for you, Harold. I waited and waited and hoped you'd see the light and clear out of that trap and come home. We waited, Edgar and tiny Nora and I. We kept the homefires burning for you. We gave you many a chance to see clear back to the path. And then, when you humiliated us finally in public, when you stopped giving us the decency of discretion and were seen with her by all the neighbors!

And they naturally began to be concerned for me. They hadn't known a thing until you went around so carelessly, you two sinners. I'd not said a word. I'd had strength enough to wait, to hope it would pass from you, to hope you would receive a sign, see the error of your mortal ways....

Oh, we waited, my little son and I. We waited for his Papa to come home to us that we might be a complete family again. And then the neighbor women came to me and tried to tell me what they'd seen, and I remember, I was vain at first, oh, I was foolish, I wouldn't listen to them. I thought they were just being snoop gossips, which they were, but they were also looking after me. They knew even before I did that he was a lost soul, that I was deluding myself with false hopes, that he wasn't going to see the error of his ways and make a correction. And they were right. You never came back, Harold.

And so we moved away, and from that day on, I was mistress of the household. I had to take care of both the domestic chores and the more worldly economy, and of course I was naïve at first, and got us into some bad investments with a few crooks.

That feed salesman, oh what a viper he was…!

Well, we survived it. We never hungered for want of anything. I baked you kids two cakes a week. We always ate the freshest fruits and vegetables we could get, and I sewed all your clothes by hand and you were always nicely dressed, and I continued your educations and helped with your schoolwork too. And sometimes I don't know how I did it. If not for Divine Spirit entering me and guiding me all the time, I might have stumbled under the load. But I never did. And you kids never thought yourselves deprived because other kids had fathers at home and you had none. You never felt sorry for yourselves because Mumzy wouldn't let you. Mumzy wouldn't put sick and wrong beliefs in your heads, so you never had them, not while you lived with me. Not like your poor little neglected children, Edgar.

Look at me, children! Come look at your grammum now, if your mother hasn't poisoned you completely against me. Look at the badge on my face. If you have any Spirit in you, you'll perhaps understand better than your own father, who says he wants me to see a doctor. Now why should I see a doctor? He's only going to try to con me into accepting some medicine or surgery that I can't will myself to believe in, even if I tried. You have to buy all that voodoo, have to believe it really works if you're going to allow it.

I can't drift that far back now. I've come too close to Spirit. I've left mortal mind too far in the dust now. I've worn my badge of honor here for twenty years. If it were going to kill or damage me, surely it would have done so by now. And look. I'm perfectly fine. Healthy as the day I was born, except for this one eye that isn't really diseased, I'm convinced, but only being slowly plucked out. It is the right eye, after all, and it was offended at least once by the sight of that floozy in the red dress running off with my children's father—

And then there was that thunderclap in church—

Bu she was too big to let out. She widened the hole—

And so it was. And so the relief is coming. I can begin to feel the easing of it. The evil vision is leaving me. It's not nearly so clear as it once---

I can't make out the color of those spiked shoes....

Well, no sense fussing in here anymore on such a beautiful day. Pick up the lesson here...

Oh, and my glasses are dirty again! Now I'll have to get Kleenex from the bath—

OOOOH, MY GOODNESS IT CAN'T BE—

Those men are coming up to my yard. Who—

Three men in suits? And that one in the middle has some kind of satchel.

WHAT ON EARTH—

I don't recognize—

They're coming up to the door. Oh, Iris, run, you haven't got your wig on. OOOH, who can they be?

OOOOH, WAIT A MINUTE PLEASE—

No time to comb it; just get it on properly—

I'M COMING, JUST A MINUTE—

Oh, hurry, hurry! I've never seen those men before. They can't be from the church, can they?

Oh, for heaven's sake, stop ringing. I'm coming as fast as I can. Just tuck this little wisp in. Can't have anyone see me without my hair—

Oh, I hope they don't start to turn away....

149

I'M COMING!

What could they possibly want?

That isn't Mr. Potter is it? That one in front—

Oh, my, they're turning away. They mustn't have heard me—

OOOOOH, I'll catch them. What could they—

Who could they—

Get this lock unfastened, UMPH, it's always so hard to—

OOOMPH, there! The bolt here—

Good, they heard, they're turning around. Just get this doorknob lock turned—

OOOH, I'm so unprepared. Thank goodness I've my robe on. What on earth could they want? Nothing has happened has it?

YES, I AM SHE—

III. Dolf

WHATZIT—

Must've fallen asleep. Still raining. Jesus Christ, how long is this going to keep up? Boxwoods losing all the new topsoil I just—

DAMN TV LEFT ON—

Waste of energy. What is this, some picture? Turn the sound on, where's that switch? Ah, here…

God damn commercial. God, I hate commercials. Looked like Alan Ladd—can't speak proper English, promote ignorance, blast the sound up above the program forcing you to—

Glad I attached this switch here, turn the sound off. Don't need sound for ball games anyway, only the news. Then you don't need the picture. Silly expensive gadgets, TVs. Won't have these around much longer when you're out of oil, at least won't have them on day and night. Damn kids grow up all glue-eyed bathed in pap and propaganda, bunch of worthless zombies, can't read or write, can't add, got those little calculators now in grade school, how the hell are they ever going to learn?

Why, Jane taught second grade kids their arithmetic—what was it—some thirty-five years? Didn't we figure it out one day sitting in there? You

153

stopped in for sherry and I asked you to marry me. Ah Janey...

We did the double crosstics in bed together. You had a good head for crosswords. Yes you did. And why did you doubt your intelligence so? You were every bit as sharp as Libby, but she had the arrogance and none of the patience, at least not for double crosstics. I don't think Libby liked to struggle with her mind. Didn't want to challenge herself with anything.

And she was going to write! Now that was comical. Twenty-two years old, just got finished at the Sorbonne; she was going to write. Of course she was! So was I, so was every other little twerp on the ship, the newborn of European universities, heads busting with grandiose ideas. Sure, sure. We were all going to be Fitzgeralds, come back and conquer the continent, sure.

So you got pregnant. You could've gotten rid of it, there was that abortionist in Trenton.... Could've asked your father for the money. Didn't have the nerve though. Marriage was the easy way out, and you knew it, Libby. The hell it was—

You didn't know what you were getting into 'for the sake of respectability' –and rebelliousness, you might in all decency add, proving you didn't have to marry a Jew. Well, did anyone ever say you had to marry a Jew? It was you thought you had to prove something. I never did understand why. You had to dissociate yourself. Brooklyn ghetto. No, I don't blame you. Only you didn't have to get pregnant. God, it was only the third or fourth time we'd—

You were too young, Libby; we always agreed there. It could've been a book instead, perhaps. Only I don't think so. I think a book would've proven impossible, a defeat. Whereas the infant, that was at least a sort of compensatory accomplishment. An excuse, at any rate. None of this Family Planning then. Kids came along, take it or leave it, that's what you got. And I was never upset about it, was I?

Well, I would have liked to have had the means...but Mother had plenty of room here. It wasn't so bad as all that, Libby. You said you loved the country. Well, you pretended to. And you had New York as well, the best of both worlds I gave you. And later, we had Maine too. And the baby never got in your way. You had your parties—

That Andrew Jackson fellow with the waxed mustache, wonder what ever became of him? Most unfortunate name. Fancied himself a dandy. Chasing you all the time, what did he think you were? All right, I agreed to it. And it worked out well most of the time. We had an arrangement. You didn't want to feel married, you said. You could've had that Jackson fellow, or any of the rest; why the hell didn't you—

I don't think you quite had the guts. Now Jane, Jane was different; our love was young, sublime, co-ed....

She shouldn't have dropped out for him! She was a good student. And she had the discipline. Could've done something, anything—

Well, she did, didn't she? Taught those kids, oh, thousands of them, we figured it out over sherry—

So sweet up at her blackboard. She had a real grace to her. Oh yes, you had the dominant personality, Libby. Maybe you appeared to have more character. Or you wanted to *be* a character.

And you were, later. You played the regular *grande dame*. After Mother died you filled the house—

Those Christmas parties! The time Bob Kooch fell off the porch—oh God! The time Madge and Willy wandered off in the snow for hours and we sent out the cocker spaniel with the brandy flask tied to his collar.... Found 'em under the canal bridge finishing off the bottle of Cutty Sark—

Bill and Madge Hennessey from Harrison—

No, no it was—

Shawnessey. The Shawnesseys from Boise, Idaho. Boise Idaho, what the hell kind of place—

There was a young lady from Boise—Boise: noisy-noisy, um, not much—

Coy-sy? No, poise-y, um…oy—oy? Oy vey! Oy-goy—

Goy-sy?

Go back to sleep Dolfi. No, I can't go back to sleep. I'm tired, but I can't sleep anymore. Jes' caint sleep no mo', caint snore no mo', seems like I been here befo—

No, don't even try; you'll be up at night. How about a cigar? Now where the hell…? Well, I thought they were in this pocket, now they're always kept right here in this left shirt—

No wait. That was after breakfast and I was sitting—

Okay, okay, so you've got to get up if you want a cigar. Guess I don't want one at the moment, too much trouble. Just sit here, close the eyes again. AHHH—

UNCLE TOBY. YOU GWINE A SIT ON OL' PAPPY'S LAPPY? THAT WOULD MAKE OL' PAPPY MIGHTY—

OUCH, HEY BOY, EASY ON THE CLAWS THERE. WILL YOU SETTLE DOWN! OKAY, OKAY! SIMMER DOWN NOW. GOOD—

Remember Janey, Toby? Remember how she didn't like you at first, how we had to lock you in the cellar that first week? But then, remember Toby, when you snuck up to our bed and she let you stay down at the foot? And that was the first time she let you get close to her, and from then on you were friends.

Well, let's say, you coexisted peaceably. She didn't get up and leave the room anymore after that. And I was glad. Oh, it was never a case of allergies, she just had this silly fear, squirrels too. Anything 'fast and furry' she would say. Fast and furry. She was a little creature, wasn't she? Smelled of lavender a lot, or else of orange blossom. Could've been a china doll—

On the canvas lawnchair in that linen suit, she was always smart. Could've been nineteen twenty-two, right there on the green. I was coming out of Philosophy one-twenty-one and she was going in for Italian and, just as they do in the pictures, we bumped into each other in the rush of bodies and I knocked a book out of her little paw. I think it was Leopardi…. And that was how I noticed her, how she was just the right height and build and we seemed perfectly matched—

After that I always noticed her, watched her…until we were formally introduced at that Thanksgiving dance. It was at the punch bowl, by Harry, and I never guessed that she and Harry—

But then old Harry did have his dash…

DAMN IT, got to empty this bladder, starts to hurt every time it fills up, must be the prostate. LET ME UP THERE TOBY—

Have to go back to the damn Doctor—what's-his-name—Hatchet? Not a bad guy, really, at least he's not insisting on an operation. And with a name like Hatchet, I should be grateful, eh?

GOD DAMN KITCHEN LIGHT LEFT ON AGAIN! Well, no sense turning it off, soon be dark. What was that doing on during the day anyway? Jesus, enough bills to pay without wasting electricity—

I'd like to know who the hell took my French toilet water—

Ahh…that's better—

Can't understand it, saw it there only recently. She must've stolen it. Next time she's here must remember to confront her. Always kept it right here behind the john. It was a gift from Janey. The cruise—she bought it in a little shop in Crete, or was it Sicily—

There was an old lady from Sicily—

No, no, that's too hard. There was a young lady from Boise—

WHO—

KIDS! That can't be—there aren't any—

No, can't be kids. The rain, hear things in the rain sometimes. Maybe hearing things inside my ears, the left one's always a little too waxy...

No, that can't be—

OH, IT'S *YOU* UNCLE TOBY. STOP THAT SCRATCHING! SOUND LIKE A KID—

No kids out there in this rain. That God damn kid, climbing in the window like that! I don't like anything, man, woman, or even cat prowling around in my bedroom while I'm sleeping. And thank God we got him the third time. Wish to hell I'd caught the one robbing the pear tree!

Worse than raccoons, neighborhood prowlers, come in the night, rip off all the God damn ripe pears. That tree had been loaded. I was going to pick them myself in the morning. For Christ's sake, kids can't keep their hands off your—

Who took off with my French toilet water, I'd like to know. Unless it was that stupid maid, what was her—Dolores? Doris? Dinah? Diane? The woman had an I.Q. of seventy-five at best.

Must've taken it for some women's perfume. Must've been she. Couldn't have broken it and hid the evidence, whole place would've reeked of it for weeks. Wonder what else she made off with. MAID OFF WITH, right.

Now, there was a young Jewess from Boise, whose bedroom at night was quite noisy, or something...her blanket blank and her blanky blank blank was blankety blank or blank blanky—

There was a young Jewess from Boise, whose bedroom at night was quite noisy. Well, how would I know about her bedroom at night? Unless I were—

Wait. There was—

No, no, I once had a neighbor in Boise, whose bedroom at night was quite noisy. Though it was perfectly true that the girl was a Jew—

No, no this isn't going to be clear enough. There was—

That young rascal! Rascals, hell, there could've been a gang of them that night. I'm not going to be one of those paranoid old farmers sits on the front porch with a shotgun across his knees for Christ's sake. If they're going to come in the night and pick off every single God damn beautiful ripe juicy pear I was saving for Sally's visit—

I'd shoot 'em if they tried it again. Still got that Luger. Been meaning, always been meaning to clean that thing up. Still have the full clip. Might as well have it serviceable. Best thing about it I'd be too old by the time I ever used it to do any damage. Who'd put me in prison at my age? Kids—

Still sounds like there's somebody out there in the rain. Who the hell'd be prowling about in this cold rain? Let 'em! Let 'em catch pneumonia while they're at it.

Even Ophelia's kids—as good as they basically are—you can't trust 'em. They're brought up—all of them—with an outright contempt for their elders. Why, I worshipped my father. And fathers carried canes in those days. He never had to use it on me.

That poor Buddy Scheidel's father beat him bloody that time, and that was a shame; the whole school agreed he'd gone too far. Now I'd never do that, couldn't, to a kid, unless maybe I caught him stealing my—

Ophelia, I never laid a hand on you. Maybe that's part of your problem. I guess we were pretty lax in disciplining you. But when did you ever need it? You were either too little or too cute when you were screwing up, or else you were old enough to be reasoned with. But we didn't neglect you either. You can't charge that. What is your beef, Ophelia? You seem to have lost the ability to communicate, with me, with the world...

I can't figure you out. You've obviously got a beef of some sort, think the world's done you wrong. What did anyone ever do to you? For Christ's sake, Fella, we gave you a good childhood, sent you to excellent schools. All right, you sent yourself to graduate school on scholarship, that's true. But then so did Libby. So did I; it's easy when you're smart.

We were proud of you then. You had a nice family life: three fine children, all good looking, whatever else they may or may not be. And so you decide the world owes you something--the world, or your husband, or me, or yourself—

Do you think you let yourself down? What the hell is your problem? Drinking yourself to death. If it's not pills, handfuls of pills—God, how could anyone take the time to swallow—

It's your wretched bourbon, your gin, whatever the hell you wrap yourself around all day. All right. All right. I can almost understand it sometimes. There is a great temptation there—we all succumb to it occasionally—of wanting to blank out, let go, get drunk to forget it all. Bobbing in your fish tank pickled to the gills, floating all day in a dark, cloudy swill, blurry images looming in and out...

Although, for my part, after the last two deaths, I haven't had to do it. Haven't wanted to let go completely. Afraid. It's too seductive. Don't want to join you ghouls just yet...

And they, he, whoever the hell it was, broke a branch off that pear tree! I tried to repair it. Doubt it has a chance. Won't be putting out green this spring despite the wire and tape. Damn kids. Damn them all—

And maids too. She had no business taking the living room books apart. Jane and I had just dusted them. Puts them back all mixed up, half of them upside down. Now I'll have to do the whole thing all over again my—

One thing I can say for Libby—and Janey, too, for that matter—knew enough to leave my stuff alone. But that Rosy with her constant meddling—

Libby resented her pregnancy, the one pregnancy I ever caused as far as I know. She couldn't reconcile mothering with her other, however vague, ambitions. I think it was a sub-conscious cop-out. She didn't really believe in herself, in her potential, or so-called talents. What talents—I can't think of any—did she bother to develop?

She didn't like the country at first. Okay, it was primitive: *dirndl*ed German women crocheting, gossiping in the kitchen... too quaint, too quaint after New York and Paris.

Ah, Paris. She'd been such a rebel there, apparently, though I'll never know—wouldn't talk about it, something sacred, a lover? Older man most likely, intellectual, one of her professors probably, American, French? Well, he never wrote her as far as I know.

And the rows we had at night! Hated being stuck at Mother's house, didn't you? You think I liked it any better? The boredom, lack of privacy.... Well, we moved didn't we? Only had two years of it. You didn't suffer so damn much, Libby. And in the end you loved it here. You, so regal on your chaise longue bees in the grapes behind the screen long ebony cigarette holder between ringed fingers. City lady retired to the life of country gentry, you made out all right....

And it was fashionable. You were always a fashion-conscious little—

Ever since Paris. Paris put it in your blood. I can't imagine you in your Michigan days, a token Jewess. What could those Midwest boys have made of a New York Jewess, feminist, smart, fast-talking, cigarette-puffing sophisticate? What did they know? But you were still a Daddy's girl then, weren't you Libby? Didn't you tell me you only fraternized with the Jewish boys? Still set apart, still loyal to Daddy—

Ah, but Paris, Libby, you were educated there. The world widened for you, no more Jew, Gentile, Goy, Yid. You found out about Communism with a capital C. Maybe just a lot of libertarian rhetoric. Somehow you found out about the other classes. Suddenly you didn't have to be Jewish—

But you took it wrong. Denial, too much denial of the physical fact, Libby. You looked like an Eastern European Jew. There was no point in converting to Christianity. Better to go without: opiate of the masses after all. Better to live, a Jew rejecting Judaism, and die—

Ah, but there's the rub. On your deathbed, Libby, you weren't so sure. You admitted it, darling—oh, sweet, sorry moment of despair! You wanted something to cling to and there was nothing, a vacuum, and it was sucking you into itself and away from all light. I had nothing to offer you, Libby, I'm sorry. I should have called somebody for you, a priest even, it didn't matter to me. But you said no it was too late now, there was no time to begin with spiritual matters, better to give you morphine, eh, *ma petit chou*, better to sleep through the transition, better not to know...

Oh, you took so damn long. And when you seemed to recover that summer, we lived on the hope—six months— It was a gift. Frieda went to Europe, you got to see her when she came back, we had the driveway paved...life was beginning again. Funny how cancer comes back after going underground. You'd even gained weight, looked almost back to normal. I had hope. I'd believed. It was a miracle...

Didn't happen with Jane. No, Janey was much swifter. But then, when I married her she had that cough. By that time the cough was so much a part of her it didn't spell out cancer to me...

We couldn't have known. And Rosy, the swiftest of all swifts. We didn't even suspect. Liver cancer— why, she never *drank*! So strange. Like Edna dying

166

of that brain hemorrhage, so sudden, eerie. Rosy looked healthy, plump, smooth, no cough—

Well, I don't know what's holding me together. Railroad train runs me down, I get up, stagger about. I'm still walking for Christ's sake; I can't understand it. The sensation of death was so certain, creeping up freezing off big chunks of me...

No doubt it'll happen again. Listen to that pulse now—now where is it? Why the hell can't I find—

Okay, there it is. Boomp boomp, boomp-boomp, boomp-boomp, boomp-boomp-boomp, boomp-boomp—

Why the hell so fast? It's because you're thinking about it now, Dolfi, calm down you damn fool!

Boomp-boomp—it's going to slow down now, it's slowing down, boomp-boomp—

See, Dolfi, just don't worry about it, it sounds fine, it slows right down to normal when you just take a deep breath—

Boomp-boomp, boomp-boomp, AHUHHHHHHHHHHHHHHHHH, that's right, let it out slowly—

Boom-boomp. See, much better now. It's back to normal, now. You can relax, relax your damn legs; you'll get a charley horse again for crying out loud!

Well thank God it's not the Eater. That I couldn't stomach. Can see why Libby's father put a bullet in his brain, if, as they thought, he did diagnose his own cancer. Nobody'll ever know. Should've insisted on an autopsy. Annie couldn't handle it though. She began to fall apart right then, I'm convinced of it. God, to go out like her, though, a bloody vegetable! Libby could barely take it, those last six or seven years, the way Annie forgot everything, even forgot her own daughter, started calling her "Mama" in Russian, then it was Yiddish, turning into a baby in the end like Benjamin Button—

I'm sure that colored her attitude. Libby wouldn't have died like that under any circumstances, not after Annie. Libby was brave enough for a woman with no religion. Finally said she wished she'd had something. Well, she saw it through, and I'm glad they gave her that shot, I wouldn't have wanted her conscious. Another three hours it took, sitting there, clock hands—cursing those clock hands. Then begging them to swing around, release me, release her, separate us!

That doctor was all right. Hope I get one as understanding. Of course there won't be anyone at my bedside—

Well, maybe there will be, if I get married again. She'd have to be a real gem. Of course, Ophelia might come, but then I don't trust her to be sober....

Lara, dear Lara, you were so young! Three little kids, my God, how cruel it was with you, just divorced—that bastard! If only you'd known. It wasn't you, it was the Eater changing you. He should have stayed, what a lousy—

Oh, Lara sitting at the piano with your youngest, the boy, what was his name? Oh, Christ I can't remember—picking out "Old Black Joe," me with the banjo on my knee, oh, I come from Alabamee with—

Then the letter from your mother; how had she known? Did you tell her about us, Lara darling? About my proposal? And you were thinking "seriously" you'd said. The children would've been so happy here. Oh, I know you were young, thought you had your whole life—thought we'd just be a few years and then you'd be free for someone else. We loved each other, what did it matter what anybody thought—

Cancer. I cause it. God damn it *must* be me! Everybody I ever loved in my life, my God—

There was a young lady from Boise. A young Jewess, a, no...I had a young neighbor in Boise, whose bedroom was often quite noisy, now it was perfectly true that the girl was a Jew—

But her "Oh-Jesus-Christs" were quite goy-sy. Goy-sy?

169

Well I still don't like it. Oh skip it. Not in the mood for composing anyhow. Haven't written anything, not even a letter in, well, not since that note to Heidi in German, dictionary on the desk, forgotten too much of my German it's terrible—

No, I regret it, I should've written more, more light verse at least. But then it fell out of favor anyway. And since the *Manhattan* lost Priestly and gained that godawful Jespers—he tried to turn the thing into another *Life* for Christ's sake. Well, the poetry sure went to hell fast. And after Paddington and Weizl died....

Nobody appreciates that gentle—that genteel— kind of light verse, light humor, light essay. Light, sophisticated, crisp, unpretentious. Everything today has got to be heavy, like a lead balloon. Everything sinks like a weight to the lowest common denominator. If it doesn't hit you over the head, isn't violent, sensational isn't macho—

It's all gotten so heavy, so crude, none of the refinement of our day. The thing was to approach delicate perfection. To be natural meant to be elegantly simple, not base, not coarse and chaotic. Organized, but not constricted, light verse was perfect for the times. Art was a delicate flower— Weizl's parable on that—

The violence and crudity of the Fascists was enough heaviness. There was enough hammering going on; poetry was precious. We used to dig for it in the bottom of the Red Cross boxes, Paddington and I—

And now it's all this Beat stuff, not even Beat anymore, I don't know what they call this hippie shit, with its groaning reiteration: "the world is an atom bomb the world is an atom bomb the world is an atom bomb—"

They had no appreciation of history. Nothing happened before nineteen-fifty. What a gang of flunkies! Unread, unwashed Bohemians. Sitting in the window across from us on Eleventh Street barefoot black beret crossed legs banging his bongos, looked like a goddamn monkey, unkempt, shaggy—

But then of course they want to imitate moneys—the new Rousseauians—only they've never heard of Rousseau—and not Henri; though he was a monkey-fancier, he certainly wasn't a personal imitator. He didn't ape apes. His paintings are intelligible, light, well-drafted, refined, a bit cynical perhaps, but delicate, controlled.

I don't know why everything's got to be two columns long now. We didn't write to be paid by the word. We never valued length over concision. Take a little gem like Paddington's "White Ducks," four tiny lines, couldn't have been more than fifteen words, very Oriental actually, practically a Haiku, so perfect, so total unto itself. Who needs this silly Goldstein stuff, four columns, and all this repetition, pounding pounding hammering his one simple idea; you'd think everyone's head were rock. Poets on the rock piles—

We wrote for an elite. And we didn't care. We knew we were only going to be read by an elite. Why pretend otherwise? Even if your verses get printed in one of those anthologies for public school children, how many of those little drug- and TV-addled goons are going to respond to my little fish? They'll take all the imagery literally and shrug their stooped shoulders and their ignoramus teachers aren't going to be of any help to them: "It's about a little fish"; "Very good John-john, you get an A for today."

Why write anything if you know you're writing it for those dolts? My little fish is at least thirty years old now, anyway. Surprised to get two-hundred and fifty for it—but it was a nice surprise. Maybe there are some others I could dust off, submit....

The educated reading public is shrinking. Why sure it is. Oh, poetry revivals, such a big fad now. And read-ins—sounds like the Beatniks, got together in those cellar bars to out-whammy each other with sophomorisms; we couldn't stay for laughing at them. Libby almost spit out her cappuccino!

Subtlety. Precision draws the reader in like quiet natural beauty. It's a puzzle, an intricacy to be appreciated formally, like sipping fine liqueurs as opposed to guzzling beer—no, not beer—apple wine, that Godawful kid stuff, or Tequila.

And paid by the line! My God, they're all monstrosities now. I read the first four lines and turn to the cartoon. I'm not subscribing anymore. This last year was on the Fergusons anyway. It was nice of Jack. He still thinks of me as the *Manhattan* intellectual. I'm flattered, I suppose. But Jack, I'm eons beyond that. Who do I know in New York anymore? Christ, the last of them, Rich, Rich died, when was it? Not last Christmas, the Christmas before—

That letter from Tammy, cancer again, of the liver, wasn't it? Or of the pancreas, I can't remember. It was a blessedly short time for you. Jesus, why must it always be cancer? Every single one I ever loved—my God, the whole universe...

All right, all right, none of that now. That's like your beat-em-over-the-head poets. Everyone in the damn country's got the same fixation. Can't even—

Got its own euphemism now, like Consumption—although that included a lot of cancer, it wasn't all TB. A large percentage, and venereal disease, VD—can't even say it; just call it "The Big C."

Well, better syphilis, better almost anything...

All right, all right, now, how did that little dancer thing by Paddington go? Wing aflitter, something glitter, something something, but bitter, bitter. What was the middle part now? Wing aflitter something, was it glitter? Yes, I believe glitter, but then what—

Let's see now, where? Oh hell, there's some more in the box on the piano, ones they gave me last Christmas. Take a whiff now: AHHHHH. Getting a might stale though... Now what about matches? Thank you birdy. Love this little brass match-bird. Brought it back from Munich last time...

The Christmases we used to have! I'd string up that Viennese man on the unicycle, get the marzipan from Frederick's, the tree at Bill Druthers' gas station, the bulbs from the attic, spend the whole day setting up the place. Oh, and the electric candles, get the damn extension cords untangled, sorted out...that year I labeled them all, always a few bulbs out, apparently for no reason, have to go buy new bulbs, go all the way to Eatonsville— Then there were the stockings....

Thank God Ophelia always took care of the stocking stuffing. I had to do the hanging though. And then the wooden figurines on the mantelpiece, my God, how did I ever get all that set up?

Libby was always busy with the food. Defrost the goose, slice chestnuts, get pickles out of the barn, what the hell else did she—

And then they'd arrive, the noise, the confusion, three kids! You'd have thought there were twenty! And we'd paint the marzipan fruit with food coloring, dust the little potatoes with chocolate powder—my God, they looked real!

And getting them all into bed was a struggle...

The guests would arrive: the Carmels, the Sweeneys, the Ruffuses, the Nortons, the Bickbys, the Froths, the Churchills, the Olgilvies, the Swanns, the place would fill up. The drinks! I'd spend the whole time mixing drinks, get those little bitter oranges off the tree on the porch. And they'd start to sing carols...

Poor piano, sticky with spilled drinks, cocktail rings. Fella would cart the kids upstairs for the last time, snow falling...

And Gerald would pass out, inevitably—you'd pass out right here on the chaise. And Jenny, you always made it here, on the rocker, and Hal, I remember you and Marion on the stairs and Lara—

Oh, you're all gone now. All gone....

***

Let's see what time it is. It must be time for a drink. Too early for supper still, the sun hasn't gone down yet. Let's see—

Oh, almost six, time for a little sherry.

What's this? Stove on! HOW—?

Well, for Christ's sake. I can't be expected— living all alone here—the meals I have to prepare, salt free, get distracted, the phone rings. God damn it, wonder how long—

Must've been the coffee pot from this morning. Yes, must've been the coffee, that's the burner I always use. All right, you're off now. Couldn't have wasted that much electricity, only one burner. What did I have for lunch? Ah yes, the liverwurst and cottage cheese, yes, okay and no coffee. That's how it happened then. Okay, okay, I'll remember next time. Sink's clean, glad I did those dishes then, and pills upon the sill—don't have to take any now do I? No, no, not until after I eat, then the nitroglycerin just before...

All right, Dolfi, how about a glass of sherry? Cold and rainy, good day for curling up—

But where are you when I could use you, someone to curl up with, keep me warm, keep the old blood circulating—for crying out loud, where are you Janey? Rosy? Libby? You God damn whores of Satan, Christ almighty—Mother, you too—

abandoning me here one after the other. Why is it I, alone, rattling around here, bag of bones, my prison and my tomb?

Oh never mind. You're all in New York for the weekend. I'll have a cozy sherry by myself then. Turn on the TV news—

I'll just get myself a glass here. No, wait a minute, there should still be the glass from this morning on the drainboard. Ah, so it is, why waste another. Okay, now an ice cube. All right. This cigar needs a light. A matchbook—

Libby always kept this first drawer here full of matchbooks. But no more. Where the hell did that Daphne, that Donna, that Dotty what the hell was her name? Where the devil did she put that carton of matchbooks I'd just bought, the ones from the A&P—

Oh yes, here on the piano, and right next to my little bird, how superfluous. One of you's got to move. Birdy, I'm putting you here on this side table. Okay. The matches, the glass, the ice, still room in this ashtray...

Shall we put on Cronkite? Oh, he's got a good fifteen minutes still. But we might as well tune in the picture here, keep the sound switch off. What is this ludicrous program? A man with his horse, talking to his horse. Okay buddy, you have a nice conversation now...

Let me pour myself a drink here. Where's that Italian Swiss Colony I just bought? For God's sake, why can't anything stay where it belongs?

Okay, here you are. What were you doing down there? I specifically left you out. Did that Deedee or Dolly or whatever the hell her name is—

Have to write her a check soon, ask her next time when she comes... Bitters, put some bitters in now, just a drop, or a 'drip' as Libby used to say. Christ, I'm taking over your habits now. Remember how I used to tease you about putting bitters in your sherry? God, and now I'm doing it. It's pretty good though; 'just a drip now, Dolfi,' you would say...

Ah, the Eastern birds book, how many times did we—

I can't bear to open it now. And Janey, too, she loved to look up birds, the towhees especially, we got pretty good at towhees.

Ah, Janey, you seemed so doomed. Told me you'd smashed everything, all of your precious trinkets there against the palm tree in the middle of your lanai. Couldn't part with your knickknacks. Jesus, you had so damn many of them. The scrapbooks—thank God you saved some of them. Added to my collection we now have a cabinet full, who the hell's ever going to—

You could've saved your precious knickknacks too. I would have gone up to the barn, found wood, made a cabinet, just like the one I made for my hedgehogs. Remember Janey, that hedgehog you picked out in Vienna? And it's the best by far—

That was a cruel joke, Libby. You must've known. Oh, maybe in the backs of our minds we all knew it. Nobody could have a cough like that for so long and smoke so many God damn Camels—

But you asked her—that's the incredible thing, you little conniver—on your deathbed. It was something out of Dickens, I imagine. And I never could get her to tell me, so your little conspiracy remains intact...

'Marry Dolfi for me, will you darling?' or 'Look after Dolf, that's my last wish, and he is so terribly fond of you, Jane' or 'Who's going to take care of him, he's so helpless'—heh, heh, little did you know, Libby darling, little did you know—'He tries but I can't imagine him managing on his own...'

Was it subtle or outright? You probably just asked her to marry me, if I know you Libby. You never minced words. What did you give me? Oh, she was marvelous for three, no, just two, two and a half years. If you could've known—

It was too bloody short. We were in love. We were lovers. That's what you were capitalizing, right Libby? You knew we were in love. My God, it'd been

179

some forty years. We never fooled around much in all that time, the tension, it was painful, precious.... Sometimes I wonder if she didn't ask you, 'May I have him now?' No, I'm sure it was you who asked her. Janey wasn't the type. She took what came to her in life. Didn't do too badly at that: three husbands, three nice homes, and her own place in Florida after Paul died. We made love there that spring, amongst the seashells... Man, she had a lot of seashells. All those baskets. It was rather charming really. Such a child, all her collections. And to think of her standing there, empty house behind her, smashing all her treasures on the stone lanai—

Always detested that word, 'lanai'—that belongs in Hawaii for Christ's sake, this was Tampa. She loved that place. I think she was happy enough there alone, especially in the winters. But she never complained about leaving. Took her pledge to Libby mighty seriously...   She was a saint, cough and all.

But then it was your turn Janey girl, and after I'd made the mistake of marrying you... I really did need you by then damn it. I was so God damn unhappy—

That cruise we took! I could look at your picture on the other side of that photos cube there in your blue knit suit, one of your clever fabrications. You were always crocheting and knitting, and yet I hardly remember you that way. Funny, I guess I never noticed it that much, but you must've been; there're drawers full of your knitting now, I wonder—

180

Frieda might be too big, but Barbie...

Well, I can't face that stuff again for a while. And Rosy—thank God you didn't leave a legacy...

The shoes I found in the back of that closet! Libby's shoes. My God that woman had more shoes than—

All right. All right. Leave them alone Dolfi, let them rest. So they had a lot of junk, what woman doesn't? Although, I sometimes wonder if Rosy didn't know she had only eight months left. She brought so damn little; it was like a vacation she was taking...

Well, I'm just as glad of it, hardly much to worry about now, and the daughter came right away, took nearly all of it. The next one I marry had better pass a complete physical with flying colors first. Like buying a horse, you've got to look at the teeth—

Could Rosy have known it? I'll never know. They all acted so bloody protective, I wasn't even allowed to talk with the doctor. Well, hell, if she'd known it she kept a pretty good poker face, maybe she'd hoped for a change—

But I don't believe that theory. Cancer is cancer. You don't turn it around. There might be a short reprieve, as in Libby's case, that miraculous summer, we were actually living again, and then the inevitable slide....

I'm just glad Janey didn't revive like that. It could only have broken my heart the more. God, I was, we were—

It was worth it, I suppose, for two and a half years, the Sunday mornings in bed with the *Times* puzzle... She, at least, would snuggle with me. Rosy wouldn't let me in her bed. She was funny that way, very affectionate on the chaise, in this chair—and she wasn't light either—but she'd sit on my lap, she'd kiss me anywhere but in bed. Well, I respected that.

They each had the big room. They had all the privacy they wanted, and all the attention. The little bell I got down from the barn, cleaned it up for Libby, served for the three of them, never could've known at the time I'd get so much use out of it.

Oh why? Why in God's name couldn't there have been some variation on the theme? Christ, three cancers, four, if you count Lara, five with Mother, all the women I've ever loved...

It must be me. *I* cause it. I'll have to warn the new Mrs. X: Caution: association with this man causes cancer! Dolf can be hazardous to your health.

Do I want to go 'round again? If so, what are my options? There's that fat Mildred. She'd want to rearrange everything, she's had no respect. And she'd insist upon bringing that colored maid of hers she claims she can't survive without. No. No Mildred. Though she'd have me in a minute.

I should give it up now; it's my turn next. I can't go through with it again. Ophelia's all alone now. She can help out if I can't manage. What else has she got to do? Doesn't work anymore, got to do something besides drink all day long, going to die of cirrhosis before she does me any damn favors...

This infernal rain! Makes me think dreary thoughts. Melancholia, Dolfi, that's what you've got, a good case of old-fashioned melancholia...

Got a future, who knows how long I might—

Why not marry again? Have nothing to lose, can't sit around mourning these three 'til the end. Find a healthy nonsmoker young enough to outlast me, decent eyesight, she'd drive the car—these hands shake on the wheel so now I—

Well, there aren't that many available widows left, let's see: Ginger's gone, and Harriet, and poor old Wanda—God, I hate to think of her suffering. And Libby used to go and see her every week, for years it seemed. Cancer of course. Always cancer. Well, thank God it looks like heart attack for me, clean and quick. Have a little sherry, sherry's good for you. A drink a day keeps the rescue squad at bay...

God, when they took Janey, I think they said something about the child's stretcher. They put her in the child's stretcher. She only weighed sixty-nine pounds. Jesus, I can't stop thinking about her—

Think about, think about... think about Ellen. Now there's a gal! If only she'd let go of her little Barney. He's no good for her, oh, sure, bright enough, but none of her spark, none of her wit, her imagination for Christ's sake. He's going to soak her dry. She needs a more inspiring consort. I know you're dead set against marriage as you put it, but I don't insist, as long as you're willing to live with me, I have no qualms, who's around to object after all? Who cares about neighbors—hell, at our age? You're financially independent aren't you? Of course you must be, you've got Ezra's pension, surely that with your social security...

And you're young, Ellen, what did you say? Sixty-eight or so, a teetotaler, but you smoke don't you, English Ovals I seem to remember. No better than Camels. Haven't noticed you coughing though, but then we haven't seen each other in over a year, and you never answered my last letter, did you? I'll try you again in time. Right now I'm too busy...

Let's see there's Mary Lou Murdick, she's too fat. Merry, perhaps, but not my type. I could never love a fatty—

Betty Vitroli, is she still alive? I'll have to get back in touch with George, though I hate to keep making him my agent, my pimp. George is in the market himself...

No, no no, not Ellen after all. She's got that hideous laugh, I could never live with—

My God, it's a horse's whinny. Worse than a whinny, it's a bray. Don't know what she finds so damn funny all the time. No, not Ellen, don't think she's all that bright in the final analysis. Who then? There must be—

Anyone, anyone, so long as she outlives me! It's my turn now to be nursed for crying out loud. Didn't I wait on you three? Didn't I cook all your special foods, arrange it all on separate trays for you? How many trips did I make up that spiral, it's not as easy making that turn on the top with a loaded tray. Times I slipped got your damn eggdrop soup all over me, Jesus, Libby. You never knew about that though. Had to start the whole damn process all over, then you'd be sound asleep by the time I'd get up with the new cup—

All right. I was glad to do it. Would've done it for anybody. All the laundry, the damn dishes, I did the dusting and vacuuming then too, plus all the outdoor chores. Couldn't keep up with it those last few months. Garden went all to hell. Never could get it back the way you'd kept it in front there. All those roses you'd planted! Can't see the tea roses on the left anymore, ivy's taken over everything. Got to get in there and rip it all out now. My God, there's so much to do how the hell will I ever—

Where the hell are my grandchildren? They could do something useful for a change instead of always running off to Maine, to California, where the devil did she say Sam had moved to now? The Dominican Republic? What the hell does he expect to do in a place like that? The Dominican Republic! Why not Paris, Rome, even London for Christ's sake, might learn to speak English—

Oh they'd be no use anyway. Can't trust 'em. Be just as much work to supervise—

Ungrateful spoiled...Ophelia never spoiled those kids I don't know how they got so—

She used to buy all their clothes at the thrift shop. I know that used to bother Libby. I always thought it was a good idea. They were forever outgrowing things, why not? Perfectly good stuff there.

What's wrong with you now, Ophelia? Last time you were here you looked lousy. How could you let yourself get so damned fat? Is it the booze? I never gained a pound drinking, neither did Libby. I don't understand you. You say you don't eat. You must eat. Gorge. You must. Oh, maybe not while you're here. He certainly doesn't hesitate. Got that big beer belly... My God, last time you two were here he drank a half a case of my—

In one day! Every time I turned around he was reaching in the refrigerator. Who does he think he is?

All right, all right, so you have a new boyfriend. What was wrong with Ed? I always did like Ed. Maybe not the liveliest guy you could ask for, but a decent conversationalist, good family man, good father. From what I could see, the kids adored him. Took you on two cruises, didn't he? And twice to Europe; you visited the Jamisons that time in London...Jamison's divorced now too.

What is all this divorce business? Libby and I stayed married forty-five years. Forty-five years, my God that's a long time...

And it took death to break us up. We had our differences, sure. We parted, not a few times. It wasn't always roses, but what the hell do you expect? You young people, everything has to be perfect. You have to have your little plots in the suburbs, your 3.2 kids, your two-car garages, your swimming clubs and your woods. You always had to have woods for the kids to play in...

You had it all set up, kept it going 'til the kids were too grown to care anymore. Girls became interested in gallivanting around with their boyfriends. All right, so it disintegrated. What did you expect? Can't live your whole life around kids, pets.

My God, Fella, you told me once you had to find a new house with woods so the dog could have what she was used to. Now come on, a dog can adapt for goodness sake. A dog doesn't need a glass door opening onto acres of pinewoods. Look at the dogs we had. Made the transition every year, nine months in the apartment, three months here. They had to adapt, so they adapted. Just the same with kids, kids can always adapt to a new neighborhood. You were happiest, you always said, when you and Libby moved to Washington during the War. A strange city, wartime, you loved it, all the soldiers and sailors on leave. You had a grand time...

And so what was your problem this time? It was another suburban development, just like all the others, no worse. That's the way you'd lived for years. Ed changed jobs and you moved. You'd had ten years in the last place, longer than any of your other moves. I admit, that could've made it more difficult, but it's the same everywhere. You could've gotten just as involved in the new place. I'm sure you would've found all of the same organizations. What difference does it make? All those suburban developments are the same. People have mildly differing accents, that's all. Remember how you complained about the stupid people and their unintelligible speech when you first moved to the old place? All right, you got used to them. Never heard you complain about them in later years.

What the hell's the matter with you? All that time spent feeling sorry for yourself! Why, all you did the last time you were here was drink. The two of you. He and his beer, you with the sherry. I know you were drinking it, even when you said you weren't. What the hell do you think, I'm blind? I had to get the new gallon jug there under the wet bar, you'd already damn near emptied it. And Ed said you won't cooperate with the A.A. people. Well, I don't entirely blame you; I can't stomach the religious ones myself. But they've apparently had a very high success rate. And you've got to see *somebody*. That psychiatrist of yours hasn't done you any good. I still don't understand why you tried to kill yourself. There's never been a suicide—well, not on *my* side...

Yes, Libby's father, your Poppi, yes, yes, I know. Damn him, cruel bastard should've had the decency to leave her a bloody note. Must've known he was dying of cancer. I would too...

Did it properly though. Bullet through the temple. A manly job. Hemingway—well, he stuck it in his mouth—but Poppi, that was the thirties, a whole different...

Bullet enters your brain you don't feel a damn thing, don't even know you're on the floor dead. That's the way to do it. You and your chicken-hearted pills! Pecking on those pills, choking 'em down with your bourbon... I can just see you, sobbing in your booze.

Where was your intelligence? You should have known it wasn't going to work; much too slow. If you'd wanted to do it, you could've driven your car off a bridge, stuck your head in the gas, run a vacuum hose from the exhaust into the rear window of your car, taped up the cracks and—

Well, you failed at it. You wanted attention, I suppose. Well, you certainly go it. That night when Ed called me—

I offered to come, but as he said, there was nothing I or anyone else could do. You were in the intensive care unit *one day*. Why, they kept me in there two weeks—

Couldn't have been too badly damaged, he said you'd turned blue. Apparently, Sam saw his dead-blue mother being dragged out of the woods on a stretcher, poor boy. Ed said he took it all right though. Strong kid. Takes after me. I think I'd have been damned embarrassed though, standing around with my school chums watching my mother, ice blue, getting herself packed into a rescue van...

'Sammy, heard your mother tried to kill herself yesterday...'

I remember Jimmy Freilisch, his mom tried to hang herself in the barn, think they said his dad found her and cut her down. Poor little guy burst out bawlin'. 'Yer mother tried to hang herself, yer mother tried to hang herself,' the kids sang. And his father had had to cut her down with a hatchet and they'd sent the maid for the doctor in the middle of the night and that's how the news got all over town...

Women. Always have to make such a mess of things. Sometimes I wish Libby had had the guts to take the Luger out. I'd tried to make the suggestion, subtly, but then I would have had to clean it for her and show her how to fire it. Hadn't been fired since the war, would've had to take it to the gun shop have one of them inspect it for me, test it first, I wouldn't want to...

Libby! Forty-five years. And you never left me. I paid for it in the end though. You may have resented me for many of those years, but damn it, Libby, I paid for it in the end, didn't I? I saw you out of this world, watched you leaving me, ounce by ounce, night after night, your cheeks...

Every time I looked over, afraid to see more shadow, leaving me inch by inch your bones, your hand, a bundle of kindling, I held you up to sip your soup...

Oh God, why can't I just forget it and go on? I lived with it once; that was enough. Lived with it twice, Janey was faster, mercifully faster, trickled away like quicksilver, seepage...

Everybody leaves you, Father, Mother... Oh Mother, you should see your Dolfi now, older than you, and tough. Two trains run over me I'm still walking around. Why the hell am I so tough? The rest of them, what are they made of? Jesus, human frailty. I don't ever want to see it happen again. Next gal I bring in here is going to pass a full exam. I wasted these last—how many—these last seven years, wasted on deaths. Should open a damn funeral parlor. Damn women always have to die on you...

Ever woman I ever loved. Joyce, what happened to you Joyce? You used to split logs out there in your winter jacket hatless, snow-dusted. I couldn't believe it when Harriet told me. Not Joyce! I said. Not those magnificent muscles, why? You were younger than I, there was no reason—

Christ, don't let me start. Morbid, that's what you've become, Dolf, morbid. Got to get away from here, do something. Take another trip. Go to Maine—Sebago Lake. You owe it to yourself to go. In the spring. The trout—

Who the hell could I get to go with me? Floyd? But Floyd doesn't drive. How would I make that drive alone? Have to stop in hotels all along the way, waste so damn much money. Floyd would be more problem than he's worth. Hell, I like Floyd, sit all day in a rowboat quite happily. He could read while I fish. Maybe Floyd has a friend...

Should write to old Floyd anyway. Or does he owe me a letter? I'll have to go through that mess on the desk. Jesus, I'm so far behind in correspondence. Let's see, there was Griffin's wife what the hell was her—

Sarah? Shirley? What the hell can you say? I wish it would stop. But it will never stop. Condolences. God damn sick of writing them, so damn many! Might as well order a box of those cards, can see why people buy—

Christ, when Janey—

I'll never speak to those stupid Elliots now. Lousy sympathy card—was that the best they could do for Valerie's aunt for God's sake, who doted on her so when she was a child? People are so crass. All those letters afterwards.

It never ends. Ray. Ray you imbecile! I called Virginia and you have to write 'And how's Janey?' Idiot. Well, I'm not answering that one. Ask your damn wife.

Thank God there weren't so many after Rosy. What the hell am I, secretary for the dead? Christ, it never ends. Still get them from people who knew Janey; I don't know who the hell they are, wish they'd just send a God damn check if they want to do something. It was in the *Times* for Christ's sake: 'Donations may be sent to the Cancer Society.' Why do they have to pester me? Had her picture there. If anyone'd bothered to read it...

Don't pester me. Libby wanted them to donate to the Humane Society. Okay, all right, I never argued with her. Libby and her adopted animals. Uncle Toby, you fat satisfied monster, don't you remember your savior, brought you in a little wet rat, filthy, couldn't even mew properly... And when you go— Well, you, for one, I don't suppose I'll have to worry about. At least your pals can't write me. You're no spring chicken Toby. You're glad it's just you and me now, aren't you boy? Quiet. We can do what we want in peace, nobody rearranging anything. Nobody except that damned Dolores, she couldn't do anything right for us.

There was once a maid named Dolores, who couldn't do anything for us, but move things about so, so—

But change things around, no, but scramble the house—

There once was a maid named Dolores—

Who? What the hell, Cronkite? Turn the sound switch there—

Damn. Missed it. 'And that's the way it bloody well is.' God damn it! What have I been doing? Sitting right here with the picture—

Stupid, now you'll never know how the hell it was, well, how was it Walt? What the hell happened today? Damned if I know, damned if I care, God damn stupid—

Uncle Toby, why didn't you say something, wake me up, stupid...

Might as well get another sherry. Still raining, must be getting cold in here, shut this door. Drafts. What did I do with that woolen shirt now? Oh, for crying out loud I don't know where anything is! Nobody puts it away in the proper— Did I hang it in the closet? When was the last time, I, I can't remember—

Oh, sure, last night. It was last night, must've worn it upstairs then. Okay, get something else here. Got to straighten out this bookcase someday, don't know what the hell happened to my Melville. Why the hell she had to meddle with that bookcase— She had no right going in there, always messing with things, just as glad to be rid of her. Always had to be meddling... that bookcase didn't need painting, could've waited until I was there to tell her how to put them back. Just rearranges every damn—

That was the night I went out in the truck. So God damn angry with her. Shouldn't have blown up like that. But my God, Rosy, you promised when you came up here. Every time I turned my back you had to be meddling. Can't find a damn thing now. The kitchen. The kitchen shelves didn't need repapering, why the hell you had to—

Now I can't find that Swedish milk pitcher, can't find the grapefruit spoons. Those were Mother's grapefruit spoons. Well, they're gone now. God damn it, Rosy, always messing in my things. Why you could never just read for an hour, had to jump up and fuss, jump up and fuss. Glad you're gone.

Look at this sable coat of Libby's. Now what the hell am I supposed to do with that? Can't give it to the thrift shop, worth too damn much. What did she pay for that, six hundred dollars? Something ridiculous. Still in good condition, could give it to one of the girls I suppose. But they don't wear those things. They'd just ruin it. Wouldn't appreciate it. Offered it to Mabel, she was too big in the bosom. Ophelia couldn't wear it now, what a grotesque—

How could she let herself go like that? Always had such a good figure. Wore the same dress size as Libby. Don't know why in God's name she got so fat. Looked terrible the last time she was here. Is he pouring beers into her? She hardly ate a damn thing, just a little cottage cheese. He ate the whole liverwurst! But she's worse than he is. Blown up like a balloon. I don't understand it, how she could let herself go like that, why she's so damned unhappy. Had a good life.

Where's my sherry now? What the hell did I do—

Oh, all right, all right---OOOOOGH! There it is again. Oh my God, this is—

Emergency numbers, rescue squad taped on the pole lamp got to—

URRRRRP. Something moved. Better, it's lifting it's—

Just indigestion, sure, it's just a gas bubble pushing up. Scares me. Sit down. Scared now of every little—

Check the pulse: boomp-boomp, boomp-boomp, boom-boomp—racing, still racing a bit, got to slow down, slow it down, that's it, let's get real slow and regular now, deep breath—AHAHUMMMMM—

Gone now. Must've been gas. Damn that chest pain. Felt just like a freight train. Next time ol' freight train runs over my chest, knock me flat in the living room, no Rosy's going to be there to call the ambulance. No Jane. No Libby. No Dolores. Even Ophelia's unreliable. Seems to have so damn many problems of her own.

What the hell went wrong with you anyway? Jesus, you went to two excellent schools. You were lively, lithe and popular. Used to bring two boys home at a time. Had everything going for you. Married a nice steady guy. Had your three healthy kids. Always lived in houses with plenty of space for the kids to play, good neighborhoods, good public schools. You had a career. That's something your mother always wanted and she wanted you to have what she didn't have... You had more than your job, Fella, you had all those community activities, all those meetings you were forever attending, your election—why, you even enjoyed something most of us never enjoy: a political victory. You were a success. What the hell did you want?

You seemed to fall apart after Ed got that job and you had to move. Well so what? You'd moved before. Ed had to work. You go where your husband's job is that's just the way it goes. Or you could've left him if you were so opposed to moving. You didn't have to fall apart like that so he was forced to divorce you. I don't understand you, Ophelia, you had it all...

All right, okay, so now what've you got? Fatso. That fat old bald-headed—what could you possibly see in a guy—

He comes here and sits down for exactly five minutes, then he's up heading for the refrigerator for another beer. My God, he doesn't even ask. Just walks right in the kitchen and takes one. Drains a whole case in two days! I buy one case of beer it lasts me two months. She brings him here for a weekend and it's gone in less than forty-eight hours. A whole case! No wonder he's got that belly. No wonder she's gotten fat too. Hangs around with a guy like that. Retired even. All he does all day is drink. All she does now is drink all day with him.

Okay, if that's what you need to do with yourself now, if that's what you want in life Ophelia. Only I don't see what you had to complain about before. I suppose this beer guzzler is better than Ed? That's your business. But now you've got this drinking problem. You don't even admit it. But it's clear you won't be any use to me. I'd have to rely on Mabel. And Mabel's hard of hearing, she'd never hear anything if I were upstairs trying to shout. Or what if it happened when I was up in the barn? I've got to have somebody. Can't live like this in constant fear—

Freight train running over my chest. Well, let them find me here. Let them find the body here. At least it's going to be that and not cancer. Every woman I've ever had—

***

See them to the grave, eaten up before my eyes. Every damn—

There must be some woman out there. Healthy. Doesn't smoke Camels. Doesn't have a family history, no breast problems. Check her teeth while I'm at it. Got to be somebody can outlast me. At the rate Ophelia's degenerating... Christ she looks terrible. Hair all gone grey suddenly, doesn't keep herself up, hardly talks anymore. He did all the talking, in between guzzles. What she sees in that guy—

And why the hell you had to go and swallow—

You could've done it properly instead of making such a half-witted attempt. Sleeping pills. Christ, where'd you get so many? The doctors never let you have enough on one prescription to do any damage. Libby could only get ten at a time. And it takes more than that—

What did you do, save them up until you had forty, fifty? I've no idea how many it takes—

Oh, I'm ashamed of you, Ophelia, so ashamed.

Well, naturally he was going to look for you. You handled everything so carelessly; of course he'd find you in the time it took—

Why the hell didn't you do something quicker? Sleeping pills, my God. Look at your grandfather. He at least had the decency to send his wife out to the store so he could blow his brains out in private. He knew how to blow his brains out. Did it right, with one clean shot. You could've learned something from him.

And death came quick and he wasn't afraid of it. People weren't then. I don't know what's happened to this younger set. Ophelia, you don't just play games with it. You've got to show respect for death. If you're going to do it, do it gracefully. Do it successfully, for God's sake. Next time, buy a revolver. Jump off an eleven story building. Drive off a bridge...

I don't blame Ed for divorcing you when you had to go and play such a stupid trick on him as that. You ought to be ashamed. You go through a dramatic drowning act and naturally you're saved, so don't act so damned surprised and resentful. It was your own damn fault that you lived. Sure you feel stupid now. Who wouldn't? How are the kids supposed to react?

Libby was never sorry her father committed suicide, especially once she got her own cancer. She used to say she wished she'd had his strength. Takes guts. A man like your grandfather, Ophelia...

And your other grandfather, whom you never met—

I remember him skinning the doe he'd shot. I remember him explaining it in patient tones: "The doe didn't feel anything, son." She died so quickly.

The bullet struck exactly where he'd aimed it, right in the skull. I saw it. She fell straight forward, knees buckling under—

And then I heard the rustle and the thud. She was over on her side and never moved. Died instantly. Didn't have a chance to know what hit her. Didn't suffer, my father said. No pain.

Jesus, I hate those archers, those idiot Robin Hoods with their damned aluminum arrows, the way they'll wound a deer and let it tear through the bush, the arrow ripping—

Oh, they make me so damn mad. They aren't Indians. They don't know what the hell they're doing. Can't hit a barn. You don't shoot, period, if you can't control your aim. Father explained: "Exactly there, you've got to hit them square in the brain. There's no excuse for firing otherwise, if you can't be sure of your shot." And they don't give a damn, wounding animals, letting them go off and die miserable slow deaths, infected holes ripped in their sides…

They should be made illegal. I wouldn't let any idiot Robin Hood walk across my property. They'll have to go around by the river. No one with a God forsaken bow and arrow's ever coming across here as long as I—

He can shoot *me*. Ha!

My father wouldn't have cottoned to any stupid sleeping pills. They say he had a heart attack too. Like father like son. I'd much rather die a man's death, like my father, run over in the chest by the ol' 109. No cancer disfiguring-slow-torture eat-em-up-from-the-inside-out... no, not for me. I'd never stand for it. Not like Mother, no. I'll go like Father. Not like Mother or Libby, not like Janey or Rosy or Joyce or Lara—ah, Lara! Not like the damn cancer-ridden women, all the women in my life. My own half-sister Heidi—

Not like every goddamn woman. Not like Edie Greensmith, not like Rubie, not, certainly, like Beth with that hideous thing on her neck. My God, like rotten fruit they are. They smell like rotten meat. Oh, for days I had to smell it, every time I entered the room. After a while I didn't even have to be bending over the bed. And even Jane—my God—you rotted too. You were always so sweet, clean, rose water and lavender—

My God, they're so weak! Now you, Ophelia, when there's nothing *wrong* with you. You've nothing to complain of. You've got thirty years coming to you, what the hell do you want to give it up for? Oh, you make me sick. You mock your mother, your grandmother. You don't even know what death is.

My father showed me. He made me. I didn't want to. He made me, and he was right. Shoved my hands right up there. The guts were still warm. The blood was sweet. It smelled clean, sweet—not rotten—it was fresh. Jane was always so fresh. Crisp linen dresses. Orange blossom. On the canvas lawn chair—

Walking out the screen door to the back lawn I saw her for a minute, a college kid on the green, young neck, clean smell of the girls at dances. Japanese lanterns, wooden dance floor, clarinets...

I danced with Jane. She was so light. That New Year's Eve on the ship, she was dying even then, but we didn't know it. So light on her feet, a girl inside an old lady's body, oh Janey—

You make me sick, Ophelia, you with your fat red face, your red eyes, nose like W.C. Fields for Christ sake. Hair gone grey always so messy now, what the hell are you trying to prove? You drink all the time now, you've let yourself go. You were a sexy dame not long ago, you used to wear Libby's clothes. Now I've got boxes of them, nothing would fit you, why you've blown up like a bloody balloon—

The kids won't take anything. It's all too good for them anyway. The silk gowns she had, the shoes! God Almighty, what am I to do with all those shoes?

You can't possibly fit in that gold embroidered caftan we bought in Crete...

So now you've got your beer-belly beau, lets you drink all day I suppose. Is that all you two do now, lie around and drink beers and let your bellies hang out at each other? I don't know where you got it from. Libby and I drank, sure we drank. Everybody drinks. But we didn't get sloppy drunk like you youngsters, we didn't abuse alcohol.

Oh sure, I would get a little tight sometimes. Everybody did. But not like you and Ed. Ed would always pass out right after dinner, lie on the floor on his back and snore. Apparently he always did that, you said he'd pass out in the middle of your dinner parties. Now *that* I'd never have allowed. No one we know ever did such a thing. No one *we* know ever got a red face and blood-shot eyes like you and let themselves go like that. I can't think of anyone we were close to ever becoming an alcoholic.

Don't know where Ed would've gotten it from, his mother's a damn teetotaler, Bible-thumping—

Jesus, that woman's a pain in the neck! Guess I won't have to see her ever again. Hope Ed doesn't feel he can't show up here if he wants. 'Course that last time he was here he found it necessary to punch an old man in the—

All right, all right! That's behind us, I forgave him, didn't I? Just don't bring your old ma up here, Ed, and I'll be glad to—

That Iris! There's another one. Cancer eating out her face, and all because of her crazy refusal to see a doctor. Stupid religious fanaticism—people deserve to die ugly, mangling deaths if that's what they—

Thank God I haven't had to watch. Seen enough, seen all I want to see for one lifetime.

My God, why did you have to leave Ed for Old Beer-belly? Ed's a perfectly nice guy. Drink was only an occasional problem for him. He was a good father, a good provider. I always liked Ed. Libby was especially fond of him. And Janey was fond of both of you. Why, she loved you as though you were her own daughter, Ophelia. She told me many times.

Well, you're not much anyone could love now. Could barely bring yourself to speak last time you were here. Mumbled a few things when I pressed you, stared at the floor. Let him do the talking. I noticed you. What the hell do you think I'm blind? Of course I noticed you. You seemed off in another world. I had nothing to say to him. I suppose I wouldn't have had much to say to you either. At least he watches the ball games...

Ashamed of you Ophelia. Yes, I am ashamed you would do such a stupid thing as try to kill yourself, and that you'd failed to do it right. You made such a mess of your nice life. There was no conceivable—

You had three lovely children, bright enough, nothing wrong with any of them. You had a good husband, a good career, lots of friends. Even your new house was nice enough. All right, all right, so you were unhappy there. You used to tell me you were unhappy in the last house when you first moved there from New Jersey. I remember it well: Everything in New Jersey was always wonderful, everything in the old place always better, the new house was ugly, you didn't like the neighborhood, all your friends were back in New Jersey...

That was in the beginning. Then of course you came to love the place. Now it's everything was better *there*...

You moved in early spring, I remember, because Rosy and I were about to be married. That's right.

You didn't even give it a full year down there before you decided to end it all with sleeping pills and succeeded in getting yourself taken to the hospital in an ambulance. You can't take it, can you? Why are you suddenly so defeatist? What has life ever done to you? You never had to suffer. You had everything your way. Ed was good to you, your children were good to you, you had no reason—

Well, I suppose you had your reasons, but now you won't talk. You won't tuck your dirty shirt in over your bare belly or comb your messy hair. I'm disgusted with you. And with him, too. Of all the young men you've brought home to meet me, never such a fat, bald one—looks older than I do for Christ's sake.

All right! All right! Enough. Enough of both of you. I've missed Cronkite again. Why must that happen to me? The commercial comes on and I turn the sound switch off, then the next thing I know, I've missed him again. Oh well, tomorrow night I'll leave it on for the commercial, torture myself, just for you Walter. I'll listen to you tomorrow night without fail. Don't give a damn about the sports or weather though. And that's gotten to be nearly two thirds of it now. They waste so much time with those idiots—

It's still raining! Can't tell if the sun's gone or not. Staying light a long time now....

A can of Chunky-lite soup. Let's see if there's any of the beef chili left. I don't care much for the chicken, turkey's okay, but too bland. I like the pea and ham, but I can make that just as well myself. Why should I buy the can when I can make it from my own peas right here? Okay, chunky turkey, no, I don't want that. Cream of mushroom, let me see—

There you are. I knew I'd bought another one of the chili beef. Chunky-lite, yes, this is the best of the Chunky-lites.

Chunky-lite. Chunky-lite. Oxymorons of the world unite! Heh-heh... Some damn ad-man must've had a good time with—

And now where's my soup pan? Somebody's always hiding my favorite—

There you are, in the right spot for once. You can't trust anyone these days. That idiot Dinah, or Dolores, or Doris, or whatever her name is, always putting everything—

Well okay. Now get it under the can opener right this time. Turn on the switch here. Get this blender out of the way. For crying out loud, what's this blender been left sitting *here* for? I never use the damn thing anymore. Used it a lot for Janey's eggnogs. They were easy enough to make. I'd always have a dollop of brandy while I was at it, fortify myself for the trip upstairs—

She didn't want rum in it, only brandy. And Libby, she had to have her eggdrop soup. How they could stand it, night after night, the same damn thing—

All right, if it was all you could get down. All right then! Can get rid of this blender now though. There's no room for it in any of the cabinets. Don't know where the hell to put it. Can't put it in the cellar it'll get ruined. Perfectly good blender, hardly been used. Must be twenty years old. Couldn't get much for it. All these gadgets in here, my God— kitchen is full of them. All these expensive—

She wanted a toaster-oven. Okay, I got her a toaster-oven. All I ever use it for now is pot pies. The toaster's superfluous though. I never use the toaster-oven for toast, although I suppose I could. Just a habit. Use the toaster for toast and the toaster-oven for pot pies. Now I got two of them side by side with the blender and the can opener here taking up so damn much space—

She had to have this juicer. An electric juice squeezer! Now how many times do I have enough oranges, even in the winter--

When Betty used to send the box from Florida—

I think that's why she wanted the juicer. For a while we were getting boxes from Betty, and from Janey, too, when she had her place in Tampa. And then there were the grapefruits from the Collinses. Why they only sent the grapefruits… Or was he the one with the grapefruit orchard? Oh, I don't remember now who sent the damn grapefruits. Betty's dead of cancer, cancer of the spleen I think it was…

What the hell do I keep this electric—

And the coffee grinder? Now I can only drink Sanka. She used to love those French roast beans from the little specialty shop in Middleford. Never use the damn thing. Suppose I could give it to Ophelia. She still drinks coffee. Or does she? Didn't take any when she was here. Drinks too damn much booze—

Taking up space here. Gathers dust. Gadgets everywhere! Give them to that damn Dolores or Daphne or whatever the hell her name is next time she comes. Get rid of this clutter here. Hardly have room to peel the potatoes now. Have to do it in the sink.

Well, what else are we going to eat now? A little cottage cheese. If there—

Yes. There's still enough to save some for lunch tomorrow. And toast? No, just plain bread. This pumpernickel's getting a bit stale. I should finish it. And where's the margarine? Here you are—

No, you're not the margarine, what the hell?

Strawberries. Better remember to eat these, put some on the cottage cheese tomorrow, now where—

It was yellow, one of the yellow plastic tubs I—

And it's not "mar-*jar*-in" for Christ's sake! Who ever heard of a "g" followed by "a-r" sounding soft like a "j"? Do you say "*jar*-ment" for garment? Do you say "vin-e-*jar*"—let's make a dressing of earl and vin-e-jar—

Shall we make a salad Uncle Toby? Look, there's your food, you keep your nose out of—

Mar*jar*ine! It's mar*gar*ine you fools! You don't say "*jar*-age" for where you put your car, you don't say "*jar*-den" for where you put your petunias. You don't say "*jar*-bage" for where you put your potato peels. What the hell's this mar*jar*ine?

Goddamn advertisements. Ruined the language. Look at that Winston ad—

All right, all right, we've been through this enough now. Put the stove on to three.

Got some grease on this knob or something. Slippery. Okay, now where's the goddamn spoon, let me see, the spoon I always use for making soups, my favorite soup spoon, the silver—

Where the hell did you go now? I thought I washed you this morning. What—

All right, if you're not in this drawer, you must be in the dish rack. Good. Always like this spoon for soups. The others are either too small or too big. This one is just right, said the baby bear—

That kid in Berlin clutching his tin spoon. Kid was no more than sixteen…. My God, I was his age in the first war….

Obviously starving. Red-brown pimple scabs on ash-white moon face, lips cracked and blackened…. Same age as Ophelia…. Could've been mine…

Christ, if only Paddington—

He was too damned clever sometimes. Too bright and beautiful. Hero of his generation, bah! Antihero. Loved young boys though. That time in Heidelberg, got him fixed up with that Corporal with the jeep—

He was grateful to me for that. Gay blade. "Gays" they want to be called now, can't get used to—

Can't use that word anymore. Ruined a perfectly decent word. What was wrong with queer? As in different, misfit—even fairy—of another realm, or faggot—little sticks, but certainly not "gay." They're some of the least gay people I've ever known. How the hell can you be gay when you've got to spend your whole life trying to find people like you while hiding the fact from everyone else…. Ruined a perfectly good word.

That boy with the spoon—

And the few that finally got the soup, barely able to stand up in line. We called in the medics to spoon feed a lot of them.

My God, what a war. And Paddington such a hero. Such a darling. Anyway, thanks to him we had that fabulous house in Dusseldorf with the girls to cook—

The night the British officers brought the Russians over and somehow they came up with rabbit. Rabbit all around. Delicious! I've never had it since. Funny how food could taste so good in the middle of war. The girls were clean. The redhead. I had her. Clean and not stupid after all, a school teacher. Taught kindergarten, or so she said. Wish we'd had more than fifteen minutes. Damn Brits thought they owned the place. Paddington and his little corporal—

And the one with the accordion, what was his name? Harry something. Had a nice voice.   The redhead sang "Lili Marlene"…

Needs a little pepper. Always needs something. Just a dash now. There. That's ready now. Turn the stove off this time. Now, that's definitely off, the red light's out. Good. Get the cottage cheese here…

Why do they all think I'm so helpless? Can cook perfectly well. Haven't burned the house down. Do my own dishes. Put everything back where it belongs. Don't need another God damn woman. Don't need anyone. Perfectly happy eating alone, thank you.

Quiet. Rain still—

Don't have to run upstairs every five minutes. Can sit here and eat my soup while it's hot. Well, my God, hasn't it been enough?

Studied hard to get the damn degree. Wrote the dissertation. Tenured. Raised a daughter, stayed married to one woman for over forty-five years. Served behind the lines. Grandchildren three. Two additional wives cared for and put to rest. Mother's place still standing. Nothing's burned down—

Got to get to those front beds as soon as this rotten rain's done. Maybe tomorrow morning if it's not too muddy. There' so much to do; got to get the mower repaired...

Frank's dead. Frank, I miss you often. No one to help out with the garden now. Have to make it even smaller this year. No corn. Takes too much space.

Get some local kids to help you she says, pay some local kids. You find me a local kid I can trust. Climb in the windows at night. Steal the silver cigarette lighters. Steal my pears. I was saving those pears for when Sally—

They don't know how to run the mowers. Would slice off a foot no doubt. I'd be sued. Idiots. Drop out after the ninth grade. There's not a single kid around here anymore that can be trusted. I used to have Petey, but Petey's gone off to computer programming school. Now how the hell is Petey going to learn to—

Have to do everything myself now. Get up early tomorrow morning, weed the front bed. Tomorrow, tomorrow's Sunday. The *Times* comes tomorrow. I'll have all the news that I can use. And there's the crossword—

Damn, can't enjoy that anymore. Used to run right up to you with the magazine. Your face would light up. Even in the end, remember? That last week, we spent most of the mornings on it, cozy in bed together. Oh Janey—

Can't finish this cottage cheese. Sticks in the throat. Glass of water. Run it a bit 'til it comes cold. Ah, damn. Got to get someone else out here to make me forget you three.

That letter! Didn't George say something about a woman—

Oh, leave the dishes, Dolfi, you can come back—

It's been so long since I read it. His last one, on blue stationery—it was Mimi's stationery. There was something about a cousin of his I think he said she was—

Must be on the desk somewhere. What a—

Jesus, look at all this junk! Got to sort through all of this. So much of it. Throw it all somewhere. Throw it out. Christ, what's this, a phone bill—September? Throw that out. And this. More advertisements. What the hell did I save this for now? Oh yes, the hedgehog. Maybe I'll still want to order it. Save this.

I know it was a light blue stationery. A woman's; must've been Mimi's. George could've gotten some of his own made up. I never used Libby's.

This damn thing! I've been looking all over for this—

All right. We'll put you in here. It must be somewhere—

Said something about a woman we both knew at Hunter…

Teacher? Student? I don't remember. I can't remember why he was telling me—

Now that should have gone to the bank. Must send it off right away, damn it, I thought I'd—

These poems belong in the album there. What are they doing out now?

Wasn't she that student we both admired, the one with the big blue—

It was light blue for Christ's sake, with his wife's name on the—

What's that?

WHAT THE HELL IS GOING ON *HERE* NOW?

Is that my ladder they've got? God damn them! What the hell do they think they're doing, walking across the lawn, Jesus Christ—

GOD DAMN DOOR, warped in the rain I can't, now—

HEY, YOU KIDS! WHERE THE *HELL* DO YOU THINK YOU'RE GOING WITH THAT—

IV. Edgar

YAAAAAAAAHAHUMMMM OOOOOOM

Vivaldi -- . . The Seasons . mustve started over again
-- . how many times . . how long have I been . -- must
have taken my watch off . -- . . now where -- . . oh
yes . left it on the sink to wash vegetables -- . mustve
eaten . . then what . -- oh yes . -- . . the kidneys -- . .
delicious . hello Cleo -- . you been napping too . .
you liked those kidneys didnt you . -- white bowl in
the refrigerator puddle of brown red in the bottom
let you lick the blood . -- . . yes and taste the fried
ones oh so delicate juicy bathed in wine -- . . then
mustve finished the bottle passed out here with
Vivaldi . that wasnt bad that Inglenook -- . Ill have
to remember that one . . you been dreaming of
kidneys eh Cleo . -- there was some scene with a
man frying kidneys . -- . . kidneys and a cat what
was it -- . . oh yes of course Bloom Ulysses . only he
had cream from the top of the milk bottle too didnt
he -- . shame you cant get those glass bottle
deliveries anymore bluewhite below yellow on top . .
and we love cream dont we Cleo . -- . . I could run
out and get us some for tomorrows breakfast coffee
-- . . pour it on cereal too . hey why not just drive
over to the Stop n Shop in the back there they have
those purple cartons half pint whipping cream -- .
would you like that . . maybe that checkout girl with
the mole would be . -- no . -- . . no she cant still be
there this late -- . . but how late is it . dark out -- . and

is that rain . . sounds like rain or is Vivaldi scratchy . - - lemme turn that off . -- . . no no just turn it down -- . . let the seasons go round again . go look at the kitchen clock -- . might as well get the watch   clock never right goddamn thing . . keep resetting . -- that dial doesnt want to hold time maybe the batteries are old . -- . . watch is always perfect though -- . . yes can taste the wine and some kidney underneath . well mustve drunk off the bottle -- . how many calories . . got to remember that enter it tomorrow at the office . -- and how much butter did we use . -- . . one stick thats one quarter pound -- . . cant go out for cream anyway Cleo remember Im on a diet . gotta remember to record that meal -- . kidneys practically nothing salad with only a little oil . . but that burgundy . -- its got more calories than white . - - . . Ill have to look it up one liter -- . . dont need any more to drink tonight if I get up to turn down the record then Ill be up so I might as well go in the kitchen and check the time but there may still be some cocktail peanuts . yes I bet there are some peanuts left and some bakers chocolate -- .   havent had dessert after all and theres no sugar in those big chunky bars wrapped in white waxed paper I can just . . better stay here awhile but what if its really late . -- it might be time to go to bed then I might as well get up and go to bed . -- . . that always seems so ludicrous   wake up to go to bed -- . . but what else is there the rain . yes thats definitely rain -- . goes so well with The Seasons . . couch cushions warm why get up just yet . -- have to spring out of bed at

222

sixthirty do the exercises shower shave dress fry a slice of sausage cup of instant coffee with no cream aaack . -- . . there should be enough grapefruit juice in the jar since yesterday   Im almost sure -- . . you want your ears rubbed Cleo that feels good . you old thing lemme look at that eye now -- . oozing . . still the red glassy look of it . -- you have to remind me of Mother dont you old gal . -- . . have to have you put down one of these days -- . . although hate to . why does she have to torture me so -- . it couldve been such a simple procedure when it was small twenty damn years ago for crissake and this never wouldve happened . . she could be whole and healthy now or at least dying of something else not so damned offensive . -- why oh why . -- . . its so idiotic your idiot beliefs -- . . your goddamned Christian fundamentalist superstitious lunacy . well now you know and now youre scared -- . you see that thing eating its way into your brain your face in the mirror hideous monster for no reason . . it couldve all been avoided so simply long ago if you werent so damned stubborn in your cursed religion . -- so what gives you the right to go on torturing us all . -- . . youre no better than Ophelia -- . . you make me suffer too much . my god its sickening -- . how can I go see you . . oh I will Mother I will I know Ive got to . -- Cleo you and that eye are not long for this world . -- . . youre headed for the vet soon -- . . I cant stand looking at you as much as I loved you old gal . and you were such a good cat such a delicate feminine thing -- . proud hunter too the way you placed the birds on the mat just so . . I know it when youre dreaming about your great hunting exploits your legs twitch and you mutter in your sleep . -- Ill give you more evaporated milk in the morning though I wish it were cream thick sweet . -- . . I could run out to the -- . . but its raining its got to be late besides were on a diet now Cleo and cream though I love it especially on the Corn Checks its in the thousands . and why do all the exercises the situps -- . which Cleo I detest . . if were going to have to write down cream . -- no weve got to do it . -- . . weve got to show that pert little blond Cle -- . . in three months or maybe even less . well show her shes going to notice a new man in a new navy blue sports jacket better than Harvey has -- . and shell look up and smile and well take her out to lunch . . how about that Cleo . -- you purr I purr . -- . . the little blondll be purring after I show her Angelos steamed mussels and a big bottle of Chianti -- . . take our time going back to the office drop her at the door while I take the car down to the garage . well be discreet -- . that damn Mary Jane will never need to know . . I can tell that blonds got class . -- she wont be the blab and gossip type likes the attention someone older to listen to her drivel. -- . . shes already confided in me after all -- . . that time she mentioned her boyfriend running off to California when I caught her coming out of the john with a damp blotchy face . hey that would be something Cleo wouldnt it -- . go up to her desk tell her about my Joyceian experience with the kidneys the cat the

224

cream or lack thereof but she wouldnt get it . . too
dumb . -- alright not dumb just unread unschooled .
-- . . its not her fault -- . . bit of a disappointment .
theyre all too damn dumb after Ophelia -- . whats
the surprise . . at least she was smart . -- that smart .
-- . . knew me better than -- . . knew more than I did
in general . always ripped right through those
double crosstics never once beat her in Scrabble -- .
well at least she wouldve gotten a literary reference
as obvious as that . . in our courting days she was
valedictorian Phi Beta Kappa . -- of course she was
always a little intimidating . -- . . couldnt imagine
bringing Ophelia to an office party -- . . Jesus shed
challenge em to a game of charades . be down on
her knees on the rug in no time acting out obscene
French puns for Christs sake -- . well what can you
expect . . theyre a bunch of overspecialized
computer scientists engineers . -- administrators
business hacks . -- . . no more renaissance men -- .
not like me . . a little bit of everything not quite
enough of anything . -- course it takes a lot more to
satisfy the Ophelias of this world . -- . . how easily
contented that blond must be home alone at night in
an apartment filled with knickknacks framed
photographs -- . . did she get rid of the guy from
California yet . TV sitcoms a few magazines talks on
the phone never has to think -- . hell no . . thinking
is work thats what she gets paid eight hours a day for
enough is enough . -- bubble head blond boyfriend
comes over . -- . . they go out for a couple of beers
somewhere with fake Tiffany lamps for crissake

listen to Country Western music gossip about mutual friends at the office -- .. if she finds stuff in that sterile environment worthy of gossip . but if her life depended on it shed never get it about Joyce -- . nobody reads him anymore anyway . -- .. cant afford to -- .. got to specialize fast might lose your competitive edge for crissake . but in my day ysee little peach fuzz Mumzy allus told us yew gotta gitchure edgeecation grow up to be a gentleman know a little bit of everything read and write . -- course spellings always been too illogical to bother learning and languages to a Midwest boy . -- .. guess not -- .. at least I can pronounce the wine list and thats why young gentlemen and gentleladies go to college . not to learn a trade but to become polished -- . but then after the War Mumzy there was no more time for Joycing around .. the competition was fierce all those guys going after the same jobs . -- there just wasnt time . -- .. everyone wanted his threequarter acre patch of lawn little bungalow babe 3.2 babies the bit -- .. and there just wasnt time . had to make up for those war years parlay those skills you developed on the ship the plane the base -- . become a professional get drafted into the Cold War effort who the hell cared if you were a wellrounded gentleman scholar .. wonder what happened to Chooch   lying in your bunk together feet to face each with a paperback we scrounged from the bottom of the Red Cross boxes the ones nobody wanted the poetry the philosophy . -- remember Nietzsche Chooch . -- .. that whole month you went round quoting Man and Superman drove us all nutz -- . . the occasional wellworn detective novel . you read all that Paddington one day remember -- . out loud . . and all the guys walking by kept telling you to shut up and threw dirty socks at you you kept right on reading that clear bellow of yours I loved it didnt want you to stop . -- never did answer . -- . . got an answer to that one letter Texas -- . . Chooch I just cant picture a Chicago boy like you whoopin it up with Texans . probably got a drawl on yew by now -- . but that blond couldnt have been born much before well McCarthy anyway . . and of course she wouldve been just starting college when no that couldnt be right . -- where did she say she went anyway Duluth . -- . . no Duke no that wasnt it -- . it was some little Catholic place in Delaware or some godforsaken . during the sixties -- . then she must be about oh skip it . . keep the blond for flirtation around the office let them wonder and twitter . -- back to Lorraine and Cherie then . -- . . at least theyre pretty safe -- . . what a pair of losers probably never get laid . well Mother Im not going to feel guilty now -- . you had your religion long before I came into the picture and people dont change . . theres no way I couldve ever changed you . -- its a miracle youve made it so long and that you havent experienced much pain apparently . -- . . Nora youve been no help -- . . youre half converted yourself . or are you -- . I wonder what you really believe anyone whos gone through life using as many damn skin creams as you

. . I suspect Nora though Ive never confronted you cant imagine confronting you   that youve been humoring the old gal all along . -- stay one foot in the fold make sure you get your rent check . -- . . oh cmon Nora shes supported you all your goddamn life -- . . okay so shes given me help too . but youve remained a complete dependent -- . and I dont fault you . . hell Id go along with her just to avoid rocking the boat . -- neither of us wouldve interfered to save her . -- . . after all shes not our child -- . . its not as if Frieda the time her heart stopped from that drug reaction what was she about seven . youd have wrestled the adrenaline out of that doctors hand had you been there -- . no wonder Papa . . I couldnt have taken it . -- Im sure flat on his back for two years every other bone snapped in two immobilized helpless no escape from your parade of bedside Bible readers preachers driving him crazy when he was powerless to escape . -- . . Id have been plotting your poisoning every day behind my bandages for that you maniac -- . modern medicine saved his life . thank god -- . Mother it was not your fundamentalist friends . . it took an eight man team national experts experimental technique hours and hours of surgery goddamn scaffolding collapsing the thud the crunch the liquid pain the enveloping blackness . -- Papa mustve been on morphine for months . -- . . mustve lain there cursing you -- . . laughing at you and your pestering preachers trying to drive him up the wall . hospital shouldnt have let those bastards in -- . what could they have imagined

228

it was going to do for the guy . -- I come in little boy for crissakes they tell me kneel . -- . . I never had anyone tell me to kneel in my life the nerve of those goons -- . ran out of there sorry Mother sorry Father but no dice . let me sit on his bed after that -- . damned idiots . . no wonder he ran off with the socalled floozy . -- hell she was probably the first sane person hed been able to talk to for . -- . . goddamn religious idiots opiate of the masses are asses   look at you Lorraine your goddamn fatass husband friend of Barry Goldwaters dubious distinction that runs off with his own floozy and you my dear still cant admit it -- . you cant bring yourself to divorce the bastard thereby freeing up your many socalled longpentup desires and talents and all that latent art all lost sacrificed because you Lorbaby are a goddamned mackerelsnapping papist idiot who doesnt *believe* in divorce you dont *believe* in it . . its friggin legal now for Christs sake in case you havent been paying attention . --

AHHHHHHA

youve just been hiding behind this religious jazz baby . -- . . I really should set her straight if Im going to waste anymore of my time -- . . we can go out to Tonios . Ill be very gentle with her not make a big deal out of it -- . I know it hurts kid . . its been my fault . -- I guess I wasnt admitting to myself how much I cared but youve got to do your part baby . -- . . sure its hard to admit youve been dumped abandoned in your pumpkin shell house kids clothes

229

pets pots n pans the whole domestic kit n caboodle and what more could you get settled on you -- . . but you oughta at least sue the bastard . listen even my old crazy mother had the guts to call a louse a louse -- . listen the Church doesnt say anything about lawsuits . . hit him in his own bailiwick take the bastard for all hes worth . -- Im going to take you out next Tuesday or Thursday whichever day you dont go to art class and youre going to hear the truth from me . -- . . why -- . . what right do I have . because Im a man who doesnt like to live in a nest of lies -- . look I wont bring up Mother again . . no examples no need for explanations youre a smart cookie the simplest way possible -- . Ill put my fork down . -- . . Lorraine you ought to divorce Mike because Mikes never coming back -- . . shell think Im about to propose . Jesus -- . I cant say that or shell think its my turn . . shit Im not marrying you Lorraine or anyone else for the time being . -- what do I want another mess for . -- . . extricate myself after twentyseven years from one nut think Im going to go jump into housekeeping with another -- . . enough crazy women in my life . Mother a religious maniac wife an alcoholic suicide -- . even you Nora youre not a normal sister whatre you a dyke . . she turned your head so against men it spoiled your chances in life . -- you shouldve rejected her and saved yourself you didnt have to get trapped in her net of guilt pity whatever you feel . -- . . I know its tough but you gotta break free of it to save yourself Nora -- . . whatre ya going to do go down with the ship . look at me -- . I was gaining more weight than was healthy got a little out of shape screwed up my skin nerves trying to keep up with Ophelia drinking too much but I got a grip on myself always have . . up now doing exercises first thing keep careful track of everything I eat . -- computer printout last week showed I managed to cut down by 234 calories lost some pounds . -- . . skins a lot better since that dermatologist -- . . think I will turn down the phonograph . while Im up -- . whee . . steady there guy not too fast here put your head down take a couple breaths . -- o n e and t w o and t h r e e . -- . . there thats better -- . . okay . steady as she goes -- . might as well put you back in your sleeve here Vivaldi . . now better go in the kitchen see what time it is look for my watch . -- rain keeps coming ought to be finished by morning what the hell day . -- . . oh yeah Wednesday -- . . got two more days of exercising before I can take a break . cmon Cleo Ill get you something too -- . why did I hang up on that massage parlor . . damn it . -- they must get a lot of those . -- . . guys call up find theyre too chicken to hear the sound of their own voices -- . . they wouldnt have asked any questions all you wouldve had to say is what are your rates . or they might think that was too sophisticated better just how much -- . theyd tell you about the different deals not in any details . . probably by the time limit the fifteen minute the half hour the hour . -- it couldnt be that much . -- . . maybe twentyfive for the fifteen -- . . forty the half hour . ask when how late theyre

open -- . go as late as possible . . girlsd be tired and
bitchy ready to go home . -- get a fifteen minute job
. -- . . the introductory thats a good one introductory
-- . . nah I couldnt . theyd talk too much stupid
professional patter -- . so youre going to get a
divorce honey . . cute guy like you . -- she mustve
been out of her mind . -- . . like at the dentist when
hes got you helpless with a mouth full of cotton
wads -- . . God therere so many of them though .
sprung up like mushrooms in the last few years -- .
never noticed them before . . maybe they were
always there and I just never . -- some of them must
be doing pretty well judging by the size of these ads
. -- . . Mafia probably -- . . but would it be
dangerous . have to pick a good location something
near the suburbs away from the red light strip -- .
bouncers with guns . . pimps . -- theyd have to be
discreet . -- . . must use a fake name of course -- . .
Mr. Alan Carter or how about Jack Larue . youd
have to be careful of course -- . theyd call you by
your name . . might not respond right away must
figure youre going to give an alias . -- how silly really
with all those different joints . -- . . whod ever find
out -- . . Im anonymous enough for Christs sake .
whod give a flying fuck what I did -- . they dont even
know me the higherups that count the ones Id most
likely run into at one of those . . I bet that Mark
Harris goes . -- he looks the type . -- . . and hes still
married isnt he -- . . you wouldnt know the way he
talks . the little blonds mine though Mark -- . I can
see she doesnt fall for your routine I saw her after

232

you came in the other day all leaning over her desk
flopping your tie at her . . you know you act like a
college kid sometimes . -- youre my age Harris old
buddy whore you kidding . -- . . she turns around to
that dope Marcy as soon as you prance out I saw her
-- . . crinched her eyes up like this . upper lip curled
that was a genuine look of disgust -- . that little
blonds got taste shes not blind . . she knows shes
the cutest thing on B . -- shes not the flirty type . -- .
. doesnt have to be -- . . I hate those coy ones
anyway . thing I like about you Honeyhair you look
so serious act smart work hard do a decent job keep
quiet youre a good secretary good as old Portia was
and I appreciate that -- . . Ill take you to lunch at
Damians tell you about some of the idiot secretaries
Ive had to put up with so youll know how much I
apprec . no no thats stupid -- . I wont talk about
work . . nothing about work thats up to her to
bring up work . -- what the hell will we talk about . -
- . . your interests -- . . of course your boyfriend .
well talk plenty about him if you want -- . . Ill be a
fatherly old confidant you can cry on my shoulder in
the future . wonder if theyd have one that looks as
good as Honeyhair -- . tight pink miniskirt with the
tips of garters showing low neckline so you can see a
little freckle on the inside of the right breast puffed
up in the wire brassiere offering itself like a cutlet on
a pink plate . . I could call what the hell time . --
only 9:30 . -- . . still early for crissake -- . . why not
just call and ask about . stupid nobody does that -- .
you just drive by get in the car windshield wipers

cold aird sober you right up drive around with the
phone book on the seat next to you trying to find a
neon façade . . some weird strip no parking in sight .
-- have to just go in and commit yourself take what
comes . -- . . pay in cash but only carry just that
amount -- . . no ID . leave the wallet in the glove
compartment -- . but what if they only take
reservations . . oh what the hell . -- leave it Ed . -- . .
try again some other time when youre more rested
when its not so dark and rainy -- . . some Friday
after work maybe .   peanuts all gone -- . I guess I
did finish em up after all . . well then what can we no
. -- no more wine . -- . . some dry vermouth maybe -
- . . on ice . yeah just a little straight up no -- . no
gin dummy thatd make you sick . . a twist put a
twist in it . -- anyway freshens it up there that smells
good . -- . . lemon trees -- . . Mother . your lemon
trees should be in -- . never mind . . how about
some pickled herring . -- that sounds like just the
ticket . -- . . on a white cracker -- . . get the crackers
here no crumbs please need a plate anyway . get
one out of the dishwasher here -- . not bad . --
elegant with the vermouth . -- . . now what was it I
was -- . . oh yes the MX Missile article . wasnt
really following it all the technical problems
something about timing the rotation around the
tracks -- . what do I bother reading that crap for . .
retired from the missile building business thank god
what a waste of talent and energy build these things
gotta haggle over the price of every damn screw for
five years stuff is junked six months after its built . --

no I stoked that fire long enough . -- . . the absurdity
-- . . spend your working life which is a helluva lot
more than your pleasuring life family friends
trimming the dogwoods walking the dog . I do miss
having Old Trusty around -- . cant get another dog
though not if Im going to find an apartment . . a cat
in an apartments okay but not a dog . -- its not fair
to them . -- . . no they can make the MX without me
-- . . Ill sit this one out fellas . its all yours -- . next
thing Im going to build is a boat . . or maybe a little
house . -- wood like to work with lots of beautiful
wood . -- . . dont want to cut it all myself though
cant afford to go that far on my own -- . . now if Sam
really wanted to get involved . but thatll be years
later   first therell be the apartment city life get one
of those old brownstones gut it -- . look into it
anyway . . it may prove too impractical . -- gotta
get something soon though . -- . . cant go on paying
for this white elephant falling apart every minute
goddamn crappy building job ceiling cracking there
look at that its gotten bigger -- . . water seeping
through the carpets no bloody foundation . windows
leak like -- . who the hell are these imbeciles a
bunch of votech flunkies slap these things together
so damn overpriced too . . this piece of shit isnt
worth the materials that went into it wont last
another five years . -- gotta unload it cant afford to
take too much of a loss gotta get Sam up here help
with the painting and cleanup hire a carpet cleaner
rent out the upper half live in the kitchen and the rec
room till its sold . -- . . get Ophelia down here soon

to pick up her junk -- . . says she doesnt want anything . well shed better take some of it or its going to the junk dealer -- . cant be bothered lugging all these handmedowns . . they were great when the children were growing up . -- never spent more than a couple hundred bucks on furniture throughout the marriage sick of these chairs and this heavy couch sagging pillows . -- . . its a good piece needs new slip covers -- . . have to place ads in the papers I guess . have people coming over all weekend what a bother -- . maybe call one of those charity pickups . . the apartments mine . -- everything will be handpicked by me . -- . . get some of that wood and glass Danish stuff nice modern masculine -- . . huh . masculine just attractive clean simple elegant spare solid dark colors but not drab rich browns dark reds maybe -- . no more goldenrod and no avocado green . . some new glass and brass lamps theyre going to be expensive . -- the few antiques guess I could keep them if Ophelia doesnt want them of course especially the clock Ive always been fond of the clock and the Chinese pot the wooden salad bowls she may want those . -- . . Christ if youd just come down here and help me with all this Ophelia -- . . youre entitled to choose what you want . but get it out of here -- . Ill rent a truck for you . . Sam can haul it . -- dump any of it at Dolfs he must have space in the barn the guest house he never uses anymore . -- . . itll be yours someday Sam possibly soon -- . . Ophelia I cant feel sorry for you with that place about to fall into your lap it must

236

be worth a couple hundred thousand if that old goat werent such a goddamn pain in the ass didnt mean to punch him that hard . took him by surprise that time -- . he certainly deserved it . . God I cant take some of his horseshit sometimes . -- torturing you like that . -- . . no wonder you grew up with no goddamn ego -- . . all right all right sound like him now damn it . you two will have to work something out -- . Im sorry I cant be your defender anymore . . hes your father Fella youve got to get tough . -- shout the bastard down . -- . . just quit taking it from a feeble old man now Jesus youre younger and stronger than he is and he should realize he needs you youre the one whos going to take care of him -- . . he cant expect to find another Rosy . God how he cons those old dames into -- . and then they die on him . . hows that for irony . -- the old bastards going to outlive us all . -- . . no hes going after that last heart attack then falling down the stairs -- . . good thing he was drunk . didnt break a knuckle -- . hes got the damnedest luck . . you gotta hand it to him hes clinging to that place . -- hell go down with his own ship start a fire on the stove one day choke to death trying to save his damned hedgehog collection . -- . . your bastard of a father never made you feel loved enough never praised you enough never gave you that sense of selfworth -- . . or maybe Ill never know . maybe he was a good father to you Ophelia -- . if you hate him as you seem to with some terrific repressed hatred . . well dont expect me to do the punching . -- you confront the

237

guy have it out with him . -- . . how many years have
I watched him bully you -- . . you cowering crying to
me . I think its about time you and Daddy had that
long overdue confrontation -- . do you both some
good   theres still love there . . youre both so
hopelessly sentimental . -- youre not like Libby
Ophelia why couldnt you have gotten her toughness .
-- . . shes the only one who could ever handle him
bossed him around like the spoiled brat he was -- . .
Dolfi shut up . thats what he needs from a woman -
- . thats what hes been used to for so long . . of
course Jane couldnt handle him either . -- now she
was a saint . -- . . he ran roughshod over her -- . .
the nastiness the contempt   god that made me sick
to see when she was dying and so defenseless
against him . and that Rosy -- . she was a total
victim . . didnt have the least idea what she was
getting into . -- oh he can be a charmer . -- . . charms
them off their feet -- . . brings them to his sadists lair
. goddamn Germanic bullyism -- . tortures the old
things to death with his brutal snarling and bitching
constant criticizing . . of course nobody can do
anything right . -- well he doesnt dare try it on me .
-- . . afraid of me -- . . probably always been afraid
of men . doesnt dare try his crap on a man -- . takes
it out on women . . well his mother mustve made
him her little surrogate hubby . -- weve talked about
it . -- . . Dolf you can be quite human a real fine
sensitive fellow on brief occasions and youve been
good with the children but then youve snapped at
them too -- . . that time Sam was playing in the barn

238

you made him cry . cant remember what -- . youd
probably yelled at him too hard . . God knows I
couldve smashed your face in but kids can take it . --
they accepted you always got over it quickly . -- . .
not Ophelia -- . . she was never the type to bounce
back . brooded for hours days -- . I had to take care
of her wounds . . Jesus give the poor woman a break
shes your only daughter your only child . -- for
crissake all you have left in this world you
cantankerous fool . -- . . but theres nothing I can do
-- . . no Ive done my bit Im out of it now . thats her
problem and she may do herself in before resolving
anything with you and Ill hate you for it if she does --
. meanwhile Ill wait in the wings and hope for the
best . . Ive got my own problems . -- Mother
grotesquely disfigured dying ever so torturously for
no reason the absurdity . -- . . Christ it could be
worse -- . . I suppose it couldve happened years ago
. shes had a long life now basically good -- . she
didnt deserve old Harolds desertion . . she bore it
well enough in her younger days we never wanted
for anything . -- she couldve had another husband
before Stephen she was certainly young attractive
enough nothing was preventing her . -- . . the
bitterness the wormy suppressed hatred she stored
up all of it so unnecessary -- . . at least she tried to
spare me from it . but not Nora -- . Nora had to
have been brainwashed against men . . she
obviously never had sufficient interest . -- for awhile
I thought she was a dyke but she apparently had
boyfriends although its hard to imagine who in his

239

right mind would ever want to get anywhere near
that prickly kewpie doll in an Amazons body . -- . .
but who knows maybe she has some secret charming
side Ive never seen -- . . is it possible . seems mighty
hard to imagine but then anythings possible I
suppose -- . God knows why men go for some
women . . not Ophelia boy she was as *for* men as
Noras against em . -- Ophelia shouldve been one of
those wild west saloon Lollies who stick their bosom
in your face when they sling you your beer who seem
to love getting grabbed by the unshaven blackhatted
types with the heavy pistols held hostage over a
poker game if theyre lucky get themselves tied onto
the back of a saddle whisked off into the
mountainous dusk . -- . . yes thats my wife theyve
got with them -- . . and I riding in the posse knowing
full well she was enjoying herself mightily and would
be damned disappointed to be rescued again .
Christ what an exhausting routine that was year after
year -- .

***

what was that Thurber cartoon no no not Mrs Harris
on the bookshelf no the one with Lida her name was
definitely Lida -- . . with you Ive known peace . what
was it man sitting next to the woman holding her
head -- . with you Ive known peace Lida and now
you say youre going crazy . . boy thats more subtle
than the wife on the bookshelf but I like it better . --
I think its in the *Thurber Carnival* or maybe one of
the others . -- . . Im sure we have it -- . . Ill look it
up . but not now -- . we had a classic Thurber
marriage she was dominant threatening shrieking
and I was the Walter Mitty dreamer she thought I
was such an intolerable slob really I wasnt so bad as
all that she was compulsively neat . . compulsive
about so many things   asserting always asserting her
control over the smallest dumbest . -- pet peeves
really . -- . . everything was one big pet peeve -- . .
resented housework but couldnt let it go for a
minute and banging about . Christ she was the
noisiest dishwasher went about everything with such
fury -- . shouldve been an Army sergeant Fella . .
God I dont miss that . -- leave a fellow alone in the
evenings to drink in peace . -- . . got to get more
vermouth -- . . here . the peace -- . I cant stand it
now too damn quiet . . no not the radio thered be
too much annoying talking in between . -- here . -- . .
the wind concertos -- . . Mozart always comforts so .
so balanced -- . no its more that hes predictable
nothing jarring alls been rounded off now at least for
me . . clarinet . -- sleepy clarinet . -- . . let me just -
- . . oh you too Cleo . good night for snuggling on the

241

couch eh -- . shame about Frieda after all that squawking never could get a decent sound out of the clarinet never took it seriously enough . . couldnt get those kids to sit still long enough really listen to great music . -- red rubberband lips stretched wide around that black plastic mouthpiece though made her a little crosseyed . -- . . oh lucky reed hot tongue licking teeth clenching down blasts of bodyheated breath coming through you dangled between two milk thighs on the piano bench squawksquawk -- . . it was endearing . I have to admit I wish shed kept it up -- . damn her . . regular Lolita . -- how the hell was I supposed to . -- . . alright alright -- . . Cleo could you move down here a few inches atta girl . much better -- . easy with the claws now . . damn that idiot crack looks like its gotten longer . -- I should try and do something about that this weekend get to that ceiling . -- . . cant sell the damn place theyd notice the crack in the workroom too -- . . got to paint over that . dammit so much to do -- . dog hair everywhere have to look in the phone book find a cleaning service what could they charge for one day . . oh the leak under the washer too . -- what about the washer . -- . . leave it here -- . . will they let me . dont really want to bother -- . of course an apartment building wouldnt need it . . anyway they all have laundry rooms . -- gotta get Sam out here to deal with his room all that damn stuff on the walls his painting sketching . -- . . hell have to repaint the whole room do something about the stickers on that door -- . . Christ gotta put that doorknob back on the upstairs bathroom . how the hell -- . its nearly dark when I get home from work deserve a little rest for crying out loud . . gotta get up early do my own shopping on the way home . -- maybe get some of those steaks tomorrow could freeze a few shouldve picked them up today . -- . . still hoping youll see her again is that why you keep stopping every day after work -- . . really Ed pretty damn childish . she probably doesnt even work there anymore -- . had a fight with the boss he tried to give her little buns a squeeze back there in front of the meat locker . . slapped him tore off her red apron stamped out the door customers be damned . -- if Id been there couldve caught her arm walked with her a few blocks let her blow off steam taken her out for a drink at Micks . -- . . check tomorrow she might be back -- . . okay youre waking up a little thawing out . its a good sign -- . twentyseven years wrestling with a woman bent on self destruction . click -- . new era clean slate . . get back in physical shape priority number one diet exercise diet . -- theres still some of that bakers chocolate in the cabinet no sugar it cant be very many . -- . . excuse me Cleo -- . . its still early I can rest a little now then get up maybe tackle that crack tonight . just a hair more -- . now thats fine . . another ice cube will make it last longer . -- lets see now it was back on this shelf the last time I . -- . . oh great -- . . here you are . theres one square left -- . hard . . pretty damn old I guess . -- still its chocolate . -- . . get a little plate or something crumbs -- . . how about a

243

paper towel . there -- . oh you want to lick the kidney pan here you go . . Im going back to the MX article now . -- soon as this damn house is gotten rid of wont need to stay home much at all spend every night out with the girls . -- . . meanwhile Im in training gotta get back down to 190 fit in that blue blazer again do those Airforce exercises every morning cut down drinking as soon as the house -- . . and all the ugly memories . soon as I get my apartment will want a lightup glass shelved cabinet like Ross get a set of nice decanters lined up golden brown and white get some kirsch wasser -- . miss that . . used to have it at Christmas always with Libby and Dolf . -- this vermouth doesnt go well with the chocolate . -- . . get something sweet -- . . we might have some cordials left . drink this up here -- . excuse me again Cleo . . get something like kirsch wasser let me see no not Gran Marnier crème de menthe horrible no . -- ah perfect Kahlua just the thing to go with chocolate rinse this out a minute here . -- . . no no ice this is just fine of course if we only had some cream -- . . okay turn over the Mozart tape now get back to the article got to remember to record Kahlua though . what is it about four ounces -- . thats got to be a lot have to exercise more on the weekends go to the club ten laps will take that off spend the mornings in the pool the afternoons fixing up the house . . got to get back in touch with that realtor what was her name Furnis Furgusson something like that . -- look her up in the Yellow Pages . -- . . get Sam down here damn him hes got to get that room in shape call Sam remember to write that down -- . . say its a sellers market these days ought to get enough money shut Ophelia up . she can pay her own damn medical insurance but she wont -- . shell find some phony excuse drink it all up . . damn you do you think I give a fig whether or not you take care of yourself at this point . -- once Im free of you you can do yourself in any way you damn please only just wait until the house and the divorce are settled . -- . . would you please do me that one little favor Jesus Im doing the best I can here -- . . suddenly got this whole damn thing dumped in my lap . it cant be done overnight you little idiot -- . probably take six months before I can completely wash my hands of you and then theyll never be that clean . . youll find some new means of torturing me Im certain of it . -- dont think youre dragging me down with you though not me boy . -- . . Im going to dance on out of here yet youll see -- . . little bimbo on each arm and your sordid affairs your endless stream of pathetic little desperate seductions . you couldve saved me from the gory details -- . oh but not you that was the best part you seemed to get more out of them from telling me than you did from . . cant believe all those suckers couldnt see right through you . -- guess I was the biggest chump of all eh . -- . . maybe it was a failure complex of some kind Im willing to admit it now what have I got to lose -- . . Christ your dissatisfaction was enough to make the most selfsatisfied guy feel inadequate . well shucks

245

Ophelia -- . I aint so bad . . not the big fucking
disaster you tried to make me out to be . -- hell Im
the survivor . -- . . look at me Im going to get some
new suits take some ladies out to dinner note I said
ladies not little psychotic nymphomaniacs -- . .
ladies . women who know how to keep their legs
crossed women who arent flirting with the guy at the
next table while youre in the john . Ill take some
ladies to the theater hell maybe rent a yacht take em
sailing -- . you dont know what youre going to be
missing Ophelia . . gave up a lot you know . -- your
choice I didnt make you it was your decision didnt
drive you out didnt plead with you to stay . -- . . hell
by that time I was numb as a doorknob -- . . didnt
give a flying fuck what you did or didnt do anymore .
I just wanted to live -- . you wanted to kill yourself
presumably and I spoiled your little plans though Ill
never know . . figure you were willing to take the
chance it almost didnt go your way . -- if not for
Trusty you wouldnt have had your white knight
rescue wouldnt have wakened a braindamaged
hideous monster . -- . . finally you had to see
yourself as you really were -- . . yes my dear the
charade was over you were no siren you were a
boozy old floozy all gone to seed . it was over my pet
no more coquette -- . you got your damn life back
for what its worth and I got mine and he . . he got
you . -- ha thats the biggest joke of all . -- . . I guess
you won didnt you sucker -- . . you got her in the
end the battles over kid . shes all yours -- . good
spoils old sport . . only youll never be able to take

care of her . -- bet you resent it already she really cramps your style now doesnt she . -- . . youve got this great big excheesecake invalid on your hands now big daddy Mr Beretsporting bum -- . . youre a bum and you always were . always will be a big welsher dumped four wives for Christs sake scattered some brats abroad never gave a damn for anyone but yourself -- . its divine justice really you should be saddled with Ophelia in the end your just desserts . . ha just try and weasel out from under her now you bastard . -- Ill kill you . -- . . you got her you take goddamn responsibility for her -- . . Im retired . Ive paid my goddamn dues -- . organized my whole life around providing this poor unfortunate womans security . . sold my soul to the gummint love that old Walt Kellys gummint . -- listened to her sob out hideous tales of infidelity packed her off in the ambulance hey buddy thats it for me . -- . . Ive earned the purple star now for Ophelia duty -- . . you can have her my blessings . just dont try any cheap tricks youve got no place to hide -- . I swear Ill kill you if you . . sailing sailing . -- first thing Im going to do when the house is sold go sailing on the bay cruise for a week even if I have to go by myself . --. . stock up on ale -- . . no too fattening . nothing but white wine tuna fish and celery stay out there till I lose that twentyfive pounds come back and conquer the office -- . oh Fella its so senseless sometimes so stupid . . we were happy together if only youd been a little stronger or couldve just let the doctors help you . -- all this waste . -- . . we could be together this nightmare would finally be over Id take time off work we could go on another Caribbean cruise you liked that -- . . we were so right for each other . you know I loved you -- . I tried to show it . . I cared and I still care .-- thats the damn problem . -- therell never be anyone who was all those things together bright sexy creative aggressive spirited . -- . . Jesus Fella why couldnt you have held up -- . . for twentyseven years I could never encourage you enough -- . . always needed more support more comforting more praise . I was only one man Ophelia -- . that was part of the problem you needed an army of psychiatrists lovers father figures . . ever since we moved from Idaho that Dr Schanke the only one youd ever condescended to work with . -- and you were making such progress and then we moved . -- . . god maybe I am to blame -- . . its always been me wrenching you away . but what was I supposed to do had to support us goddamn family -- . could never do what I wanted could I . . had to prostitute myself . -- one lousy time I ever tried to strike out on my own start my own business . -- . . Jesus you couldnt take that for a minute -- . . wonder if I couldve made it if Id been married to someone else . what the hell -- . I was alright with going back to the federal teat . . what difference did it make . -- had to work . -- . . not the sort of guy perhaps needed security myself -- . . its just as well it failed left me to concentrate on you and the kids . at least work was meaningless no competition for you four -- .

you think it wouldve been better more glamorous
say with a guy like Jules . . you couldnt have stood it
with Jules for a year . -- the guys a workaholic youd
have had to compete for his attention all the time . -
- . . you think he wouldve stood your having all
those damn lovers with his reputation on the block --
. . hell he wouldnt have had the patience for you . I
was the only one lucky me -- . only it gets to be a bit
much sometimes even for Saint Edgar . . yeah sure
you broke me . -- finally got to the point where I
sincerely did not give a damn . -- . . should have sat
there a few minutes longer -- . . shouldve had
another drink what the hell my ass was covered Id
called the cops hadnt I . couldve passed you by
dragged Trusty back to the house waited for them to
find you -- . scared shitless they were going to pin it
on me somehow . . Jesus you never thought of the
rest of us you selfish little . -- never thought of
Sammy how he might have to live it down the sheer
insult of it all . -- . . the need to punish -- . who . me
-- . or were you thinking of him . . the fucker didnt
come rescue you in time . -- you actually thought hed
follow you here or physically remove you or what did
you think Ophelia . -- . . of course well never know
will we -- . . all you thought about was your own
childish misery your own inability to love yourself
thats what it was if you want to get technical you
understood it better than I did Christ it was your field
. oh face it your lack of ego Dr Schanke was right the
tragedy was you tried to build one it just wasnt good
enough -- . all those successes of yours and nothing

was ever enough . . you remained empty unfulfilled
nobody could have loved you enough I finally got
that through my head . -- it wasnt me Ophelia it
never was me . -- . . I was just the unfortunate
chump who couldnt see it -- . . or if he could wasnt
driven off by it . youre never going to get that
ignorant sonofabitch to take care of you in the
manner to which youd become accustomed -- .
goddamn tramp whats he got some teachers pension
. . how you gonna live on that eh Fella . -- you gonna
sit around watching his beer belly grow now waiting
for Dolf to die so you can move in there together . -- .
. bully for you -- . . hes a freeloader and a fiend if he
tries that . course its not my problem if he does -- .
idiot cant live forever . . got to be worried about
outliving him now hey you two could always
engineer some sort of suicide pact . -- no hed never
go for it . -- . . leave you first go to his daughters or
one of his exwives to die -- . youve not bought
yourself any security with this one Fella . youll never
be secure -- . youll face death someday alone like
anyone . . terrified . -- dress rehearsal not
withstanding . -- . . and youll call out my name yes
you will and I wont hear it no I wont not from my
yacht in the turquoise waters of the British Virgins no
Ill not hear your cry -- . . oh Cleo you poor old gal
commere you . cancer eating out your eye there
just like mother no we cant have you around too
much longer -- . one of these days going to be taking
a ride to the vet sweetheart . . dont cramp my style I
might find a condo I like that wont take pets . --

youve had a good life what are you something over
eightyfive in cat years . -- . . still Id miss you -- .
remember your kittens Cleo . I know when youre
dreaming about your kittens yes I do -- . you make
those same maternal mewings to them you lick the
air as though washing their coats yes you do . . get
rid of you someday . -- this junk furniture . -- . . get
those damn handbags out of the closet there -- . .
Christ she had twenty of the damn things . left em
all like the clothes half the shoes -- . couldnt have
had the decency to take out your own garbage . .
here what am I supposed to do with this junk haul it
all off to the Salvation Army . -- Jesus you fall apart
on me cant take responsibility for your half of
twentyseven years . -- . . youve been nothing but a
headache the last three or four of them Ophelia and
now that youve played your little game its time you
did the big girl thing and honored your half of the
agreement if you dont cooperate with me this time
Im going to haul your half out to the dump dont
want your goddamn pocketbook collection never
open this closet here -- . . just see how many of the
goddamn things shes . Christ this is amazing -- . its
really . . will you look at these . -- got to be . -- . .
well Ill count them then top shelf brown leather
brown plastic two black leather with gold clasp three
brown vinyl with monogram four black suede five -- .
. second shelf woven plasticcoated basket six yellow
cloth seven . whats this goddamn empty gin bottle
-- . red knitted what was that eight white plastic nine
pearl evening ten whats this wad of dirty

251

handkerchiefs . . slob . -- Ophelia you goddamn slut . -- . . matches piano bar   whats this somebodys lighter didnt know you smoked Ophelia -- . for the love of God spare me any more of the sordid . red leather with shoulder strap ten or eleven pink beaded cloth -- . whats that thirteen silver evening bag didnt I give you this one . . dont remember you ever using it damn still in good shape maybe one of the girls . -- put it on the chair there think about it . -- . . this was from Greece Libby gave it to you mustve been Libby -- . . whiskey bottle . charming -- . green fake leather fifteen Christ youd hidden your stashes everywhere wonder how much I could find . . will inevitably find . -- once I have to clean out the whole . -- . . look at this mess and theres more -- . . this is a nice one never saw you use it . maybe one of the girls -- . oh to hell with it . . you dont deserve these things Im throwing the whole damn lot of em out right now just gotta find a trash bag big enough goddamn mountain of bloody handbags spoiled brat . -- here under the sink must be a . -- . . yes good and its a big one -- . . twenty goddamn pocketbookets for one woman what the hell did you think you . I guess they just accumulate dont they twentyseven years well its good riddance to them now you had your chance you said you would come get your stuff its been weeks Ive seen no evidence of your -- . to hell with you then . . this is it out of sight out of . -- its going in the trash now never answer my goddamn letters youve had your chance I can take it as a no response youre not coming back for any of

this now its too late run up there leave everything on my hands send you checks got your car the color TV .
-- . . you didnt hesitate to take the brand new TV -- .
. cant get you to haul off the rest of your junk pocketbooks weigh a goddamn ton . Christ smells like cat piss in here again you still using this heat vent as your toilet Cleo -- . Jesus fucking Christ give me a break . . thats it youre going to the vet . -- I cant keep cleaning up your shit . -- . . Christ youre losing control of -- . . what . commere now Cle -- . look thats BAD . . BAD KITTY . -- you dont do that anymore now what are you regressing . -- . . outside -- . . I know its raining . now go out and do something outside and Ill let you back in Christ cant clean up cat shit every goddamn day sticks to the shag rug hate this ugly carpeting -- . going to have all polished wood floors no more cats no more carpets .
. get some paper towels now . -- Jesus Cleo why do I have to have a cat thats stinking up the place . -- . . bad enough with you Ophelia lying around never washing those last few months good riddance I say --
. . you can stink up his place now how you couldve let yourself go like that . spray some more Lysol -- . there thats good enough . . after all got to call in a cleaning crew at some point . -- damn the rain feels good . -- . . anyway nice and stormy out and sobering batten the hatches put out the storm anchor nice to be in a cozy harbor on a night like this -- . . alright Cleo come on you . lets get another glass of Kahlua -- . no wait nothing more sweet . . how about some Scotch yes a little Scotch would be just

right about now . --   cmon Cleo weve done our jobs for the evening let the rest of it go till tomorrow never use that closet anyway . -- . . now Cleo youre going to stop this infernal pissing and shitting in the dining room -- . . what if Lorraine comes over to dinner or what if the blond . having cat piss radiating from the heat duct oh wonderful a real bachelor pad think theyd take pity on me and clean this place up probably get a big kick throwing out all Ophelias junk for me wouldnt have to face it by myself . now look heres the nice new kitty litter I bought you   you get used to this its your last chance -- . were going to have to have you put down . . cant stand the vet smell the look of betrayal in their eyes as the needle plunges in the last sad look Father why hast thou forsaken me . -- Christ I cant stand it . -- . . Cleo dont make me do it -- . . here cmere youre my gal now . you just get a grip on yourself use the litter box like a good kitty we might even be able to have the vet sew up your eye or something -- . here . . here look you want a bite of cheese . -- Ill have just a nibble you may have this piece . -- . . thata girl at least you still eat well enough -- . . unlike Ophelia got so sick of trying to feed her wouldnt let go of that bottle long enough . yogurt -- . thats all shed even consider . . Christ Im sorry Ophelia Im sorry life dealt you a cruel blow Im sorry your job at the bank was so unsatisfying Im sorry that therapy center folded Im sorry the AA people didnt do you any good Im sorry none of the doctors could help you Im sorry you ever came down here if you hadnt wanted to and I never

insisted you did . -- it was you insisted Sam needed
you Trusty who would feed the cat . -- . . you
couldve stayed up there with him nobody prevented
you from making that decision but yourself -- . . we
spent many nights discussing it as I remember . Im
not sorry I pulled you out from under that bush what
the hell was I supposed to do Id found you it wouldve
been criminal to leave you there -- . what was I to do
with the dog standing there barking the police about
to arrive I had no choice I wasnt your goddamn
accomplice after all youve got your life back now and
its your problem what youre going to do with it
drink yourself to death in your lovers apartment fine
anything you want just leave me out of it you got
him now . arent you happy baby -- . well neither am
I . . I didnt want to lose you this way but you left me
no choice you cant make me responsible for your life
now just because I did the human thing and pulled
you out from under a bush in the nick of time no way
baby that life is yours its never been anyones but
yours its about time you figured that out . -- you
cant live through other people you cant pretend the
whole world needs you and therefore you exist to
serve it . -- . . that doesnt work your children need
you somewhat when theyre babies but not when
they grow up thats a fact of lIfe -- . . Im sorry you
cant accept facts of life but theyre there and theres
nothing I can do to protect you . could do -- . Im
sorry Im no longer responsible thats crap youd think
I was   got no reason to have a guilty conscience over
this   youd set it up this way so when you fell right

255

into it I just let you have what youd bargained for .
half an apartment up there in the slums if that was
so precious to you we talked about getting an
apartment here remember we couldve saved a great
deal of money but you insisted we had to have
woods for the dog you had to have woods for Sammy
-- . Sammy was going to college in a year   you
couldnt accept that either . . well Im sorry I couldnt
have prevented the kids from growing up any more
than you could have . -- I think thats fine they each
have their own lives now so do you and I thats fine .
-- . . you drink all you want now nobody will bother
you nobodys going to drag you off to hospitals
anymore now you dont ever have to try -- . . I guess I
was losing patience but my God how many years had
it been . how many thousands -- . you know Im still
getting those bills . . dont worry you wont ever see
them but I know how much its been . -- well if youre
not going to cooperate in your own cure then screw
you the AA people are right theres no one in the
whole damn world can help you if you wont help
yourself youve got to hit rock bottom before you can
come back up . -- . . maybe if he dumps you now -- . .
maybe if you find yourself out on the street shopping
cart in your hand instead of all those pocketbooks .
maybe then Ophelia maybe then

***

cant believe she bothered to sew these cushions back up should have ditched this thing lumpy   zipper sticking in my neck -- . . there thats better . feathers an inch thick on the living room floor like goddamn snow phone ripped out of the wall kids staring wideyed in the morning light -- . Jesus H Christ glad I dont remember that one . . mustve had to throw out most of the feathers anyway . -- how had she done it . -- . . mustve used a knife or something couldnt have ripped these up with her bare hands thick slipcovers but then I dont think any of the slipcovers were torn -- . . mustve taken the trouble to unzip them first . that was just like Ophelia -- . destructive as long as it didnt cost anything . . what a damn comedy . -- oh well itll be easier this way send Sam up with a UHaul dump it all on her front steps   get me some of that swank Scandinavian stuff all smooth lines nothing lumpy invite Lorraine over offer her a glass of Scotch . -- . . no no vermouth sweet vermouth Campari   Lorraine drinks nothing but Campari never cared much for the stuff myself -- . . shes attractive though certainly does keep herself neat and nicely dressed I liked that red thing she had on the other night   it wasnt like most of her clothes softer sexier . was she trying to seduce me -- . funny to think she might want it worse than I . . better watch out for that dont know that Id like her so much with her clothes off too skinny be all bones no rolling curves all angles . -- like her drawings of stick people . -- . . juvenile most of them even the one of the man -- . . shes caught

257

herself in the illnevergrowup trap . this damn youth cult -- . cant fool me though shes definitely over forty still like Margot the perpetual coed some of them can get away with it petite thin ones she must be a size six for Christs sake sometimes I wish she had a little more of Cheries buxomness . . Cheries got too much Lorraines got too little . -- put them together yes and youd have the little blond only theyd have to be blond and one third their combined ages . -- . . well Im not sure Im ready for a thirty year old have to be in your sixties before you go that far -- . . someone intelligent sympathetic someone who survived marriage well . they both have botched it as much as I did suffered God knows you two have suffered -- . that New Yorker cartoon of the Russian Bureaucrat in the art museum looking at the still life of flowers he hasnt no . . it was send him to Siberia he obviously hasnt suffered enough . -- Ive always liked that one . -- . . got to get that out show it to Lorraine -- . . no Lorraine wont get it takes herself too seriously would think I was making fun of her art god forbid . Cherie show it to her -- . yes Cherie and her joke books . . that says something you sit on their john and discover they have one of those joke books just like the Rubensteins next door god I thought you had to be Jewish . -- well Cherie you said it was a gift so maybe it isnt you and your stuffed alligator . -- . . yeah baby thats cute but youve been living alone too long scare men off with a thing like that -- . . or is that the idea . look youve got to make up your mind either you want to swing

or you dont -- . and Lorraine so silly sometimes I
cant be playing party games . . I guess Im not Ivy
League mentality just a Midwest stateschool boy   for
a woman who graduated from Swarthmore   Cherie
you dont impress me a great deal you didnt even get
my reference to Rube Goldberg   youre not that
damn young . -- Ophelia was bright   I took it too
much for granted in retrospect they are a very rare
commodity indeed women who are both sexy and
bright intellectually assertive types . -- . . you two
always taking your cues from me   why dont you
volunteer an opinion of your own -- . . who am I
some great critic editor of your thoughts . take you
to the theater cant even tell me what you think -- . I
knew you didnt like *The Door Keeper* Lorraine but
was it because you didnt understand it or because
you found some part of it objectionable . . Ill never
know you didnt want to discuss it   and why go to the
theater if you wont discuss the play . -- take Ophelia
to a bar afterwards over a cognac shed go on all
night   she could be a lively stimulating date if she
held together . -- . . always overshadowed me at
parties men found her so stimulating she was hardly
the gazeatmeandlisten type   get some guy into a
fight -- . . Dick coming to me demanding an apology
from my wife . cant remember what shed said to
insult him that night -- . damned funny really guy
wants me to force her to apologize   damn wimp
demand it of her himself not my fault if shed got you
in a verbal hammerlock . . well thats that . -- you
girls have a high standard to live up to though I

guess Id settle for less if it was predictable not liable to selfdestruct . -- . . Lorraine you might be interesting if you took your drawing a little less seriously and read more   you dont seem very talented to me your sticky people too childish somethings missing there I cant start getting involved with that let your teachers steer you in the right direction all this crap about your artistic personality though thats plain silly Ill not indulge you in that bunk -- . . you want to be an artist be one but dont moon over the prospect so   youre no ingénue . ah crap it wouldve been nice if youd kept our theater date for tonight   I wouldnt be standing in here staring in the sink   give me that scotch bottle Ill do the goddamn dishes tomorrow   not going to stick my hands in there now -- . empty cocktail peanuts jar . . where do we keep empty jars now Ophelia always saved peanut jars where   not down here . -- oh there you are   why the hell was she saving all these got so much cleaning out to do   gotta buy more garbage bags   call about a special trash pickup . -- . . hows that plaster patch doing   must be set by now -- . . yes you look ready to sand . not going to start sanding now do it first thing Saturday before swimming -- . call Joan Fergusen in the morning was that her name   lets see   no I dont want to let my fingers do the walking now . . oh yes her card right here where I left it on the counter nice not to have things moved on you   wont be having trouble finding stuff now one small benefit of living alone . -- Fergusen that was her name   Fialty Realty . -- . .

thats real cute Joan lemme write down the number here remember to take it with me -- . . so stupid to forget the little black book yesterday when I was so looking forward to printing out the first color graph of the diet see how we were doing here of course today was out . goddamn ONeil had to keep us prisoner in his meeting fuckin idiot cant put together a report to save his life -- . alright ONeil so you wasted another goddamn budget day idiots . . idiots once again Im surrounded by idiots story of my life goddamn idiots everywhere how the hell is anyone supposed to get anything done the least bit meaningful worthwhile . -- well heres to ya suckers all . -- . . gotta write down all those calories too now what was it kidneys -- . . oh wait till morning youll have a clearer head . plenty of time punch it in the computer at work it usually comes back to you then anyway -- . 460 plus 855 yes thats it . . get out of here this fluorescent lighting too much like the office . -- this is better a little Berlioz . -- . . oh thats the problem dummy gotta switch it to phono here -- . . okay now where was I . the rain did I let Cleo ah there you are feeling cozy now are we -- . move over old gal let me finish that article now where the hell was I too technical tired . . how about Artificial Knees here . -- no Id rather Liquid Helium . -- . . damn you Lorraine theaters just getting out now thought we had a date you bitch you cunt you Jesus cant waste my time thinking about you now dont need your company to put myself to bed after all -- . . just leave me alone all you damn broads

good for nothing imbecile cockteasing . but not the
blond she wouldnt do a thing like that   shes serious
a little bit afraid of me thats good she wouldnt dare
maybe shes scared because Im old enough to be her
father   hard to imagine that   couldnt have been a
father at eighteen some guys -- . but theyre total
idiots . . but shes not repulsed always gives that little
shy grin   what does she see stained teeth flab over
the belt . -- look in the mirror shaving you never did
have a strong chin   maybe not a weak one either but
nothing to distinguish it   hair receded oh thats okay
she likes eggheads and its still rather curly in the
back   its the body though too illdefined   got to lose
some . -- . . I know take a cruise grow that salt and
pepper beard come back ruddy salty older perhaps
but it would be better to look even older if shes
looking for a father figure why not a regular Captain
Kangaroo for you my dear -- . . did you ever notice
the peach fuzz . oh so succulent -- . would I dare to
eat a peach . . she didnt like my pointing it out
youre an animal too you know look at this covered
with a fine coat of fur   all humans are furry its
beautiful fur dont you think . -- scared her with that
one haha   the big rabbit eyes   pulled her arm away
but she likes it Im different . -- . . women want
wisdom   must be bored shitless by that greasy kid
she hangs around with   probably only wants to show
off what he knows and what could he possibly know
-- . . cars . does he talk to you about cars or his
dreams how hes going to start his own company one
day make it big -- . dont you listen to him sweetheart

262

that hardly ever works   guyll sell out sure as rain
spend the rest of his days turning gray in middle
management flirting hopelessly with his secretaries
youll get fat and bitchy darling kidsll wear you out
fast . . its now or never sweetheart . -- come away
cruise the Caribbean with me Ill teach you the
constellations teach you how to read charts you
could do it you know   we could schedule our
vacations together take a chance live dangerously . --
. . hey what possible harm could I do   youve still got
your youth your freedom   I know youd never marry
me hell itd just be a nice education for you peach
fuzz -- . . stroke that cheek shed slap me for sure .
but she keeps coming around   there must be
something she wants cant be money obviously could
do better than me -- . I dont know   its the best thing
going though . . Lorraine and Cherie bound to turn
sour on you real fast theyve got to be half crazy to
begin with dont ever want to go through that again
got to find one thats still fresh hasnt entered the
despair zone yet still alive still optimistic . --
optimistic . -- . . havent even thought of that word
for God know how long   always makes me think of
Old Dale Carnegie God were we ever that naïve -- . .
funny now Ophelia how the tables are finally turned
eh . here you with old granddaddy up there yeah
youre stuck with the old fart now   dont tell me your
troubles   hey you wanted him baby you got him   a
deals a deal shouldve let you go years before cat in
heat dragging all your toms around -- . Cleo you
were much more of a lady than she was . . really . --

its my turn now dear . -- . . thought I didnt have it in me   look just a couple months separated and Ive got three of em and therere plenty more where they came from   just get me in a nice sexy apartment outa this white elephant boneyard of family relics -- . . Christ this hideous lamp turn that off much better . much better -- . what the hell take off the shoes too might as well be comfortable at least . . eh Cleo settle yourself back down girl   thats it here let me rub your tummy . -- furry little blond like to get my hands on that peach fuzz   fannys a little large but otherwise shes got a lovely shape   not too big in the bosom dont like too much tit . -- . . Cherie might smother a guy   can imagine her controlling motherly she does remind me a bit of Mother -- . . God Mother would turn purple if she heard me heh heh . Cherie and Mother -- . but if you think about it they both like to treat you like a baby all that fussing she does . . Id be so fat shed be baking cakes all the time . -- its always like that the ones that dress the most aggressively the little wouldbe floozies the ones with the soft big hearts . -- . . oh shed be fun for a few weeks but shed quickly turn into Mother   her skins too fleshy and soft   anyway Id be afraid of rot   cant stand to look at Mother dont want to go out there -- . . no you should have had it taken care of years ago I begged you to damn it . how is anyone supposed to stand looking at you   dont even have the decency to wear that eye patch   Im sorry Mother but youve asked for it   its too late now theres nothing I can do a simple little incision for crissake   if you werent so

264

damned paranoid about doctors put so much mumbo jumbo in your head faith healing idiocy what you want me to do a few chores   hire somebody for Christs sake Im too busy -- . got to answer that letter anyway damn her . . maybe tomorrow try to remember to bring it in   do it just before lunch   reward myself with the scotch . -- excuse me Cleo gotta get up a minute you stay here now Ill be right back . -- . . flip this record over too -- . . damn her thinks she can get me out there now well dont you dare try and come here   Ill come out as soon as I can   listen you have Nora get her to come out she owes you   shes single Ive got responsibilities   I guess you think I can just take my whole vacation out there and to hell with me and my life   to hell with sailing to hell with the little blond . so thats your opinion -- . I see . . well forget it no . -- no ice this time bartend   Ill take it neat . -- . . maybe Christmas alright I said so last time maybe Christmas   Christ Christmas is going to be strange now   of course last year it was hardly worth recognizing   now there will be no question of going to Dolfs   at least Ill be off the hook   kids can go if they want -- . . I might just be on that cruise arm around the little blond other one over the tiller Papa Hemingway yessir thats me . Big PapaIll take em for a ride -- . oh now Cleo presenting yourself   you really want it at your ripe old . . all right   thats it roll over   belly fur still soft as a kittens yes at least Im no stupid Tom cat cant tell one hole from the other   I know what you like Cle . -- yes thats it isnt it . -- . .

yes yes little blond out there curling up to Big Papa
here cruise off into the goddamn sunset together -- .
. damn them all ought to leave em all now anyway
whats in it for me   havent I suffered enough . damn
missile article read it at work tomorrow doesnt make
any sense anyway spend all that on big decoys might
as well be papier mache . -- its the little guys that
count precision instruments theyre the ones that
count Ive made the damn things ought to know
stupid   big missiles cant do a damn thing . . before
its too late . -- give me those little guys could really
do some surgical strikes for you   mount a few right
up there on the bowsprit youll see . -- . . how ya like
them fireworks sweetheart -- . . whoosh there goes
one send it straight to off to . to -- . ah I see you
youre in my sights Barruco better duck Ive got you
right at the end of your dock now target the shoes no
more dock water fizzes no more you you little
conniving blackballing bootlicker thought you could
cut me out   okay okay nice shot . .   lets see now . -
- cruising underwater submarine launches the most
successful keep em flying low to the ground send the
next one out to . -- . . ah yes its your turn Daddy-o
wait till Ophelias out of there wouldnt have the heart
-- . . but you getting into that old jalopy in your
parking lot yes yes see you in the target now see
your little black beret now what the hell you wear
that thing for think youre some sort of goddamn
French existentialist or some such nonsense -- . . let
you get in   start to back out just to be sure   any
strikell do it fizz flash on my screen the last bits of

molten steel and rubber black and greasy on the asphalt you are no more . beret blown into the bushes -- . next shot okay were hot now line er up get this one off to the coast . . sorry Mother but its better that way Ill save you months of agony look youre sound asleep never knew what hit you fire engines come and put out the last flames cant even find you mustve been a direct hit thats good now if only Dolf . -- Ophelia could move in shed be set for life or death whichever she prefers hes driving along the river wonder if the bastard can still drive maybe have to get him out on a little walk wouldnt want to damage the property there he is going out the drive waitll he gets on the wooden bridge there okay right in sight heatseeking very sensitive hes the warmest thing around get him before the bridge collapses just have to knock him down hard itll all be over . -- . . sorry about the bridge dear you can have the county fix it -- . wasnt your fault . nice thing about these little missiles nobody can trace em back to you can launch em from the back of a pickup try another . -- try try the office . -- . . sure wait till the blond gets out wait till everybodys out except the diehards want to make us all look bad damn martyrs shouldnt be in there anyway at this hour waste all that electricity heat never stop to think of the taxpayer -- . . alright get the right windows now you sure thats it only want to hit our floor no need to send the whole thing crashing down get it right in the window there better make this one an incendiary payload just to be sure . sorry about that

-- . guess it did wipe out over half the total space oh well cant be helped . . move on now . -- how about that damn nigger insulted me the other day go fuck your mother man yeah old gofuckyourmotherman who didnt get a handout from me trick or treat is that it cant be grateful he didnt get a kick from me shouldve had him arrested by the building security anyway had no business hanging around the parking . -- . . aright alright -- . . hes too small gotta get a bigger target get a bigger payload this time get him and his buddies where they hang out pool hall maybe or more likely alley behind a liquor store get it right in there see em jivin around the trash cans there stinkin up the place lazy drawling slobbering . sorry hate to take a chunk out of the back of the liquor store now all your neighbors can loot the place hey have a party on me what do I care -- . never wipe em all out anyway like black flies . . how about the crowd that hangs out at the park spitting always spitting soon as they see you goddamn superstitious send one right down they all look up at it monkey eyes fixed on the descending glow scratching heads what de hell could dat be blam . -- now yall know heh heh . -- . . Im on a roll now for a big one -- . . gotta have a big one if were going to get those Arabs . goddamn Arabs bastions of barbarism warrior tribes fundamentalist dictatorships have no business in the twentieth century bunch of ghosts anyway riding horses into battle horses against tanks who do they think they are Gods chosen no doubt -- . so sorry I meant to say Allahs chosen . . damn greasy olivefaced brutes like to rip off those dresses they wear   how the hell . -- they must have to hold them up around their waists to piss   refuse to join the rest of the human race . -- . . okay okay   wait for their holy pilgrimage get em right at Mecca   right at the Kabala there they go marching round and round blast that rock right out of there   wouldnt have any place to go   scatter interbreed   lose themselves in the rest of the Mediterranean races   better Christians in the long run   drop this bloody Islam stuff   look what its doing to our blacks   no theyre as bad as the Nazis Arabs think they have a racial superiority   need to destroy the others   cant tolerate anybody different   -- . . wham . so sorry look at the size of that crater -- . get all the big wigs too . . the rest of em   okay now okay thats about all we need to do for one day . -- here go back down under water here watch the screen   wait for further orders   wait till you see Lorraines ex on the screen . -- . . thats it swaggering down to his yacht   doesnt see me   of course only a few leagues out   waitll he pulls out from the dock   waitll hes rippin along   salt spray in his fat face bouncing along in that topheavy fishing fantasy Im sure you never manage to fish in   -- . . whoosh . crack -- . a few bubbles   gasoline rainbows on the water half a life ring bobs up   saying est Revenge . . serves you right asshole   serves you goddamn right Lorraine and I surface stand on the bridge   a sailor pipes out taps for you buddy   the sun sets   oh I love it . -- precious weaponry . -- . .

gotta send one over to the little blonds boyfriend
someday sabotage his motorcycle how shed fall into
my arms in her shallow grief -- . . whats that Cleo
whats with the claws . alright alright you damn
cats are as bad as kids   bad as most dames never
can come anyway -- . alright Ill let you out in a
minute gotta get up now and wash my hands anyway
. . damn cat probably just too old now used to like it
for much longer . -- doesnt smell like anything . -- . .
dont want it on my fingers though -- . . where the
hells the scotch . nothing to do -- . too early to go
to bed . . nothing on the bloody boobtube of course
no dont bother checking the listings again . -- cant
start any of these damn house projects now gotta
start fresh too tired anyway . -- . . no no bills please
you can do those Sunday morning like you planned
last time you did em at night you got three checks
back in the mail no signatures remember dummy no
bills not now let em wait -- . . no phone calls . no
dont even think of it   shed lose all respect for you
might even be out on a date   oh Cherie come and
crush your little boy in those motherloads will ya
shed probably come if I sounded desperate enough
God damn no -- . not going to do that would never
get rid of her   itd be worse than signing a marriage
certificate . . after all I have my pride . -- alright
Cleo go out but youll be wanting in again in ten
seconds . -- . . look at that rain cant go out there
now get into another damn accident still paying for
the last   still feel the impact God that feeling of
complete and utter loss of control there was nothing

I could have done no steerage no brakes rainy night
like this -- . . says she wasnt hurt no evidence of her
being hurt . wait youll see theyll come up with
something pinched nerve whiplash psychological
damages for crissakes -- . its not over its never over
. . they could reopen it anytime theoretically got a
new car out of the deal oughta be happy with that
she didnt strike me as the type pretty robust not the
chronic complainer kind hope to hell I never hear
from her again . -- next time they might try the
breath test . -- . . boy was I lucky walking the yellow
line now thats my specialty officer I always walk the
yellow line watch me now whoa there steady boy
look you dont have to prove anything youre drunk
okay youre drunk I know it I am -- . . so can I have
a wee bit more of the scotch whiskey here and in the
privacy of my own home consenting adult that I am
get blotto till I go to bed not hurting a soul . see
close that door now look at this you dummy rain all
over the carpet now -- . alright so what itll dry out
just leave it here sit down . . look what you got
here the lamp the phonebook the telephone pad a
pencil youre all set up and your mind is set up too I
know youre going to try it again you expected to do
this all night now why not go for it do it consenting
adult privacy of your own home youre just going to
ask remember . -- God knows youre not going out on
a night like this drunk forget that . -- . . its just a
point of information for future reference FYI -- . .
okay then at least youll know and some other
evening a dry one you can try it . Lorraine stands

271

you up again youll be damn motivated to try it -- .
so go ahead its anonymous theyre not tracing your
call   youre too small anyway who the hell gives a
fuck what you do in the evenings just get the ass in
on time say your yesses and go home in a leisurely
manner a few minutes past rush hour   silly theyve
nothing on you   Barruco or no Barruco this is the
government . . hell nobody gets fired from the
government all the flotsam and jetsam end up there
. -- youre secure buddy   secure doing what any
normal guy in the throes of divorce would do so dont
be shy . -- . . hey maybe girl will answer -- . . alright
put on the glasses . lets see -- . there are a lot of
these oriental ones   geisha types wood floor paper
walls Id like that puts it one culture removed like
that Nagasaki whore so desperate might have been a
mother trying to feed her kids but once I said yes she
turned professional cool stylized detached but not cold
she was perfect an oriental gem didnt even give me the
clap disappeared into the ruins couldnt help looking for
her in the bar again never saw her mustve been proud all
that GI dough gone on to another sailor . . how they do it
I cant imagine not so terrible if the guys fairly clean
doesnt get too obnoxious doesnt bite your tit or sock you
in the jaw cant be pleasant though all those diverse
pricks some of em lousy with germs girls better be clean .
-- cant imagine they wouldnt be around here got to be
well cared for   whod stay in a job like that if there was
any risk probably get medical insurance sure they would
probably get regular checkups might be on low dose of
antibiotics no need to worry   theyd sure speak English
of course they would here . -- . . nice thing in a way didnt
have to speak to that girl couldnt have gotten involved in

her troubles if Id wanted to nice and nonverbal
anonymous   still I couldnt help caring about her
goddamn city in ashes digging around for her relatives
Christ what a time to have to prostrate yourself to
strangers conquering heroes   they adored us   thought
we were gods   maybe she was thrilled with the access
she enjoyed to us big white superheroes -- . . okay alright
there the Geisha Club . nah -- . looks too commercial ads
too big . . better go for one of the more discreet ones
probably a lot classier . -- Jennys Girls now that sounds
more like it Jenny some plump hen of a madam call girls
maybe . -- . . address given probably old fashioned
brothel nothing specified in terms of services   would
have to know what you were getting -- . . rather go for
one in between that spells out services but doesnt
overadvertise . like this here how about Kozy Kittens -- .
little quaintsounding say they have massage might as
well get a massage too while Im at it . . always wanted to
try that get me relaxed anyway do they do it right there
on the massage table   private rooms . -- well of course
cant have a big locker room orgy atmosphere for Christs
sake . -- . . personal services escorts -- . . well personal
services sounds intriguing cant get much more explicit
than that in the goddamn yellow pages . try Kozy Kittens
-- . hell locations good would only have to drive about
fifteen minutes not hard to find do they say anything
about parking . . no well you cant have everything   hate
to have to walk too far along that street though maybe
theres a lot in the back sounds like a back entrance here
anyway   could always drive by and find it first the day
before . -- doesnt say anything about appointments none
of them do . -- . . I guess its not like going to the damn
dentist -- . . look are you going to call em or arent you .
this is getting stupid either do it or dont do it make up

your mind -- . says theyre open till midnight . . well no
time tonight anyway not in this rain . -- just call and see
how they sound drive by tomorrow on your way home
from work eat a good dinner relax a bit then go over
there . -- . . would have to wait in some kind of waiting
room if they dont give appointments read stupid
magazines Esquire Penthouse -- . . actually that might
not be so bad at least get you in the mood . take a
chance   you do want to know what they charge dont you
it could be a goddamn total ripoff if youre not prepared --
. okay alright Ill do it just think a minute what are you
going to say exactly . . oh I dont know maybe theyll have
a recording . -- try it dummy just dial it once okay 345 .
-- . . no thats not right -- . . its 354 6211 is that right .
6211 -- . okay its ringing . . Jesus wake up now Ed . --
AH SORRY   I MUST HAVE THE WRONG NUMBER

V. Freeda

HMMMMM.

But why our genitals operated on?

We were both having some sort of operation. Robin was going first; then it would be my turn. Some kind of sterility operation....

And there was something about basketball.

We were playing basketball together, yes, basketball. Basketball with a balloon. It was an orange balloon; we were hitting it with our palms against the dorm room door. It was all lightness and giggles. We were children, so free, so perfectly comfortable with each other, our sleek bodies stretching upwards, our bodies like mangos, smooth, no distinguishing lumps or bulges. Then came the sinister intrusion, darkening, fear of the knife, smell of the hospital, paper gowns. Aching, we clung to each other, naked, vulnerable...

Oh, it's fading too quickly. Just let it go. But I want it, to fondle, to examine. The taste of it, like raw rubber, like a balloon in the mouth, a condom, operating gloves...

It feels like being carved off from a Siamese twin, or coitus interruptus, like being ripped from my siblings, ejected out of the nest, from that pseudofamily we had there, oh so fleetingly. Basketball buddies. College pups.

Weird, though. Painful. There was that aching rawness to it, that early springtime gnawing hunger, vampiric and scathing. It must have been the succubus again...

Initiation rite? Sacrifice? Was it from another life of mine?

I wonder, why Robin? Is it because he symbolizes sexuality for me? Is it because all memory of him is coated in the thick toffee of boy candy? The perfume of his damp armpits soft black curls skin stretched so tight over young sinews a-sweat like a shorthaired pup...

Oh, Greg, he's functional. But he's not in love with love. Never was. He's not a love addict like Robin, sitting on the bed strumming and crooning the poetry he respired so naturally his sweet breath imagination I could drink for days, standing outside his window counting stars daring myself to climb a fire escape. Who knew *who* I'd find in his bed?

Not Greg. Can't imagine him ever swept up in it, whole heart whole mind. Love is only a part of life, after all, an avocation, if there's time left over when work is done, a reward, delayed gratification, right Greg? You of the disciplined being.

Why me? Why did I have to be cursed with this excessive appetite, this bottomless yearning for the unattainable, always elusive, Robin Hood out there that really doesn't exist—at least not in ninety-nine percent of the male population. And the ones that's got it—well, they're the last ones you'd want to trust your life to....

Okay. Get up now. Gotta make that apple pie. Got all the apples to slice yet. Take the dough out of the fridge must be rock hard; how long was I asleep?

Oh, that's not bad. I've still got an hour and a half. Just barely time to get the thing all the way baked though. No one wants a half-baked—

Pie! That's a good one! Pie, me. I am pie. All I am is one big thinking two-legged pie. Frozen pie. Tucked deep in the back of the bin. Nobody'd ever get a scent out of me cooling on the rack. I'm frozen. Frozen in space and time. A mastodon in an iceberg. All this glorious, well-preserved meat, going to no one, not even to the scavengers of life, the Robins. It'll simply dry up. Never to flower, never to bear fruit, never to go to seed, never to live, only to stand suspended: a life's held breath.

Why am I so afraid to live? When am I going to rush into the fray and tear off my god-designated piece? *My* slice. There's got to be one with my name on it. I'm afraid even to look for my own name. Maybe they have it spelled wrong. They

279

always do. I should've left it as Frieda. This double "e" is stupid now. The liberating sixties are lover, for Pete's sake! (For the sake of Seeger, where's my piece?) We lost. We're no freer. At least not Freeda. She's more bound in ice than ever. She lit a few times, but never sustained the flame. She sputtered.

Oh shut up Dolfi! I'll mix my metaphors if I choose. You can't pull that trip on me now. Look what you did to your only daughter, your pathetic Ophelia. Sick. Cruel to name her like that. Advertisement for your Shakespeare book no doubt.

Shut up Dolfi! I'll be your Libby now. Wish I'd said it to your face. I'm such a coward. Just ran out of there. Hopped in the car and screwed, without a goodbye. And now you're going to die on us and I'll never get a chance—

So be it, you hardly deserve any better than you dish out. What petty nonsense, really! Getting all bent out of shape because I use the wrong basket to put the apples in. Just sitting there up in the barn. How was I to know that was your precious potato basket? Pommes, not pommes de terre.

Jesus. I said I was sorry. The way you flip out through, over the stupidest….

And you got Ophelia all upset too. I was only trying to help out. I guess it was too much for you, having the two of us there. I guess old people like privacy when they're decrepit and presumably dying. God knows, you'll probably outlive us all; your old vinegar veins'll keep the vitriol pumping like rocket fuel.

I can see it now that I'm out of there: your pathetic flare-up attempt to keep some semblance of control over your household, two women trying to run things, getting into your precious orchard, using the wrong baskets and then threatening to take one of them off the bloody property in the trunk of her car—thief! Your own granddaughter, is, I confess, a potato basket thief. (Who in their right mind would ever mistake a potato basket for an apple basket, now really?)

Okay Dolfi. I'll write you a nice letter in a couple of days as if nothing went down. It's easy enough to play dutiful daughter, dutiful granddaughter, family peacemaker, diplomat among cursedly antagonistic island nations.... What else can I do? If I don't write you a goddamn letter before you die I'll feel guiltier than ever.

As though all the adults in my life have the eternal right to blow up at me, curse me to my face, (Ophelia dear, you've spent hours at it, albeit presumably non compos mentis), and I, of all people, apologize. Is this masochism? Am I as sick as you all? Apparently so.

This dough'll have to sit about twenty minutes just to get soft again. Oh well, it'll take at least that long to peel and slice all these. Look how wormy you are! I'll probably have more in the sink than in the pie. Undoubtedly so. Look, some of these are virtually useless, might get one or two slices....

Ain't it the truth though, wormy apples! Hard, green, sour (although, I must say, I like the tanginess of some of the good ones), and bruised, fermented around the open gashes... some metaphor. Fed on ashes. Vitriolic ashes. The distillation of years of spite and anger, resentments, ire, fertilizing—more like poisoning—the very soil that fed you, little green demon fruits. Ironic that you all make such a good pie.

Me. I'm such a pie. Made from you all, wasn't I? I guess good things *can* come from bad genes....

I'm a mutant though. That's why you all can't relate to me. That's why you all seem to hate me so much. You look at me and see an alien in your midst. An intrusion. Like I'm spying on you, exposing you with my very gaze, a mirror in which you must see your hideous corrupted faces, in which you must face the "Ism" itself, the thing that's possessed you.

And I dance around so free. (Was that why you named me Freeda?) Do you secretly admire my freedom? Are you glad for it? Do you want me to escape as badly as I want to? Are you cackling in perverse triumph at your creation, climbing out of the cauldron, a regular Venus—with no space for a penis. A sterile beauty, evidence of her creators' genius, unable to claim her life for her own and apply the genes forward. Who would dare anyway? The chances of another one of you surfacing would be too great....

Ophelia, the necrophiliac witch: she scrounges gravesites for remains of male carcasses, her wild hair tangling in the bones, her yellow teeth protruding like her swollen belly, a ravaging appetite let loose.

And Dolfi, gnarled little troll bent under your bridge, snarling and ranting at any and all trespassers, your ears bristling at the faintest noise of an intruder, your back teeth grinding, your filthy fingers itching for eyeballs to scratch out.

Oh, and thinking of eyeballs: Iris, you Medusa-headed Cyclops you. You and your hissing vanity, so convinced of your beauty you imagine yourself sporting a halo instead of an oozing socket. Self-appointed priestess, my ship slips easily by you as you cling to your doomed rock, wailing your mumbo jumbo prayers as the winds snatch them from your lips. Ineffectual, blind, you writhe.

Edgar. Wouldn't want to leave you out. You're needed for the fourth gargoyle on my roof. You're more difficult to picture, though. More of a Hieronymus Bosch character, clearly suffering from the torments of a power greater than yourself. A tragically contorted naked damned with his head stuck up his ass, that's you. You're a human snail, curled into yourself like an ingrown toenail, unable to hear, see, speak, feeding only on yourself, digging deeper deeper and deeper inward until your head literally disappears up your rectum. There, in the dark, brown, self-smelling comfort of self you sleep as your legs carry you about among the lost, arms reaching out to balance. You get around.

And I don't even need to be on acid to imagine you, my dear gargoyles, although you are a bit like hallucinations from a bad trip. Up in my tower there is one window. I can't look out without one of you blocking my view.

Primitive. Man ingests hallucinogenic drug and envisions his gods. Naturally, they come out looking pretty grotesque when he later sculpts them in wood, clay, or stone. Aztec, Mayan, Hindi and Aborigine, wherever pagan gods are sold...

How else can man, so alone, so desperately dependent on the forces of nature, on the whims of the rains, the moon, the clouds of insects that burst upon his crops—how can he see past these powers that rule his days? How can he imagine benevolence while staring every waking hour into the face of a sun so cruel, so merciless, a sun that ticks off the hours of his desiccating hide as he cooks, a helpless roast in Earth's rotisserie?

He knows it's only a matter of time, and the handful of dust he weeps into, hoping to glimpse the wriggle of a young pale root sending the promise of harvest—harvest, love, life, quiet children—the handful of dust will so soon contain himself.

Greater gods are the luxury of more secure souls. More secure, more secularized. If and when you take time out to think of the singular god, oh, he's just a nice guy, a friend you can talk to, right? A familiar. One of the family, a rich uncle, perhaps. God's certainly not a grotesque. God's not a snake-panther with bugging frog eyes and wildly curling tongue that comes to you in a psychotic dream to demand a complicated blood sacrifice. God's not a tree that talks to you as you curl, exhausted from fearful flight, at its harboring roots. God's not a pond into which you gaze and receive reassurance of your existence. God's not a bird that carries the soul of your mother to warn you that you'd better dig a deep hole and climb in before a wind storm knocks you down...god has no pronoun.

No, these old gods aren't good enough anymore. They were too practical, after all, too bound in the earthly reality of eat-or-be-eaten.

We can't cling to these superstitious ways. We must move on, old gargoyles of my childhood, old terrible yet familiar demons I loved, worshipped and depended upon. Now, I must give you up and convert, eh? Convert and join the conquerors. You are failing me, the longer I cling to you.

I'm a slave now in a real civilization, don't you see? And they'll feed me, and they'll let me marry and give me useful work, and all I have to do is trust their one god, their god of the unseeable, the unknowable, of the abstract from whence comes the other great abstractions of their culture, their dazzling gold, their compelling leaders, their work for which each man is valued.

Don't you see, Mom, Dad, grandparents, I want to enjoy my slavery. Let me go and see if I can one day buy my way to freedom. I'm good looking, strong. Maybe one day, maybe, if I'm good and go along with it all, maybe, just maybe (and I have to hope) they'll let me join them, and I can put on the robes of the beautiful people and walk freely in their gardens, picking their fruits, and they'll be as much my gardens as theirs for I will have earned my place in them.

This is what life feels like from here. It feels like betrayal, too, for I have loved you, my pagan gods, as I have loved the wild glory of your woods, the place where I've been dwarfed and humbled as a child. Please understand, I'll carry you all with me in my heart, but I must go now and labor in their fields. The sun will not kill me for they will see that I have water, shelter, and clothing, and I trust them to want to take at least this much care of me. I want to trust them. I'm sorry if you gods cannot.

Damn. Why the tears? Isn't it enough to get to spend Thanksgiving Day with friends, new friends, instead of old family? You should rejoice. Should, should, should! I'll say the dreaded S-word, hear me, *should*!

This'll be the first time you've completely escaped them. Not even a phone call. The phone's off the hook, remember? Yes, it still is. Dare I leave it off? What if Greg—

Greg won't need to call. He's working away oblivious. Will he notice when it's three o'clock? I hope he set his watch alarm. We'll just have time to change. He'll probably want to change—no, he never does. He's only been in the library after all.

But he'll have to change. I'm going to dress up. I'm going to wear that long blue skirt. He'll change. He'll want to when he sees me—

What a workaholic! Even on Thanksgiving Day, *jeesh*!

Here's a little live worm. Well, howdoyoudo? Here, I'll put you in with the peelings and you can eat all you want in the dark, cozy garbage bag. At least these apples are organic. Hey, I can tell them at Dave and Suzy's party: "You happen to be eating an organic (except for the flour, I can't vouch for it) apple pie made from apples I hand-picked at my grandfather's orchard last weekend...."

They'll never know the real story. What these apples really cost me. How could I tell them that? How could I ruin a pleasant Thanksgiving Day celebration among the beautiful Normals in their regal robes? How could I be so uncouth as to tell them how I dumped the apples into the trunk, threw the basket at his feet, jumped in the car and blasted out of there, catching, unfortunately, a glimpse of my mother's twisted face, a mass of wounds...the old troll at her heels, about to turn his wrath on her no doubt?

I can never tell them anything true about me. That's why I feel so unreal, like a myth I invented about myself. Really. Who would ever want to hear it? The car wrecks, the bloody brawls, the telephone cords ripped out, the couch cushions splayed and ocean of feathers in the living room, the slamming doors, kids pushed around and cursed at and worse, neglected and ignored, the squeals of lusty cocktail party games with gargoyles mashing other gargoyles up against the bathroom doors, the pouts and tiffs, the jealousies, all the ugly, shameful, realities of pagan life out there in the jungle, the forest, the swamps. The land of the Ism.

It'd disgust them. Like trying to convince someone that roast squirrel was really tasty. Well, you can certainly come to enjoy it if you're hungry enough. Don't knock it!

Time I brought that record of drinking ballads to school show 'n' tell. Boy, was that a faux pas! I was so hurt. The teacher wouldn't let me play them past the first foul word. How was I to know that language was unacceptable in their hallowed halls? Those were my lullabies. Curses were our prayers. I loved that music. It was warmth, it was family, it was the scent of the home burrow—and they told me it stank.

How can you go to school prepared to answer the question: "What's your father's favorite hobby?"

"Finger-fucking cats."

How can you talk about any of this with your friends? Friends you're not anxious to invite to your house anyway. What'd they think if you started complaining, or even, just, describing—they'd think it was all so sick, a real turn-off. Goodbye they'd say.

And it never helped when the well-meaning pious ones candidly explained that you were going to hell for lack of religious upbringing. And they'd spin off their Catechism-memorized descriptions of hellfires and devils' pikes and little children roasting forever and ever and a day....

And all you had to turn to was pure, white, blank paper—yes, another incarnation of the trees you loved in the woods....

But after so many droughts, plagues, dust storms, floods—in short, after so many years of dancing your rain dances, sacrificing your unwanted treasures, the gods (with a small "g") started pissing you off and you walked out of that old garden and took to the streets where you could find similarly exiled rats like yourself to bed down with, where nobody wanted any more motherly love and had found the drugs to help them forget the womb entirely...

Not the womb that opens into life; the drugs put you in the womb that opens into death. And you could spend a lot of time freely, openly, romancing the Big D, just, as I imagine, Ophelia did, or does....

Oh, it's exciting for awhile, but then it becomes frustrating when you're knocking on Death so long and no one answers. So you turn back to Life the only other way to go. And you find it teeming with your kind, all pressing toward the feed, a swarm of cohorts, and you don't feel like getting in there and hustling, so you set off along the sidelines, walking the narrow ridge between Life and Death. Dylan said it better:

> Came to the high place of darkness and light
> Dividing line ran through the center of town
> Hitched up my pony to the post on the right

290

Went into the laundry and washed my
clothes down...

Slicing apples to make a pie should not elicit
such depressing thoughts. (There's that 'should'
word again Freeda! See, they're in there, always
monitoring, always critical....) It's just that these
apples, well, organic or not, they're pretty
depressing. Look at this one! Why did I even bother
putting it in the basket?

I know why, at the time I was desperate, felt
like a thief, felt his beady eyes on me from the
kitchen window; knew I had to fill that basket fast
before he changed his mind...

That's just it. No Normal would bother with
these apples. They'd go to the farm, put their feet
up, read a few books, smile and ignore the gargoyles,
soak up some sun and free booze and not sweat it.

'Course I could never relax there. Have to be
busily engaged in a constructive project at all times
to legitimize my very existence, *yessirree*. Ophelia
must've always felt that way. Maybe if she just did
the right thing all the time they'd decide they loved
her enough after all and wouldn't resent her for
fucking up their youth like that, forcing them to
marry when each thought—oh, how vainly—that
they could've done better somehow.

Especially Libby. She was practically a J.A.P.
She must've known she was meant for richer, tastier

game than gnarly old kraut-sucking Dolf. Despite all his pretensions towards English literati, he could never be English. Why do all Germans aspire to be English anyway? If they're true Aryans, after all...

Well, they made it, forty-four years, despite the advent of Old Ophelia. Where'd she get this self-abnegation complex? Or was that the Ism? I wouldn't be surprised if the Ism had ruled their household too.

Of course, they were coming down off the twenties just like we're coming off the sixties now. It must've been hard to pretend to moderate. Can't imagine either of them going a day without drinks and smokes. And they say Libby was dead drunk when she gave birth...

Poor Ophelia. She was a great compensator, boy. She compensated herself right into public office, right to the top of the heap in her little research unit, right up over her head in commitments, none of them to herself. "Everyone come take a piece of me, liquidation sale, everything must go---"

All that frantic living just another manifestation of her compulsive dying. The tarantellas. She spun herself out. She wanted to time it so she could go, if not at her peak, at least not far from it. Now look, poor thing, tumbled down so low, can't even see her own shadow. She's completely lost herself and there's nothing but the hideous gargoyle mask. Truly a zombie.

My mom the zombie. God, it's got to be funny, it's so damn sickening! Black humor. *Night of the Living Dead*—a parody of literature.

Literature. What a joke! How can I possibly write anything like the stuff? It's supposed to be beautiful, ennobling, uplifting, spirit-filled, aesthetic symmetrical, glorious, transcendent, vital... Holden Caulfield I ain't.

Holden, poor brother, took it all upon yourself, didn't you? Felt responsible for the whole damn mess. Save yourself, save yourself! Flee, I scream—Holden just stands there, martyr to the cause. Get out of literature entirely you dunce! Save yourself before they eat you up, sentimentalize you into pure neurotic bathos, boy, would that be phony? Holden, look ahead, Man! Look to, say, Rudy Wurlitzer—there was a writer. Look how he saw it all taken apart, scattered abroad like so many old cigarette packs, the atomic fallout it had all become.... So what'd he do? Accepted it. Celebrated it, man, made it his own damn landscape, peopled it with human debris, lots of flotsam-jetsam types just barely existing as personalities, but real. Boy, you would've loved them, Holden. Wish you could've lived long enough.

Sure, I can make a pie with these apples, a damned tasty, healthful pie, one I'll be sure to be complimented on. Sure, I can sculpt a rose out of garbage. I can make a mosaic from these shards of broken glass. Sure, I can take this broken accordion and compose a symphony on it. But will anyone be moved? Will anyone connect with my tentative missive here, my feeble tendril venturing forth toward light I can only imagine exists? My collage of metaphors, muddying with overwork? Or is it—

"It's too amber," the freshman wrote. And he liked that, goddamn idiot assistant faculty member, and your "all strung out in Michigan." Began to feel like good ol' Jim Morrison dropping out of film school...so you didn't like my poetry but you liked *his*? What did *he* do, show up after class and suck your—

Luscious teenage and college boys. Fleeting young lovers, the one compensation for this interminable torturous youth I'm stuck in like a mental corset—

Where have you gone? You're all gone to me, you know. There's no rummaging back in the past for any clues to me you might hold. You've slipped away into regions too black, too dangerous for me to follow, I guess, really, too sick. And I loved you all, in my own crippled way of course. Each in your turn: I obsessed over you, relished the tastes and smells of you, loved you in my maternal smothering way like wayward sons, or cuddly puppies, those of you who were not so brutally afflicted. Now where are you?

The first, divorced, last I heard. That must've set you back. And the sweetness of our love, our first love, holding each other wet from sea spray, you still in braces, the pure symbiotic thing as close as siblings your skin eventually tasting like my own, salted, tanned. And I paraded my freedom—god knows; I only had Ophelia as model! And they say women go for men who have the essence of mother, not father....

I tortured you in order to weigh and measure our love, to assess the damages. It was only in the hurt of it, the loss of it, that I could see it, fully perceive it, being a left-brained individual despite artistic pretensions. Well, I had to have you in my head as well as my heart. Had to test to make sure you really meant it. And that kind of analysis involves destruction, don't it? Picked apart and scattered like a daisy. That was my first love.

From then on I lurked in the shadows with my guilt pouncing on less desirable prey. Always something missing after you. You see, I've thought of trying to contact you for years, tell you all this. You were my first love and I'm so grateful to you, you can't imagine how I treasure you—the you that survived me and my ravaging.

Oh, that you be restored to wholeness and heal from all your wounds, the wounds I set you up to receive from her? That you came, after me, to seek those savage spoilers like myself? And I, as I was saying, I, too, turned downward away from the light and sought out the maimed and moldy types. Sure, it was cruder and more obvious how a big smothering tit need be supplied to those young walking wounds, to staunch the flow of adolescent angst, the horrible raw aching longing appetites I couldn't hope to fill; I wanted emotional death for us all.

You see, years later, I'd accuse my man of using me as his emotional sounding board, same as I once used a bunch of normally sensitive boys at a time I was denying myself a normal adolescence, so repressed with rage was I...

Oh analysis paralysis! I hope you fall apart, from shredding every thread of life with your own rasp heart— "Ode to Freeda," I just made it up. You're all either divorced, or dead, or drug-addicted, or lost to society somehow I'll never trace...

And yet it's not so different from the young girl who adopts all the wounded animals in cardboard boxes tries to save them, right? I shouldn't be so hard on myself. Each of you gave me something precious that was uniquely yours to give, and if you all collectively can accept this apology, well, I've kept all those things: your music, your favorite places, your games, pet names, your jokes, your laughs, your smiles, your touches; they're all safely ziplocked in those plastic baggies in my brain, the ones, now empty of seeds and stems, that store—all neatly sorted—my you, my sordid past.

Sordid? Yes, because it was only selfishly lived. I razed enough boy territory in my time. I, mind you Ophelia, have made my modest mark, and now at tender years of young adulthood, renounce my wicked ways and go on the wagon, oh, for a long time. I don't want to disappoint you Mom, but it ain't my gig. They just turn pathetic on me. I can't stay wowed long enough. I'm too narcissistic, perhaps. What really drives me restlessly pursuing after is myself.

Where the hell did I get lost in the shuffle? Why, since I was young and loved the woods, the meadows, the sky and sea, why have I felt so unrequited? They didn't call me 'Nature' back in high school for nothing. People sensed it in me. (They didn't have to see me lying deep in the meadow during Phys Ed behind the football field, right hand in my gym shorts, face to the sun….)

Boys found out, when I insisted we do it in the woods, or, worse for y'all, cold-assed darlings, on the grass under the open sky, exposed. You see, while all that madness rocked the house and sent out poisonous fumes to drive us little chickens scattering abroad, well, I sought the solace of living things I could find that didn't speak. So did Sam, probably, so did Barbie. We all had to get out…

The tall pine would hold me in its branches, rock me in its fragrant arms. I'd hug its trunk and cry. The warm meadow would caress my skin with penetrating sunrays, its winged things do fairy dances for my amusement. The stream would cool my ankles and wrists and give me its moss tuffets to sit upon as I'd search its pools for creatures shy and hydrophilic like myself. Your sea water held me aloft and tossed me like a playful father and matched its color and the water of my eyes that I so rarely tasted then. As part of me you contained me and whispered over and over and over that you were always there for me, even when far away and out of sight or sound I would scatter beach rose petals on your back as the ferry pulled out from the island every summer, and later, I would try and write poems to you, but oh, you were so much bigger than my poems could fit you and so much wiser; I hadn't much to say. Still, you gave me everything I ever imagined as life and more, because you never made a promise you couldn't keep and I clung to you—every aspect of you, treebark moss and sand, mud and rock—sang along with your birthing winds that introduced me to this planetary ride. I can't get enough of you Earth Mother.

And to think that those little boy toys were supposed to distract me from so great a love? They hadn't a chance! And every one of them—save one—was scared of you. And that one, thank god, was never spoiled by me because he had as much interest in me as I in him and the mutual love of the non-human glories dwarfed our coexistence so, we were no more joined than two pebbles on the beach. Yet I wonder about you, too? What happened to you? Are you still true to yourself? Are you as frustrated as I by city life? Do you ride away on a bicycle at a furious pace to reach the beach, as I do? And which beach do you walk barefooted on and where's the sun in the picture, and what big rock do you choose to sit upon? Or am I mis-imagining you to be a soul brother here?

You took me to your favorite salt pond in early afternoon when we were supposed to be working together and it was suddenly terribly important to you that you share this place with me or, maybe, you just wanted a swim yourself and couldn't see how to do it unless taking me as accomplice. Anyway, we drove to your salt pond, stripped—I suddenly overcome with a rare fit of modesty—for once, I was the modest one! And dove in sleek and splashless, racing across the cold clean wet turtleful pinegreen pool to the other side where sunny white rocks formed a toe-poking beach. And I stumbled along after you, so surefooted, a true man of the Earth, long Indian hair and browned skin. I saw you, a genuine native of this land of yours, and I the white-skinned intruder, exotic element clumsy from sudden importation—oh why don't I have a home of my own like that?

Oh well, you took me back across the pond and never spoke or touched me and I fell asleep in the car and then discovered my teeshirt was on inside out.

How inexpressibly thrilled was I to find myself, a few weeks later, beside you along the beach road, miles enough to feel it was a true passage, again, into your realm, at last sitting on the beach with you, talking a little, comfortably, and sharing joints, then, working together sidebyside and getting covered with ash, riding the pick-up down to the beach and washing ourselves in the steep surf, the surf that scared me a little for its sudden depth, no easy entry or exit, all stumble down in foam and coarse grit. Again, you kept your distance, even that night side by side in a tent, inches, yet miles apart, neither of us crazy enough to cash it all in for some cheap physical approximation of natural grandeur: smelling each other instead of the pines, hearing each other's breath instead of the wind, feeling the presence of skin and bones beneath one's flesh instead of firm, supportive, flat, enduring earth. Was that your reason? Or were you simply calculating it wasn't somehow worth the risk?

I'll never know, as I say, you've flown, and gods bless you! Keep flying, because there's nothing more precious, nothing more right and free and clean and healthy and good and sacred and fulfilling and eternal as that you've found, and I've found, in the landscape, in the living.

I spend my time between the living and the dead. I race back and forth so much, a cosmic errand girl, always translating, trying to serve, not aware of my own voice, repeating the messages of others, back and forth, a slave. Growing up is supposed to free one to be oneself—oh, yeah that's so easy to say, but how to grow up? How to realize that little girl so dependent on plants for affection is the only person there, *is* the holy one, the one who knew, always knew how to go looking for it when she needed it, the spiritual strength, the lost ingredient in family life so void, so bent on doom.

I found it then, and find it again and again, when I take the time to look, but lately, I haven't known how to take the time to look, as though the time weren't legally mine to take. I've promised it to you, Greg. I've promised it to the boss. I've promised it to those who psychically prey on me with their constant interruptions of my life to announce suicide attempts, new cancer deaths, job loss, divorce, and other intrusive matters.

Why don't you fuckers just find yourselves another messenger/translator/newsgirl—eh? This one's lost the foot-wings. It's all a drudge. I resent each step back and forth, the screaming intensified now so I can barely make sense of your words, lose the message anyway. It's gotten meaningless to me, and I'm not free. Now, even when riding off to the beach, your invisible chains clink behind. The rock is uncomfortable to sit on, the waves wail crazy laments, the birds threaten with their swoops, the beach roses prick me with their thorns and the sea is cold.

A pagan's got to be free, y'know. You'll have worn me down so with your despair, I can't remember my prayers, I can't talk to my gods in peace without your sick messages crowding in, confusing and distracting me. It's my obsession, I know, but how to come up for air?

***

So, my self-pity's no different, better, or worse than their self-pity. Call me Son-of-self-pity. I've no right to draw these hideous caricatures of them, to condemn them so in their ugliness. It's like making fun of blind people. It's like calling cripples names. Ungrateful wretch. How could I spend so much energy hating these poor sick—

But isn't hate just love in reverse? Could I hate them any more than I've loved them? Loved them all: Ophelia, for her wit, her glamorous young body when she and I were young, her intense, dark, needy love. Edgar, for his patience teaching me things, his love of the ocean, his love of music. Iris for her—

Oh, this is stupid. More Pollyanna outa me— rings like a tin anvil, don't it? There's no way I can conjure up enough wonderful warm memories to counterbalance the painful, shameful ones. The Ism is us. The Ism has won. The Ism will never be a Wusm—it persists in me.

I can't elevate myself above them, that's for sure. I'm their seed, no better, no stronger, not likely to live even as long as Iris or Dolf, already spending myself dry on negative thoughts, negative practices, idle slow wounding of myself and others, pretending not to care. I'm not strong, Mom, Dad, grandparents; I'm not well. I'm sick and suffering just like you. The only difference is, I see it better than you do. Your sickness has protected you from reality, mine is still too new to have taken away my awareness, yet.

Maybe I didn't get a heavy enough dose. Maybe the genes only brought me so far; there was a mutation, perhaps, and I got a healthy gene or two thrown in, and I couldn't go all the way under, and I'm therefore cursed with the *knowledge* of my illness, which is sometimes worse than the illness itself. Worse, because it implies a responsibility. I'm not dumbly, numbly suffering here. I'm not half dead, with big chunks of me gangrenous or putrefying. I'm not sick enough to be one of you. We're separated now, like those outside from those inside oxygen tents. There's no way our two worlds can safely intersect.

It's like you're all dead already, on the other shore. I can stand on the beach and wave, send messages in bottles—of course, bottles—you'd be sure to pick them up. I can remember myself putting messages in bottles at Barnacle Beach. Many must've found bottles, all with the same message: "This is it." What was I trying to communicate then, as now? "This is it?" As in—"Is that all there is?" What a cynical kid I was/am. Was cynicism my crutch? Was it my way of handling the sadness that came with watching those I loved and depended upon slowly dying from an unnamable disease that carried enormous connotations of evil, evil that spelled damnation, the same fiery place my little innocent Catholic friends described to me? And you were all hurtling into the pit and I couldn't save you and if I held on, like drowning men, you'd take me with you.

If you ever had any humanity—and you did—sure, you all did: Dolf at the piano ragtiming folk tunes with me, Iris showing me her lemon trees with pride, and sewing me handmade dresses when I was little—

You had your human times; and you were once young and gay and attractive and the sun shone on you and you laughed freely and you dared to love yourselves if only shallowly, narcissistically—you lost it, and went on existing. That's why it's so hard for me to love you all. You're not able to love and accept yourselves. You're just as frightened and sickened by your own declines as I am—more so. What kind of example is that for a kid? Four nearest relations dying at once and not one of them bravely or with dignity. How am I to hope for better for myself? You show me what I'm made from. I'm not encouraged. You've shown me that, in the end, life is pitiful, torturous, and empty.

Now I suddenly realize where that ancient emotion comes from—the one in which sex and death combine in the form of a vaguely imagined young man who is both fatally attractive and fatally ill, and I'm drawn to him like a lover but he is not able to love me and only wants to consume me and cover me in his sickeningly sweet, cloying, suffocating scent. The feeling is more than a vision, a smell, a taste; it's a seductively powerful nightmare from which I struggle to awake. It comes upon me from time to time, usually in connection with some person that passes me by in life, some face, some figure, that pierces my consciousness like an icy needle leaving that drugged reverberation of lustful doom. The death siren. It's you, all of you.

And they say you can feel the day you're going to die. It's got to be one of the three hundred and sixty five, or if you're like Lenny, and happen to die on leap year's extra day, three hundred sixty-six options.... And Carlos Castaneda talked about meeting Death on the road, or in the form of a swooping bird. Could this cloyingly familiar feeling I get be my foretaste of death? Am I nearer than I dare admit? Are these beloved zombies of mine not on a far shore at all, but simply on the other side of a thin veil, a tissue, a breath apart? And when they really do pass through to the other side, is it going to make any real difference in my life? Is the long-awaited day of freedom from parental mental domination a mere illusion I've been kidding myself with for years? Is there any difference at all whether they're on this side of the veil or the other? I'll still see them; it's a pretty transparent veil. I'll still hear their voices and be nagged by their characters alive and well, tucked in my fertile skull. Oh why worry about any big goodbyes, any resolutions, any amends. They're still going to haunt me just fine, thank you, and I'll have the rest of my life to struggle free enough of their grips around my throat to utter any words of forgiveness, to choke out any heartfelt thanks for bearing me and bringing me to this healthy young adulthood.

Healthy and adult on the outside, shriveled and sickly child on the inside. The child that cowers, the child that whines, the child that fantasizes endlessly and tries to fly free and despairs and spaces out. The child that clings so desperately to these ragdoll shadows of loved ones trying to suck, suck, a drop of milk of human kindness that can't be tasted, but the child would rather die sucking than let go and look for another tit. Are there emotional wetnurses? Didn't other adults show me they loved me from time to time? Did they love me, or did they take pity on me 'cause I was such a sweet child? I had to be a sweet child or I had no chance of finding parental substitutes.

I'd wager most children in traumatized situations become very sweet and well-behaved—at least there's a chance that someone might hear their pitiful cries from the silent heart. The mouth could never be the vehicle. The mouth had to be kept under tight control.

The mouth, after all, was *their* weapon, and it could be used to betray. They were watching your mouth…. If you opened it to complain, or worse, to state the simple truth that you guys are a bunch of sickos and you're killing yourselves and each other—well! That could mean *war*! You would fall prey to all their witchy vengeance and you would inevitably lose, because their curses were propelled by hellwinds, and yours by a mere child's puny lungs.

But you survived! Don't ever forget it, darling, you made it! You grew, physically, anyway, and leapt through a bunch of hoops without tripping up or getting whipped—you came through! You dragged your scarred and stunted soul through the labyrinth and out into the light. And now, like a butterfly just hatched, you have a chance to spread your wings.

But don't wait too long, or your wings will dry up and never fully spread. Please don't wait forever to feel strong enough. Trust, darling, trust that now's the time, now might as well be the very moment to risk it—

Look! The phone's off the hook, there's no one to jostle you. It's raining softly and there's the scent of cinnamon, clove and ginger in the air. Take a deep breath now, darling, and push! Push, like giving birth—push and give birth to yourself—get those wings up, infuse them with warm, strong pulsating blood—your blood, healthy blood, blood clean of chemicals, blood coursing with vitamins, minerals, and hope—

Go for it, straighten your shoulder blades! (Didn't Edgar always say that: "Stand up straight, stick out your chest, you've got some nice tits there, why don't you flaunt 'em?")

Jesus Christ, Edgar, I'm a butterfly! How can a butterfly be tawdry and buxom? Instead of sexy, why couldn't you say I was beautiful? Was that too ennobling an assessment? Was it impossible to see my beauty through your tainted old yellow eyes of lust?

See what I mean? I'd be ready to spread those wings, and along would come a hot wind from the hellpit and practically knock me off the leaf. It's taken all my energy to hold on and get steady again, and the wings would be drying all the time, and it was a race with the hot wind to see if I would ever fly off freely.   And so far, I haven't flown—

I'm still a ball of potential, but getting to be an old ball. It's not so charming anymore; people don't so easily apply their hopeful imaginations to you. You start to look desperate, hard to save. The last stage is pity, and then they turn away, or worse, they step on you, not willing to watch a beautiful butterfly die on the leaf...

I'm just as morbid as Ophelia. See Mom, chip off the old shoulder.

Ahhhh. Look at that nice, sweet pie filling, nicely browning in brown sugar, spices, just right, well, maybe a pinch more ginger—I like it hot (some do): that's perfect. Spices, a fine net of jewels encrusting the firm, tart apple-meat chunks: a fruit stew. No one apple stands out anymore, all are communing, pooling their resources, all equals now. The pieces that came from the wormiest ones indistinguishable from those that came from the cleanest, reddest, healthiest ones.

If you could carve the hearts out of all of us like this and mix them all together, you'd never know whose heart was whose, they'd all be the same— some bigger perhaps, but all hearts, all for the same purpose, all swimming in the same red blood.

It's time to turn to the crust balls. Oh, good, you're nice and soft. Get some flour here and the rolling—

Wait, don't get floury just yet. Put on a tape. Music. That's what's been missing. Music to lighten the heart, to guide the movements, to roll out the crust by. Music! How could I have not noticed all this silence? I guess silence has never bothered me. Anyway, what shall it be? No, not that. That's too harsh. How about—

No. Don't want to think about Lenny right now, it's too all-consuming; I always cry.

Good. This is perfect. John Fahey's "Dance of Death." And this goes out to all you dying gargoyles...

Plain and obsessive guitar, driving like raindrops, plunkity-plunk, gentle yet powerful—

Ah yes! Love that opening chord!

A little louder. But what about the phone? I always think I'm hearing the phone with this tape on.

But the phone's off the hook, silly. Look at it. It hasn't moved since your nap. But what if Greg—

What if somebody from my past, someone sentimentally reaching out to old loves on their parents' phone at Thanksgiving, someone like Robin—

God knows, Robin would never call. Not in a million years. How'd he find me here anyway? He wouldn't have the wit to track me down. Whereas I could always find him, or anyone else if I had to. I bet I could. Old flame.

I'm determined *not* to be an old flame. A haunting, pesky old girlfriend invading the private lives of past lovers. Hell no! I have my pride. Does everybody feel the way I do? I can't be the only one who occasionally dwells intensely on an old love and wishes to hell I could contact him somehow and reconnect with those old smells, tastes, skin, hair, breath, fingers, lips, music...voice.

Not Greg, though. Oh, he'll ask about them through others but I can't imagine him ever calling one of his old flames. Were they ever really flames?

Oh, I guess they must've been. It's just so hard to imagine Greg ever inflamed by anything. Old Mr. Stoical. Had to be. It was his only choice growing up as he did. It was the manly way to be. Midwestern stoicism! Bull stubborn and stump silent. Show me, show me, show me, but don't tell me, I don't wanna talk. Silent. Even if I started talking pornographically dirty to him—

No, I can't imagine it. Can't imagine him getting off on the language, let alone reciprocating... He's got to concentrate, he's got to apply himself, see the act through, so determinedly, a project completed, a chore. Abandon? Whimsy? Imagination? Passion? Oh, I mean outside the passion of hard work. Passion in the form of wild emotion, ecstasy coming out in bites, slaps even. A sudden full wet surprise kiss, like Robin's last greeting on the green? No, not Greg... Some are lovers, some ain't.

Oh, it's probably all out-of-proportion important to me because I confuse sex with love, or at least, try to express love through sex instead of through a million acts of kindness and generosity that add up to the truest, deepest—

See dear, I see us like walking wounded. We each just barely escaped from the Minotaur and now, holding onto each other for support, we trek the dry deserts looking for an oasis, looking for water, for sustenance, for rest. God knows we don't want to set the whole thing up again for our own perverse replay—our own labyrinth, our own, dual despair! Despair for one is bad enough. Let's not let it multiply...

But I want to have babies Greg! My whole being cries out for babies to move in and through it. Fate is whisking me inevitably toward it: Family. My fate. I'll never escape. It'll either be their family or mine. An individual I am not. I'll never be solo, walking alone. My fate is too deeply intertwined with those of others.

They call it the human family, Greg, don't you see? This phony post-adolescent individualism thing is a myth—it can't last. It appears for one purpose, to shine a light on one to attract a mate. We come up to the surface, flash a light, then, our new mate glommed on tight, we descend again into the murky deep. We multiply, divide ourselves, split the beautiful luminous image of ourselves into a million light fragments, each one illuminating one of our fellows. We can't contain all that energy for long in one being. It's not meant to be. You think you can go on glowing your aloof male glow forever, but you're wrong, Greg, you're already fading. After all, you've begun to share the spotlight with me. Move over big ego. Your party's been crashed....

I know it's not fun, this inevitable coupling process. It's not fun, but it's done in the service of eternity. It's only natural, Greg, for beings to want to come together and reproduce and shepherd their young to maturity. Even trees continue to shade their seedlings from burning sun until they one day break through the ancient canopy and claim all the light they need. Oh, Greg, let's take the proverbial plunge and risk the mess. Surely it'll be better than what our poor parents have endured....

Well, that's pretty. A little eggwhite here, and here. I just hope it doesn't bubble too much and turn the edges black now and explode the lattice. It's almost 2:30! There won't be time for it to finish baking, and I'll have to take it out for a while before I can handle it to put it in the car. It'll have to finish baking over there. But what if Suzy has no room in her oven? Maybe I should call her....

But the phone—

No, don't touch it. Turn the tape over; get rid of any unnecessary silence here.

Look, it's not that big a deal. They'll want to wait awhile after eating anyway. It'll cook fine over there too. It doesn't have to be perfect, Freeda!

Yes it does, yes it *does*!!! It has to be perfect! Everything I touch, everything that has my name on it everything I am, do, say, make, has to be perfect!

Freeda, relax, that's just the Ism in you. No, Freeda, dear one, it doesn't *have* to be perfect.

But it's me. It's made from my family's apples, as I'm made from them. Those apples have been fed on the ashes of my ancestors—it's more than just a pie! It's me, an offering. I'm offering myself up to them. Up to the Normals, the adults, the society I want to join. I want to make a good impression. I want them all to say what a wonderful pie! I want to be well received in their house, a stranger, taken in. I want them to take me in and give me a place at their table. Oh, gods, please make it a good pie.... I trust you. You will....

I'd better get dressed now. Greg should be closing his books—if he's paying attention to the time there—

Put the phone back? No, not just yet. If I want to be one of them, I'll have to be serenely beautiful. Yes, calm. I need time to collect myself a little more, to concentrate on dressing. It's got to be just right. I'm not sure about the skirt now. It's a little too dramatic, a little weird. But it's me! I'm a little too dramatic a little weird. But they don't have to know that...

Maybe the black one? But that's not the spirit of Thanksgiving. It's too ordinary. Wear the blue one, Freeda, you'll have a plain white shirt on. It won't be too much.

But what if I get some food on the shirt? It'll show too much. I'll have to spend the rest of the party...

Well, how about this black blouse then?

But that makes it even more dramatic. Better the white.

All I want is to feel good. Just as bad as my dear progenitors, really. Just make me feel like you're plugging the hole inside, the cavernous pit that betrays my incompletion. Plug it up tight and meld with me and be my love that I may feel complete for a moment, warmed by your life, back to the womb, eh? The need to physically combine: Part mating instinct of the adult animal, part childish longing for physical satisfaction. We all have it; some admit it a lot less than I.

It's just that, well, I can't spend my life trying to plug holes in me by grasping at the nearest compatibly shaped people-plugs. Gotta stop them holes myself, somehow. Why don't we each have a medic assigned to us? Sometimes we have to staunch the bleeding alone. Is the hole a wound? Or is it just a vacuum, where something was left out? I don't think I was particularly wounded. Actually, I used to feel pretty contented with myself at times. When I was small, and could fill myself up easily on the goodies around me: the lawn, the spider plants by the cellar steps, the crab apple and its robin's nest, the pictures in my fairy tale books, (which were actually Ophelia's fairy tale books—somewhere we contain the same set of pictures, of course, and share the crab apple, spider plants and grass as well),

I must have been contented. We started out as though growing from the same image-trunk, Mom and I, but I've branched off on my own now.

The things I've found since to fill me—the things you can't know, Mom, because I've found them all on my own—well, they only seem to fill as much as they can be shared. I can't seem to keep anything for myself. It's all a bunch of empty calories, if I'm not getting built by it, if it doesn't add up to a recognizable whole.

I don't know what to make of this trash heap of beach combings I've collected, exploring on my own. I don't know how to fashion myself into anything intrinsically useful. Beautiful, maybe, but useful? Giving to others? Able to forget myself in the passion of my work only to surface from time to time and notice how much, how sturdily, I've grown from hard working? I come up so often to check myself out, my work is constantly disrupted and I don't get that magical swept-away feeling that tells you you're really succeeding at it. I'm too anxious about myself. And much too self-obsessed. It's getting to be boring to be me. Pretty soon I'll find myself stranded on an island of Self just like the gargoyles. I'll fall into a pattern of mad craving and voracious consumption of garbage just to keep the hole filling, filling, like a running toilet, and then, of sheer exhaustion from the Sisyphean task, I'll expire...

Mr. Sisyphus from Mexico way, the old man with the cart. He walks the streets in the hot sun, his bare head crowned in white tufts, bent in a permanent stoop, his hand welded to the iron cart pull, his feet shuffling at a steady, unvarying gait. Mr. Sisyphus, I call him, and I love him secretly as I pass by in my fast car. And some days, with no change of expression on his Buddha face, I see him carrying an actual load, usually of folded cardboard boxes. Someone, perhaps, is letting him work for them. He's doing an honest day's labor, hauling cargo in the dusty road. He'll trundle along and get there, unload, perhaps reload, and trundle back along his path. He is living. He is the essence of dumb life to me. I love him with all my heart, a real live parable in my neighborhood. And a total mystery—completely impenetrable.   I doubt he even has a voice now, if he ever did. Every day I see him I feel my own cross turn to fluff and I laugh and cry and sing his praises silently to myself and thank him for bringing one of Iris's foolish visions of the Lord into my happily receptive purview.

Oh, Iris! I love you so. You and your corny, sentimental religious mumbo jumbo—your particular, mystical teddy bear. I know you don't really believe you are one of the chosen, but you value the times you were touched by the divine. By sharing those episodes with me, you let me into the magical world of all your potions, charms and incantations. You remind me of the dark, fragrant voodoo shops in New Orleans where I was afraid to ask—

From you, I gained permission to pray.

Ophelia, your teddy bear is sexual love. From you, I hate to admit it, I learned to make love—not to *love* I still haven't learned that--but to be a romantic lover, yes, that I've mastered, thanks to you.

And you, Dolf, what teddy bear have you shared with me? Books, perhaps, and, especially, words. You showed me that words could be selected like beach pebbles for their particular beauty. You pronounced them so they bounced, and I heard them like drum beats, like music notes, thanks to you.

And Edgar, what on earth kind of teddy—

Let's see, you must have one. Ah, I think I know. Nature. You gave me access to Nature, to love her, as you pointed out every fiber of silky hair on a woman's arm, every wasp that nibbled gently at your cuticles, every dogwood you topped and lovingly doctored with tar, every wave that curled and came toward us as we bobbed together, me once so trusting in your arms....

It's hard to believe you each held me once; you each kissed my fat cheeks and idly twirled my yellow curls. You each loved me, as now I grasp at a chance to love you. But you are sick babies, and it's

319

much harder to love a sick one sometimes. Beauty is so easy to love. God loves the damaged goods just as much, they say, and I'm not a god. But I know now, thanks to you, Lenny, and you Iris, and you, old Mrs. Gallagher with your African violets and your husband on the iron lung (was he as despised by his own children then for dying of the Ism in the lungs?), I now know the gods love you old gargoyles so much, and you'll all be well taken care of and there's no need for such fearfulness.   Please, if you could each only be a little braver, a little more trusting. It really *won't* hurt; I'm not just saying that. In the end, it will feel wonderfully full; the holes will all fill up and brim to the top and you'll sink, happily, peacefully, of the newfound weight of fullness, and you'll dream yourself into another life, like you'd just eaten a huge Thanksgiving turkey dinner and stretched out on the couch—

Oh please, don't cry so long and loud, hush my babies, hushabye. You'll soon be asleep, so peaceful, and I'll gaze at each of you with such contented love, with the same face you looked down at me when I slept in my crib. I'm not unwilling to swap roles now and parent you, but you're each like Alice's baby in Wonderland, so busy turning into a pig and squealing away from my arms—

Forgive me if I drop you each.

Greg. Dear old Greg. Practically an anagram for Edgar, aren't you? Did I succeed in finding Daddy in you? Are you going to grow up to spawn a family in front of which to stretch your martini-soaked carcass every night at eight p.m.? Are you going to discover the joys of cat torture? (Perhaps you already have—you stroke me the way you stroke that cat of yours, mindlessly, with heavy fingers, worrying my furless skin.)

Catlovers. What about people? Are people too problematic for you? What are you so afraid of, my passions? My emotions? My ardor, and my sensuality? Or do all these very human things in me make me look like an animal to you? You, who have purged every drop of martial blood from your veins, you who have opted for the unfeeling life, you who therefore have to adopt feeling folks like myself, or Ophelia for that matter, to employ as your emotional mouthpieces... You think you can play us like accordions and push our buttons as we exhale your bad feelings for you? You, twin wunderkind who shit ice cream! You, two family golden boys worshipped and babied by mothers who martyred themselves and claimed you as their due!

You're secret misogynists. You like to catch a woman like a cat, scoop her into your lap where you can hold her if she struggles to flee, and stroke her into a purring silence as you grin your insidious little boy grins that say: 'Aha! I've got you now!' And, comforted with this fantasy of control of another being, you, too, begin to purr and drift into blissful oblivion.

But. Society loves you chumps. You mama's boys are what they call nice guys. So what, you say, if we finish last? It's nice to be nice. It's important to have everyone like you, at least not dislike you, and to be congenial and easy to get along with and not one to seek out or create conflicts, oh no. You just want it to be peaceful and quiet and purring away smoothly so you don't have to hassle too much and can spend your days locked away in newspaperland with your background music, cat on lap, drifting, sweetly, as though cuddled on mama's warm breast, a comforting nipple always nearby when you want to go sleepy....

Your skin is fine, milky white, your bodies soft over muscular frames, your eyes narrow and pale, you have soft, vulnerable teeth. The major difference is your hands. Greg's are so big, his fingers stubby, little mallets each. Edgar's are also short, but much slimmer. He used to play frustrated surgeon with them, extracting our splinters, and even our teeth. The cold needle-nosed pliers tasting of oiled metal, touching our red children's tongues as they gripped our loose—

Will that be you with our children Greg?

No. Not you. You're not the merry sadist type. You'll go the way of your martyred ma, your alienated pa: Drifting outward, like a raft past the breakers, your face covered with a magazine asleep, you'll drift, and wake up one day far from family's shore. You'll leave us, because you'll find we're too much trouble really, too messy, too noisy and demanding, too much hassle and conflict, too uncomfortable an environment for you, oh shining idol, for you who belong in a serene marble temple on a hill, oh most worshipped one. You'll never quite get over it. Your wife doesn't think you're the be-all-end-all your mother did. How dare she!

I can feel it already, Greg, not even married to you yet and being taken, well, a bit for granted. You really think the whole female world is going to go on admiring you forever without rest? Even we humble supplicants need to take a break!

See this pretty lattice crust I'm making here, Greg? This is us. See how it covers the sweet hot insides like a roof, yet lets out steam? And with the steam, mind you, Greg, comes the fragrance of the spices—ah, the spices of life, Greg, would you not have them rise, or would you place them so deeply under all the apples that they'd never titillate the nostril, to announce the presence of the Pie?

You see, Greg, women are the architects of the relationships of the world. We make them, lovingly, expertly, as we make the meals we all eat. I'm making our duo here because, though I see that you come from the same stock as Edgar, spiritually speaking, that is, you have some real advantages over him for me, and I feel it's a step up, really I do. For one thing, I don't see you drinking martinis...

We're siblings, really. Too much alike. We both hated our households growing up, but could never really leave because we were expected to save them, or at least to redeem them, somehow. Oh, and we bought it! We actually tried, and tried, to straighten the whole mess out. We'd roll up our sleeves, time and again, and clean up their messes—oh, they were never our messes—we didn't make messes. We'd try and fix it so nobody'd ever notice it'd been broken. We'd get sneaky. It was too much for us to keep up with. We'd sweep under the rugs; we'd patch it best we could and turn the cracked part to the wall. We'd scrub the guilty stains 'til we tore the cloth, then hide the evidence. Hide. Lie. Fake it. We became experts at deception. Nice guys outside, seething monsters of rage inside.

I know you, Greg, you're another one like me. We both lose it at the same time and those rage bombs are going to knock us both for a loop. I'm leery of your anger, too. And it's not all me, dear, one half is you. The question is, can we ever grow up together and find a way out of the mazes of our families to create our own, unique, and presumably more salubrious formula for the conjugal life? Can we? Will we? Do we care enough about each other? Can we go through the initiation rites of adolescence again for the sake of our relationship, but this time go through them together?

Pure, angelic, virginal, me! Perfection on the outside, reeking shame, disgust, horror and

resentment on the inside. A regular Dorian Gray.
Eh? Who knows, perhaps most of 'em are the same.
Crack open an apparent Normal and find—a worm.

And these apples make a delicious pie!

***

It's beautiful, isn't it? Look at the hand-woven, intricate design, the marvelous colors, the unusual bell-like flare at the hips.

"It was my great grandmother's," I'll say, "from Russia."

I'll be virginal, white and blue, with a golden halo. I'll bring purity and righteousness to their scene. I won't drink and get loud and get sleazy with the men. I'll help in the kitchen, carry out the dirty dishes, smile sweetly and keep quiet. Greg can do most of the talking for us. They're his friends, after all. I'll stay in his shadow, as much as he'll let me. He'll probably introduce me to people with whom I'll have to converse, gaily, wittily, with great interest in their topics, divulging little about myself. Mysterious, half hidden, keep-them-guessing.

It's enough that they'll have me to look at and admire, they won't want to, won't need to go much deeper. I am what I appear: Lovely, shy, and sweet. I have an interesting family, and I'm proud of it. I bring family history forward into my own life. There. I've got it on. The perfect mask.

They'll never suspect, never dare probe. It was obviously an inspiringly interesting background she came from, let it go at that. They'll never see the gargoyles. They'll never know the cumulative generations of black despair—the suicide of the husband of the woman who brought the skirt from Russia. His self-shooting in a Brooklyn apartment, not even a note to her. And she, sweet great-grandmother who used to smack her lips along my bare arm murmuring "Ah, babushka," or something like that—she who lost her mind and wandered years about a dark apartment filled with tarnishing samovars, yellowing silks and dusty carpets all from another time and place now lost to us all...

And the farmhouse, walls thirty inches thick, where Dolf sits waiting his next heart attack. Dark, and damp, the ceaseless molding of thousands of mite-filled books, Libby's hand-hooked rugs, trinkets collected on their many cruises, the cocktail room smelling of sherry and bitters, his cigars, and faint traces of the old cocker spaniel, now buried beside the brook. And the brook smell of moss and clay, fern and black loam, the smell of boxwoods crowding the front door, the smell of giant sycamores shedding their bark upon the driveway, the smell of apple blossoms and lilacs in the orchard, the beloved smell of ripening dusty concords on the porch screens, bees buzzing in the vines...

It was my summer paradise once, and now, that old troll won't let me romp in the gardens of my birthright, my inheritance. Why do they all have to be so selfish? Why do they have to cling so to their little domains? Are we young ones such threatening invaders, confronting them with unsettling visions of change—how the place will look one day when you're gone, Dolf, how we, your grandchildren, might decide to fix it up?

I know, I know. You created the place. You and Libby. You put in all the boxwoods, all the gardens, you arranged the rocks to form fish ponds in the brook, collected the antiques to fill the rooms, collected the trinkets, the books, the cooking pots, the vegetable baskets…. It's yours all yours, and we, young vultures, should at least have the courtesy to wait in the wings while you do your swan number solo, taking the spotlight for the final time. Yes, our very presences in the flesh are enough to drive you all to a frenzy of resentment, anxiety, distrust. We, who threaten not only to take it all apart and rebuild it out of recognition with no respect for the years of your personality pumped into it, but we who will no doubt send the swallows reeling with our blasts of rock ' roll inanities, our conversational drivel full of bad grammar and "y'knows," our beer cans and pop bottles and cigarette butts and candy wrappers and chewing gum—aauuugh! You cry in terror of our hordes. We'll undo you and all you stood for in five minutes time. That's why you get so pissed at us.

I'll just stay away now, Dolfi, don't you worry. I won't be seeing you again. Stubborn pride will keep me away. I know you won't call for me on your deathbed. What was I to you, anyway, a mere grandchild, an unfocused, amorphous ball of dubious potential who seems lately to have done nothing to distinguish herself? Who can't even speak and write grammatically after all your attempts to correct her?

328

It's no wonder, you say, with her mother gone to pot like that. What was she trying to prove anyway? Suicide attempt. Bah! you'd say. Weakness! It's just cowardice. Why I've suffered just as much as she has—more—has she lost three wives to cancer?

I hear you, Dolfi. Now shut up!

***

You're all taking a fine time dying!

So now we listen to your muttering, your faltering, your endless self-pitying laments. "The Streets of Laredo," over and over, the romance of your own deaths. In love with death, entranced by it, fascinated, you savor your dying as though the Big Boss had given you a last, indefinite vacation.

Very instructive, you're determined to teach your ungrateful children a thing or two about decrepitude:

"First of all, dear, you must respect the decrepit person. He is the one who has suffered a great deal and has thereby lost the ability to suffer gracefully. It is very hard for the decrepit person to bear the presence of one so young and wholesome as yourself, so please keep your distance at all times, and do not look directly at the decrepit one but hide your face and lower your voice and hope not to intrude too much upon his consciousness. Whatever you do, do not demand anything of a decrepit person. They are in no condition to give. For your own character development, spend a certain amount of time, as often as possible, in the presence of decrepit persons, listening to their litanies of complaints. It will help you to stay humble about who you are and your chances of doing any better than they in the end. Above all, carry their images with you wherever you go, and repeat their negative phrases ad nauseam in your brain to counteract the possible growth of glad feelings or positive notions that might be budding in you..."

Oh my, what time is it?

Greg should be here any minute!

I hope he doesn't make that crack about my wearing makeup again. This eye shadow is a little too much. I'll wipe this much off, now put a little white powder over the top here...

I'd better hang up the phone. Wouldn't want him to know I spent all this time with the phone off the hook. "What if my mother was trying to reach us—you know she always calls on Thanksgiving, and we'll be out later..."

No, you wouldn't say that. You don't really care if you talk to your mom or not. If you feel guilty, you'll call her tomorrow. Dutiful son.

And I, dutiful daughter, what's happened to me? All this time studiously ignoring the vain attempted incoming calls from Dolfi, Iris, Ophelia, no doubt possibly, even, lonely old Edgar down there in the empty oversized nest....

Amazing! It's been four hours since Greg left, and I've done it! Kept the phone off the hook! Kept them from invading my day, from poisoning me even more with their decrepit oozing insults. Funny that you all want to talk to somebody now, somebody powerless, somebody neutral, somebody upon whom you can dump all your miserable self-loathing, someone who can't hang up on you, who can't ever really leave you in fact—someone, like a child...

Greg, you're late. You were supposed to be here two minutes ago. I know, you'll walk in any second. You're the one who wanted to go to this this thing, more than I. Oh, I'm grateful for the invitation. At least we don't have to spend Thanksgiving alone together in some depressing restaurant, or worse, here, without any defense against the phone.

The phone! Maybe I'd better put it back. If you have any trouble and try to call...

But then, I could be talking to someone. You'd just have to wait and try again. Fifteen minutes more. That'll be fair. I could be talking to someone for fifteen minutes. Old friends-- would that make you jealous! Only it wouldn't—because you don't get jealous, especially not of my little punk college friends, as you would refer to them in your mind... You, the haloed, Mr. Perfection, not even a jealous bone in your body I bet. You just take me for granted, that's all. Imagine me so sick, dependent, wouldn't dare do anything, and even if I did, it would just be one more piece of evidence that I was the sick one, I was the one with all the problems, see, can't even maintain fidelity to her live-in lover-- pretty, eh?

What about you? Are you so goddamn one hundred percent faithful? I wonder... Or do you think you're so clever and superior you can sleaze around behind my back and I'll never figure it out? You've got me, and everything, and everybody, so under control, right?

No, you don't think that way. It's pure selfishness is all. You just don't think about anyone else, male or female, as a living breathing, complete, thinking-independent-thoughts type individual, unless, for some obscure reason, they press themselves so close up into your face you can't ignore them any longer. That's it, isn't it? You'd like the whole world to just sort of hang back and give you a wide berth so you can sidle on through, unmolested, unpolluted, untouchable, eh?

Well, you've got this much gunk stuck on your shoe now, and you're not shaking her off that easy! Cloying, dependent, that's what I am in your eyes, right? I'm that albatross around your neck, the one who exposed her feelings to you in such a way, well, you just *had* to feel responsible, and then, since you'd made a commitment of sorts, you just *had* to carry her along. She's not such a bad accessory after all, kind of a status symbol in some circles. Not god's gift to gentility, but not ill-mannered, either. Liable, on social occasions like the one anticipated, to put her foot in mouths and generally boggle conversational opportunities, embarrass you a bit, but not so much that it isn't also a wee bit charming, at least in retrospect.

She's just solid emotion is all, a bowl of orange Jello. Uncontainable, she wobbles about, exposing first this piece of psychological underwear, then that, until you've been forced to see more of her than you really bargained for....

She's not cool.

Well, what do you expect from Ophelia's daughter? Ophelia and Edgar's daughter— correction--granddaughter of Iris, of Dolf and Libby, first grandchild, prodigy around the cocktail tables, little family pet well-trained in the performance of verbal tricks to amuse drunken elders? She performed well in that context, of course, but where could she take her act from there? It was not generalizable to the outside world. Her skills were of no value to society. She was like a rich man's geisha suddenly set free to look for work in the secretarial pools of Tokyo. Character? What's *that*?

How could she build on something that was never hers to begin with? How could she grow in those pelting hailstorms of constant criticism that later, after Ophelia's suicide attempt, became storm breakers of witches' curses: "I hate you Freeda, go to hell, you stinking whore, you disgust me, get out of my sight..."

Now is that any way for a mother to address her eldest daughter?

Oh, but dear, mother was so sick. Mother was raving, simply raving, she didn't even know you were there...

Still, she'd look right in my face and say those things, day after day, and, yes, I could tell myself it was the Ism talking, sure, I knew I needn't take it personally. But what was I, a fully-equipped mental hospital?

I was worn out in no time. Blew out of there like a wet autumn leaf, stuck to your shoe, Greg, and thus arrived here, at your bachelor digs, taken in out of pity more than love. Rescued, rather than admired, cared for out of a sense of professional duty. I mean no more, no less, than a cooperative patient to her competent nurse.

Yet, a nurse is not always a diagnostician. You didn't realize that I had caught it by then: The Ism. Brought it with me, right into your home, infected, doomed...

Like a consumptive of the Romantic age, I glow with a certain fatal intensity. I wear the rosy blush of the emotional fever that is devouring me, wearing me down, as my eyes grow wider and my body shrinks to childlike proportions and my whole being cries out to the pity in those about me, those who still believe in my sweetness and innocence under the creeping consuming power of the Ism.

Sweetness and Innocence! Hah! It's the Ism we're talking about here, not a mere microbe! There's no innocence. I've stared death in the face now and felt its hot poisoned curses burn my cheeks. I've run from it, but it's come with me. I'm doomed to share their fate.

One day, my dear Greg, you'll find me cursing, raving at you that way. I'll attack you with a knife, a pen; I'll rave around the house destroying precious things of yours. I'll hate you with the fury and passion of self-hatred that propelled my mother's curses and that will loose the cave load of biting bats from my, these, sweet, innocent young lips...

I'll poison our household, our love, our bed. I'll not be able to contain the rage forever. And, like a volcano, it will spill, hot and searing from my infested brain and harden upon all it touches so that it may never be removed...

You think I can get over all this in time? Get over the first twenty-five years of my life? Start fresh? That *you* of all people, have the power to cure, to save, to make it all different, to surgically remove the pain and rage at their very roots?

I doubt it, Buddy! You ain't no Mother Teresa either. You think you can nurse this case night and day without catching it yourself? Look out!

Oh, we've talked about it. Sure, you think you're immune. You think your ability to transcend the limitations of your own family life is proof positive that you're untouchable from now on, that the Ism can't have you because you've learned to control yourself, to keep your emotions all tidily gathered up under your skirts so not one thread of them will ever get tangled in the Ism... that by simply freeze-drying yourself you can enter the contaminated area and remain unscathed. You can wander among us afflicted mortals and have no reaction to our inner storms. You can watch with dispassionate detachment; as we writhe, you can hold down our tongues—

What a life! You little self-appointed saint, you. Now I know how Ophelia felt when I was, oh so innocently, trying to help her—Ha! Go to hell you little devil, eat shit, you hypocrite! Think you're so much better that the rest of us! Think you're outside the Ism, well, you're not! You sucker—you got drawn right back in again. Your temporary freedom was only an illusion.

Escape the Ism of your family, run right after it in the form of your future family. You have to mate with the Ism, you have to keep it about you. It's the only place you, or I, feel at home. It's all we know, Greg, the Ism is life for us. It's what makes sense of it all—the lies, the denial, the suppressed rage that comes bursting forth at times, the ingrown self, the pitying self, the false self that wears a mask to the world. The empty self, the fearful self, the self we wake up with in the middle of the night to find it hasn't changed, it hasn't left, it's the same one we've carried along since childhood, the same one we can never fully know or trust because we've never been able to work it free from the entangling, strangling vines of the family disease. How can two such incomplete people possibly love?

It's not loving we're doing, Greg, it's got to be something else, something less...

I think it's snuggling. It think it's the feeling of closeness we enjoyed with a few childhood friends, or perhaps with our siblings at times, the feeling that we could bear the presence of another because by rubbing up against us, pressing us into a wrestling hold, the other gave us a sensation of ourselves, that we, too, existed, because we took up space; they had to push against us, and we pushed back. We felt equal, we felt included. We felt safety in numbers. Defined by the borders of another, of others, we were not alone. Alone, we were nothing—unable to find ourselves at all, just whistling in the proverbial dark.

I don't know, Greg, I just don't know. Is this enough of a feeling to marry upon? To start a family with? Won't we just increase the snuggling pleasure by adding more small bodies to the pile? Isn't this a bit suffocating? Would they, the small bodies, get enough out of it to escape the Ism one day themselves?

With our genes, we could very likely produce a candidate or two for the Ism. We could easily end up like Ophelia and Edgar ourselves, couldn't we? What have we got that they hadn't got? We, who for all our long years of expensive education are just starting to compete in the bigger pond, have, as yet, nothing to show for it. At the same ages, our postwar parents were well into their third child already, four bedroom house around them, two cars, all the features of success in American life that we, collectively, lack, and they, constantly, remind us we lack. We, who have so many more to compete with. We who start out with so little character, so little identity, so little individuality as our mass culture constantly reminds us. We, who are forever young, forever immature, forever children of the forever dying Ism-inflicted older generation, we who failed to find nirvana in drug experimentation, we who lost our chance to be war heroes, we who have produced nothing but some excellent rock music, who, as our elders and best critics never let us forget, are no more than potential—promising, but by no means guaranteed...

We snuggle together like two puppies in the snow. We keep warm by each other, but not warm enough to hunt. We starve, slowly, as the Ism devours us from within.

We can't win, Greg. The best fruit we can produce are some small, wormy ones, that, if we're lucky, even the birds will reject.

Better not to marry. Better not to breed. After all, our forefathers' critical voices within us will never hush, and we'll never be content with the so-much-less that is to be our lot—with our one car, our two bedrooms, our big bills, our long hours, our drawn, worried faces for our children and our lack of hope for their future.

Paint it black! Paint it black you devils!

Greg, you're eight minutes late. If I were Ophelia, and I practically am—no, I'm *not*—I'd be having a drink right now. I'd be passed out before you got home. You'd have to wake me and fix me up again if you wanted to take me to this party.

Thank god! Thank god I'm *not* Ophelia! Thank god the Ism in me is, so far, dormant enough to spare me from drinking now. I may even have a chance, who knows? If only I weren't driving myself so crazy containing all this rattle in my head. Who could I possibly share it with anyway? Greg? He won't listen. He's Ulysses with wax in his ears. He's found his way to shut it out, and he won't unplug for me.

Maura? She understands alright. But she's pretty far gone. I feel like the rage is already blowing too hot from her; I can't get close. Her dad tried to kill her with a shot gun. He ran away. She's never seen him since she was fifteen…

Valerie? Sure, she understands, but with her the obsession is sexual. Of course it would be. Her drunken uncle raped her, oh, several times she says. When she was only ten. God, how could he have gotten it in? It must've hurt like hell! Little girl in crumpled nightgown shivering, blood-stained, fetal positioned on her bed too terrified to cry…

God, Valerie, I wish I could make it all better. I wish we could all take our compassion and put it to use to kill the Ism somehow. We all feel so much for each other, and yet, we're all so small and alone, we can't come together 'cause the Ism always comes between and pushes us apart.

And Peggy, you too, sexually assaulted by your own dad! God, how can you forgive him? And he still drinks, just like Edgar, never paused for a moment to say, "I'm sorry…"

And Lenny. Your dad beat you over the head with a beer bottle and threw you into the street. Fourteen years old! You had to go back. You couldn't tell anyone, oh no! How could you tell anyone a thing like that? They'd be scared to be your friend, scared to snuggle with you, afraid you might pick up a beer bottle yourself.

And Sam, my own little Sammy, watching Ophelia slide into the ambulance, stark blue and marble cold. You must have secretly cried out with joy for the end, but it was only a false alarm, and you saw her delivered, again, bloated and wrecked, unable to write, speech impaired, but competent to curse you for months, years...

And dearest Barbie, you who got slapped around by Edgar, thrown down on the asphalt driveway by the father flesh that bore you and carried you in his arms. You who were locked up in the hospital and made to pay again and again for the sins of the family: Oh, black sheep! No wonder you strayed as soon as you were big enough to jump the stile.

But we're not only victims! Wake up brothers and sister in the Ism! We're not *only* victims! For crissakes, I'm one-third-of-my-life old. I've survived! I've gotten along, somehow, maybe not with full consciousness, maybe without any sense of control or direction, maybe by sheer groping, but hey, I'm *here* aren't I?

Look at me, I'm grown up! I'm dressed nicely to join some grown up friends, some friends who will eat a nice meal together, who will talk pleasantly and not argue loudly or fight or stalk off to sulk or lock themselves in their bedrooms or go sit, like Ophelia did that time, in a bed of poison ivy, or throw up, or pass out on the floor, or piss in their pants on the couch, or punch a fist through the plate glass window, or throw ashtrays, or get down on their hands and knees and give each other pony rides, or make out in the bathrooms or in the dark halls, or under the piano, or crack up their cars on the way home—

I'm going to a nice party with nice people to have a nice time, escorted by a nice boyfriend who drinks in moderation, and occasionally. And I'm bringing part of the dessert offering. And I made it out of apples grown in the old family orchard and have learned to make the best with what I've got.

No, I'm not going to be rich or have a lot of possessions that say I've arrived. No, I'm not going to be a boss and join the managerial class and boss my kids around and give them a sense of worthlessness... . I'm going to go with *my* instincts and try to work my way free of the Ism, now that I know it's my right and responsibility to do so.

What do I owe the family Ism after all? There's nothing and no one to protect. The last of my forebears are dying off (as they constantly remind me) and I can't protect, can't save them. If they die ungracefully, that's too bad. The world will know the truth despite what I do at this point to cover up.

I'll air the Ism in my family. I'll not go on hiding it, protecting it, for that's exactly what it wants me to do. I'll declare the Ism from the rooftops, if necessary, to force it into the light, to expose it to the one element it can't bear, to force it under the killing rays of truth. I'll fight it in me. That it will never devour me, I'll fight—

But fighting's what Greg's doing, and it's not working. The Ism's more powerful than that. Fight it, you always lose. What am I but one little speck in its universe? I, alone, can't force anything into the light.

What am I talking about? I simply can't beat it. The best I can do is accept it's there. After all, it'll still be there in our genes when we have kids, if we have kids... I can't erase my genes.

I can't hate my ancestors for being sick, either. It was probably in their genes too. They just fell into the inevitability of it. It felt good to drink. It was like an elixir at first, not a poison. How can one believe that one's life-saving medicine is really a killing poison? Who's going to stop when it feels so good, when all the magic of it seems to work, year after year, until ever so imperceptibly, it starts to turn the other way and undo all those good things?

They're not at fault. I must forgive them with all my heart. And Maura must forgive her dad, and Peggy hers, and all the many others living with this Ism, we must all forgive them, they know not what they do.

But we must forgive them, as well, for knowing not what they do. Their blindness to their own words and deeds is just another dimension of their disease. They don't want to not know, it's just that they're so pickled, they *can't* know the reality about themselves anymore. We must forgive them everything, their whole twisted , tormented lives of confusion and obfuscation brought on by slow poisoning. It's like saying we must forgive the Roman Empire for failing to retain its power due to the massive lead contents of their goblets. It wasn't their fault. They didn't know about the effects of lead. Or maybe a few wise men did, but they couldn't change the habits of an empire...

We must forgive ourselves, most of all. We, who were born and raised with the surf-song of the Ism in our ears, the fumes of the Ism in our nostrils, the woolly darkness of the Ism over our eyes. We who have struggled to the surface like wounded divers, only to find ourselves too severely maimed to signal for help, we must forgive ourselves our weaknesses before the strength of the Ism. The Ism, after all, is far more powerful than we...

We, the walking wounded, children of its many victims, we must band together, to snuggle our way back to warm, back to trust, back to light. It's alright to snuggle, if that's the best we can do for ourselves at first. It's alright. It's only natural. Real love may come in time....whatever that is.

Oh, if only it were so simple as taking a drink! But I can't drink. I mustn't drink. Especially not now. I'll get crazy. I'll get evil. I'll spend the whole party prowling the kitchen for more booze. I'll get incoherent. I'll get dizzy. I'll wander off looking for a place to discreetly pass out. I'll black out. I'll curse someone in a blackout or break something, or throw up all over someone, or out the widow—my famous college trick. At any rate, I'll become obnoxious and an embarrassment to Greg. I'll be cranky and rebellious on the way home. I'll pass out in a smelly heap and wake up with a wretched hangover, perhaps more vomiting, full of shame and remorse for ruining the party for myself and Greg, for offending others. I'll sheepishly ask for a blow-by-blow description of my actions during the blackout and Greg won't want to tell me, so I'll get angry and attack him until he's angry enough to spell it all out for me, then I'll punish myself for hours, days, drinking at last to blot out the self-disgust, and it won't go away until I get completely plastered again and black out and throw up and off to the races...

I can't drink. Greg says it plain: "You can't handle alcohol. You know you can't..." It's not an option for me. Constitutionally, I'm not built for the stuff. One beer and I'm already losing control; three beers and I'm on the floor. How dear ol' dad could put away three martinis in a row before blacking out, I'll never fathom. No, the Ism's got me too strong. I can't go that route of regular oblivion. Drugs were just the same. Never could feel good enough, never

346

could enjoy a simple high without all the subsequent, attendant fears and anxieties and irritations and palpitations and sweats and discomforts that signified death. It all added up to a sense of poisoning. It was clearly self-abusive. No, I can't even enjoy a simple pill, like Valium... How nice it would be if this would all go away with a little pill...How neat...How impossible for me!

God. Now there's a hope. I know some people can get it with God. I only imagine the fanatics--but it must work on saner, more mundane levels too. I don't know how to begin, though. It feels so forced, like the time that insane "Christian" boss had me down on my knees calling out to Jesus---AAAUUUGGH, what a nightmare! I was only half drunk, or I wouldn't remember it so painfully clearly.

No, if it's meant to be God, it'll have to come somehow outside of religion. Maybe somehow in the sunny meadow, or the dark, whispering forest, or the wind-singing beach.

I'll keep looking. I know it's there, somewhere, when I'm ready inside...when I've decided to forgive all and start anew, by myself, alone, Greg or no Greg. Jesus, at some point I've got to live for *me*!

He's thirteen minutes late. I'd better put back the phone.

The pie smells marvelous—don't dare peek at it though! At least by his being late it's getting more baked. Smells so pungent, so spicy sweet! An offering to the gods! Incense! Incense created for the gods that I may recycle my ancestors into the heavenly hosts they're meant to be now for me and my children and their children and on and on... A promise, a hope, a good act. And I was the chef. And it's to be shared, like broken bread, and feasted upon, in a festival of thanksgiving.

Mom's corny toasts on Thanksgiving: "And what are *you* thankful for today, Freeda?"

It is Thanksgiving, after all. I don't have to leave it to the pilgrims and the Mayflower-descendent certified-all-Americans like Greg; I can co-opt Thanksgiving for myself. I can be Thankful for me.

Yeah, Ophelia, that's what I'm thankful for. As crippled as I am, I'm alive, goddamn it, and I know it right now, 'cause I'm not drunk. In fact, I'm looking pretty good, and I'm about to go share a meal with some friends, and it's all normal, healthy stuff, and I'm not going to blow it, 'cause I want to enjoy it! I'll drink rich, cold, unfiltered apple cider and it'll taste wonderful and I won't even miss the wine.

I'm grateful for me. I haven't done anything wonderful, yet, but I'm pretty wonderful. At least I'm pretty special. I really wouldn't want to be anyone else right now.

Like Maura. She's probably still in bed. She can't have gone home; she must be planning to go to a party too. Or maybe she's stuck at the apartment. That's right, Roger was flying to his folks' in L.A. I'd better call her…. Maybe she could come along with—

No, that's not appropriate. I know Greg wouldn't want me to invite her. But just a friendly call—

Greg'll probably walk in just as she answers. That's okay. He'll need time to change for the party anyway. It won't hold us up.

It won't hold us up, but it could bring me down. I feel so good all of a sudden. "All-on-a-sonnet," they tell me. That's how I said it as a baby. Mom loved that. The power of a child to create natural poetry. If only, Mom, if only my childish incantations could have broken the spell and freed the princess inside the witch…

You loved me then, Mom and Dad, I know it. You were proud and pleased with your first sunny, curly-headed baby, who gripped your fingers and nuzzled your breasts…. You loved me, as any parents love a child, and still do, only it's so buried, I can't hear you shouting it; it all comes out crazy, but I know that's what you really mean to say.

You love me so much you're trying to push me away so I won't catch the Ism from you. You're trying to throw me out from under the wheels of that truck that's about to run you down, I know. You're trying to protect me from yourselves, but it's too late, we're all in this together. I've already caught it. But I'm determined—and this is what you must believe—I'm determined, dear ancestors, not to let it do me in!

Seven-six-three—no matter what, I'm not going to let her bring me down. If she starts to get negative, starts whining about old Roger again, I'll just breathe in the pie smell, smell the pie, and listen. I'll listen a little while, then I'll wish her a Happy Thanksgiving…. Smell the pie…

Four-two-nine-one… Smells divine, really—

HI. IT'S FREEDA. SO HOW THE HELL YA DOIN MY FRIEND?

Victoria Floor lives in Princeton, New Jersey.

She would love to hear from you:

victoriafloor2@gmail.com